THE ASSISTANT SECRETARIES

THE ASSISTANT
SECRETARIES

PROBLEMS AND PROCESSES OF APPOINTMENT

Dean E. Mann
with Jameson W. Doig

THE BROOKINGS INSTITUTION · WASHINGTON, D.C.

353
M315

THE BROOKINGS INSTITUTION is an independent organization devoted to nonpartisan research, education, and publication in economics, government, foreign policy, and the social sciences generally. Its principal purposes are to aid in the development of sound public policies and to promote public understanding of issues of national importance.

The Institution was founded December 8, 1927, to merge the activities of the Institute for Government Research, founded in 1916, the Institute of Economics, founded in 1922, and the Robert Brookings Graduate School of Economics and Government, founded in 1924.

The general administration of the Institution is the responsibility of a self-perpetuating Board of Trustees. The trustees are likewise charged with maintaining the independence of the staff and fostering the most favorable conditions for creative research and education. The immediate direction of the policies, program, and staff of the Institution is vested in the President, assisted by the division directors and an advisory council, chosen from the professional staff of the Institution.

In publishing a study, the Institution presents it as a competent treatment of a subject worthy of public consideration. The interpretations and conclusions in such publications are those of the author or authors and do not purport to represent the views of the other staff members, officers, or trustees of the Brookings Institution.

237160

Foreword

LAMENTS ARE HEARD about the shortage of men qualified to fill the positions of under secretary, assistant secretary, and deputy administrator in the federal government. No systematic study of recruitment processes and the type of men who fill these positions has heretofore been made. This study is intended to illuminate and evaluate the system by which these offices are filled, as a basis for future improvement.

The study covers 108 appointments during the Truman, Eisenhower, and Kennedy administrations. The 108 appointments were chosen at random according to probability sampling procedures. To provide a detailed analysis of the recruitment process, the political executives themselves, the cabinet officers who selected them, and other key participants in the selection process were interviewed.

Extensive biographical information on the much larger number of men who filled undersecretarial and assistant secretarial positions was collected during the course of this work, as part of a broader study of federal political executives from 1933 to 1965 which also will include agency heads and commission members.

Jameson W. Doig, now on the Princeton University faculty, was chiefly responsible for the investigation at the beginning of the study. Dean E. Mann, who is now a faculty member of the University of California, Santa Barbara, directed the project, beginning in 1960, and prepared the manuscript.

The study was done under the general supervision of George A. Graham, Director of Governmental Studies at Brookings. Interviewing was done by Mann and Doig, with the assistance of Mrs. Margery Rosen Boichel, Roger H. Davidson, Laurin L. Henry, Andrew J. M. Pierre, William L. Rivers, John Schott, Miss Frances M. Shattuck, and Bruce Smith, all of whom were on the Brookings staff at the time. Other interviewing was done by Emmette S. Redford and James A.

Robinson. Miss Deborah Bliss, Miss Suzanne Kirsch, Mrs. D. Lawrence-Toombs, George B. Looney, Mrs. Loma Moore, Mrs. Elizabeth Patton, and Mrs. Linda Polsby were responsible for secretarial work. Miss Barbara P. Haskins, the editor, also contributed substantially to resolving difficult questions of organization in presenting the research findings. The book owes much to her diligence, skill, and judgment. She was assisted in work on the manuscript by Miss Frances Shattuck.

Thanks are due to the reading committee, consisting of Roger W. Jones, Wallace S. Sayre, and Richard F. Fenno, for their advice and counsel, and to Joseph E. Winslow whose criticism was helpful at several stages. We are also indebted to the 350 interviewees for their cooperation and forthrightness.

The Institution is deeply appreciative of the financial support of the Carnegie Corporation, which made this study possible.

The conclusions reached are those of the authors and do not purport to represent the views of other Brookings staff members, officers, or trustees.

Robert D. Calkins
President

May 1965
Washington, D. C.

Contents

ix

1

Introduction

THIS BOOK is about an important group of political executives in the government of the United States: the second level who are appointed almost without exception "by and with the advice and consent of the Senate." About 650 executives held these positions during the four administrations of Franklin D. Roosevelt, Harry S. Truman, Dwight D. Eisenhower, and John F. Kennedy. They were responsible for the formulation and implementation of policies that had nationwide—even worldwide—significance, but the majority exercised their power in relative obscurity. Little is known about them as a group, where they came from, how they were recruited, how well qualified they were, and how efficient in office.

These second-rank officers have increased greatly in number and importance since Roosevelt's day. As government obligations change to meet society's current needs, as they become increasingly complex, the selection of the under secretaries and assistant secretaries becomes more crucial for effective federal operations. The number, the workload, and the responsibilities of these senior officials will probably change appreciably in coming decades and their role in politically sensitive decision-making become more prominent. Public concern over these presidential appointments is likely to grow. Indeed, more interest is being taken every day in the type of men chosen to run the government—and why they have been chosen. The purpose of the present study is to obtain a more accurate picture of the selection process for these second-level positions during preceding administrations and to gain some idea of the qualities of the men who have served as under secretaries and assistant secretaries. It is important to know how the system has worked in the past and what forces have influenced the recruitment pattern in order to appraise future needs and to suggest better ways of countering the major difficulties in finding and retaining competent and qualified men for high office.

Role of Assistant and Under Secretaries

"Appointive positions" in the federal government cover a wide range of differing activities and responsibilities, but those at the under secretary and assistant secretary level are a relatively coherent and unambiguous group.[1] The men who fill them are identified with the party and the administration of the President they serve (although they need not have been previously "active in politics"). They are presumed to speak for the secretary and the administration in their respective departments, and it is assumed that they will stand or fall with the administration. Nearly all are presidential appointees, holding office at the pleasure of the President and subject to dismissal at will. They expect and are expected to give leadership to the government. To a large extent they share with the department and agency heads the functions of political leadership in the executive branch. Under secretaries, assistant secretaries, and those of equivalent rank in the agencies have all this in common although their duties may vary from department to department, from agency to agency, and from administration to administration.

The allocation of responsibility and the determination of relationships within a department or agency depend in large degree upon the personality and experience of its chief. No two secretaries operate in precisely the same way; consequently, no two secretaries will organize their assistants in exactly the same way. Paul Appleby exaggerated a valid point when he observed that it is difficult for a department head "to bequeath anything of administrative value to a successor. He tends to build a structure wholly reflective of his own way of working, and its very novelty and history invite early abandonment of it."[2] No incom-

---

[1] The term "appointive positions" refers to positions filled at the discretion of the Chief Executive, outside the civil service laws, and generally with a policy-making "political" connotation.

[2] "Organizing Around the Head of a Large Federal Department," *Public Administration Review*, Vol. 6 (1946), p. 209.

ing cabinet member or agency chief has complete freedom in adjusting his managerial organization to his own style. There is, moreover, a tendency for the existing pattern of relationships to persist unless some crisis intervenes that leads to major reorganization similar to that which occurred in the State Department during and after World War II. Divisions have also been added or eliminated according to the current importance of certain subject areas. Witness the creation in 1957 of a Civil Rights Division in the Department of Justice.

The degree of relevant experience required of assistant secretaries, many of whom head divisions in various government departments and agencies, depends on their chiefs. It has been common practice for some time, however, to recruit men with a reasonable mastery of their subject for specific posts in the Treasury and Justice Departments. A relatively specialized background has also been particularly helpful in certain areas of Defense; and the provision in February 1962 of an additional assistant secretaryship in the Department of Commerce assigned to science and technology by the secretary perhaps foreshadows a similar demand for more assistant secretaries who know their relevant ABC's in other subject areas as well. Unfortunately, however, a large number of these political executive positions involve matters so disparate in character that no one individual can hope to bring to the position experience which is related to each subject. Technical skill may make only a limited contribution to job success. Thus, legal experience may be necessary for an assistant attorney general, but it is less obvious that an assistant attorney general for the Civil Rights Division must have had extensive experience in civil rights litigation in order to qualify for the office. In fact, for other reasons, active prior participation may disqualify him for such a post.

Regardless of the functions an assistant secretary or under secretary performs for any one assignment, he can never afford to overlook the political nature of his appointment and his role as a government organization man. This means that as an efficient subcabinet officer, he should meet certain minimum—extremely stiff—general requirements. He should possess a high capacity to master and understand complex programs; executive skills to be effective in a large organization; and acceptability to party officials, important interest groups, and certain congressional leaders. He should be tough enough to accept constant and frequently hostile surveillance by members and committees of

Congress. He should have some gift for public appearances and—last but not least—he should be a man of integrity. Besides all this, a certain proportion of these officers should add political strength to their respective administrations as attractive and respected public figures; and a few, at least, should be able to command support in party circles through their patrons.

For an incoming President and his recruiters to find—or retain in office—executives who meet these requirements is a hard task indeed. And there is no immediate prospect of its becoming any easier in normal times. That there are a number of men in American society who qualify is beyond doubt, but they are generally successful individuals in their own right who have already reached the top of the ladder in their occupations, and who are already socially, and probably politically, prominent. The majority would be unlikely to gain much in a practical or career sense from accepting such a political appointment below the cabinet level and with a meager salary measured by business and professional standards. The "best man available" tends to be the major criterion for the average recruiter rather than the "best man for the job."

Problems of Recruitment and Retention

The conditions under which political executives must be recruited in the United States are directly related to a political system that permits a change of administration every four years.[3] The fact that there have been only five party overturns since 1900 (in 1912, 1920, 1932, 1952, and 1960) in no way guarantees that they will be as infrequent in the future. As the top management of the government is now structured, in addition to the President and his cabinet, well over a thousand men of importance in the federal government face at least the possibility of being turned out of office after each presidential election. The staffing problem for the incoming President appears most acute at the time of administrative changeover, but this is the period also when there are more eager candidates for government service in the party ranks and when there are many capable and enthusiastic supporters for new policies and new programs. Later, as the administration ages, this

[3] The problems presented by political overturns in the twentieth century are discussed in Laurin L. Henry, *Presidential Transitions* (Brookings Institution, 1960).

source of political executive talent is reduced to a trickle and it becomes increasingly difficult to attract the desired type of recruit, especially for the key positions in the second echelon.

Indeed, although their essential role in government is acknowledged, methods of selection for the many under secretaries, deputy secretaries, assistant secretaries, and assistant agency heads needed to run the government have verged on the haphazard. Failure to secure the most desired appointees has been common; and among those appointed, tenure is often so brief that a number of incumbents have scarcely become more than casually acquainted with their jobs during their terms of office. This rapid rate of turnover compounds the problem of recruitment and has led, in many instances (especially late in a President's term of office) to vacancies in key political positions, thus short-circuiting the line of policy command and forcing subordinate career administrators openly into the political arena.

Recruitment

Filling these second-level jobs is much more than a routine recruitment job, no matter how arduous. It is one aspect of the struggle for political advantage, involving complicated relations (and frequently competition) among White House, department heads, Congress, major pressure groups, party organizations, and the shifting combinations of personal and political interests which they express. The "shortage" of political executives that seems to be indicated by difficulties in recruitment and unfilled public offices does not necessarily mean a shortage of either political or executive talent in the nation. It is rather a shortage of willing individuals who can somehow pass through the screen of varied, vague, and often conflicting eligibility requirements established by the numerous groups who often exercise veto power over appointments to these jobs. It is also a shortage of able men with sufficient dedication to public service to sacrifice secure and possibly affluent positions in their own communities for a somewhat precarious existence in Washington, which may expose them to more public criticism than they have known before. In short, there is no pool of men who are prepared, available, and identified as potential under secretaries or assistant secretaries. They have to be found.

This search for the right combination of experience and personal qualifications necessary for successful performance in political executive positions is often a difficult one. Inevitably, those involved in the search, or who are evaluating the records of those who are willing to serve, have to make judgments on the basis of some standards. These standards may be vague and imprecise, such as an interest in foreign affairs or a broad business background; or they may be quite technical when, for example, experience in debt management or in agricultural extension work is required. In other cases, the standards are political in character when active service in a campaign or active support of a senator is the ruling factor; or they may be related to the personal characteristics of an individual who has a brilliant mind or who is exceptionally skillful in his handling of people.

Personal qualifications and experience are only two of the criteria, however. Equal in importance are the needs of the agency. The abilities required in the high-level positions should complement each other. As one White House officer in the Eisenhower administration explained, all of the qualities required to manage a "cosmopolitan activity" must be considered in making any one appointment.

Retention

The time and attention devoted by department heads to the recruitment of their second-level personnel are a heavy tax on already overburdened schedules. But the energy invested in recruiting is returned with interest when the appointees prove to be conscientious, effective, and dedicated public servants. It is even more rewarding when capable executives devote an extended period of time to the public service.

The short tenure of many subcabinet officers creates serious obstacles to effective political leadership in federal agencies. Concern over turnover in the national security field prompted the Senate in 1960 to pass a resolution which stated:

> . . . it is the sense of the Senate that individuals appointed to administrative and policymaking posts should be willing to serve for a period long enough to permit them to contribute effectively in their assigned tasks. . . .[4]

Even though the rate of turnover has sometimes been exaggerated,

---

[4] S. Res. 338, *Congressional Record*, Vol. 106, Pt. 12, 86 Cong. 2 sess. (1960), p. 15705.

short tenure and its effect on a political executive's efficiency in office still remain an overriding personnel problem for the President and his department heads.

Men with long experience in the highest levels of the government have appealed for a change of the "in-and-out-in-12-months philosophy," referred to during the course of the hearings before the Senate Subcommittee on National Policy Machinery in 1960 by Roger Jones, long a distinguished career officer in the Bureau of the Budget and at that time chairman of the Civil Service Commission. Mr. Jones continued:

> . . . Whether we like it or not, the complexity of the job we have to perform today—and in this I can speak with complete authority—does not permit a man in a major policy post to make very much of a contribution, short of 1 year. It takes 6 months—literally that long —to get his feet on the ground, and another 6 months to get to know how the system works and to deal with the major issues, so that the full impact of his training and experience and everything else can make a contribution.
>
> There are thousands of personnel equations which have to be learned. There are thousands of methods of doing things which have to be mastered and which are quite different from those they have had before. After 12 months he is in a position where he can begin to make a contribution, and his contribution goes up in better than arithmetic progression thereafter every month he stays on the job.[5]

Jones warned that the frequent changes in policy officers had two effects on career officers: either they would refuse to commit themselves to any kind of policy or they would become careless and lackadaisical about their obligations. And Robert A. Lovett, Secretary of Defense in the Truman administration, testified:

> . . . It takes a long time for an able man, without previous military service of some importance and experience in government, to catch up with his job in this increasingly complex department [Defense]. At a guess, I would say he could pay good dividends to the Government in about two years. Meanwhile, of course, he is becoming a more valuable asset each day. To lose him before, or just as he becomes productive is manifestly a serious waste of the effort that went into his training.[6]

[5] *Organizing for National Security,* Inquiry of the Senate Subcommittee on National Policy Machinery of the Committee on Government Operations, 86 Cong. 2 sess. (1961), Vol. 1, p. 439.
[6] *Ibid.,* p. 17.

Availability

Despite the recruiter's desire to find the "best man for the job," he may not find such an obviously well-qualified person available. The American political system provides no systematic training ground for high executive office, and no clearly defined group from which to recruit political executives. Unlike a parliamentary system in which future subcabinet officers are educated for office in their parliamentary careers, the American system depends largely upon the private economy, the professions, or the universities for its political executives—proving grounds which differ from government service in important ways. The Task Force on Personnel and Civil Service of the second Hoover Commission pointed out:

> The capacities which are so essential in political executives are nowhere systematically developed in American life. American society has not bred executives for political leadership. America has not been Government-oriented during most of its history. Men have been preoccupied with their own affairs, their own business, their own group. It has been assumed that some ambiguous "they" would look after public affairs, or that representative government is an automatic process that needs little or no attention.[7]

Those responsible for recruiting political executives must range throughout American society, seeking to lure men and women from secure positions and lucrative and often exciting careers in private life. The area of recruitment is broader in the United States than in countries with a parliamentary system, but the problems of obtaining effective public servants are more severe because of the numbers required and because of the absence of a large enough group of people who regard a subcabinet appointment as an important career experience.

Those who might naturally be interested in executive service—civil servants and professional politicians—are generally precluded by the requirements of their own occupations and because they lack the necessary qualifications for political executive office in the eyes of those responsible for selection. The civil servant is often not seriously considered in executive selection for the very reason he is an effective civil

[7] Commission on Organization of the Executive Branch of the Government, *Task Force Report on Personnel and Civil Service* (1955), p. 40.

servant: his lack of public character and party identification. More-over, a foray into the political ranks may irrevocably commit him in the eyes of future administrations, resulting in an abrupt end to a prom-ising public service career. The practicing politician, on the other hand, is always identified with his party. Most frequently he looks to elective office, usually legislative office, for advancement. Needing a home base in his own constituency, he is reluctant to leave for an ex-ecutive post in Washington unless the position is sufficiently promi-nent to offset his absence from his own political arena. Recruiting officials, seeking people with some administrative experience and pol-icy expertise, also tend to look with suspicion on those whose chief qualification is commitment to the party.

The private sector, then, is the government's most fruitful recruit-ment source; but it is a difficult task indeed to pry the right type of man away from his home community and his own flourishing business or profession. Self-interest generally runs counter to a sense of public duty. Few who are qualified can maintain in Washington the standard of living and the level of participation in society to which they have become accustomed. The alleged failure of twentieth century America to produce statesmen of the stature of Washington, Franklin, Jefferson, and Hamilton has sometimes been attributed to the apotheo-sis of private enterprise and the adulation of those who seek first their own private interests. As David and Pollock suggest: "The basic difficulty seems to be motivational, and it probably reflects a failure on the part of the total society to instill a sufficient desire to contribute to the public service."[8]

Purpose and Scope of the Current Study

The existing system for appointing political executives has evolved during the course of the last century and a half. Its characteristics are not the result of fiat. Whatever its shortcomings may be, it has proved broadly acceptable to the contending interests and to the public at large—an advantage that could be sacrificed by ill-considered changes.

Nevertheless, changes in the recruitment process for political execu-

[8] Paul T. David and Ross Pollock, *Executives for Government* (Brookings Insti-tution, 1957), p. 27.

tives seem to be warranted. The "shortage" of qualified recruits for high-ranking executive posts just below cabinet level becomes more acute with each administration. It seems essential, however, that any suggestions for reform should be preceded by some analysis of the conditions under which present and past recruitment efforts have been carried on and by an assessment of the success in office—or lack of it— of those appointees actually chosen. Such an analysis is the purpose of this book.

The focus of the study is on the second echelon: on how appointments were filled at under secretary, assistant secretary, and deputy administrator levels during the period 1945 through 1961. A sample of such appointments was selected for intensive investigation from all ten cabinet departments and from seven of the agencies. Every effort was made to ensure its representative character.

It was decided not to draw a random sample of a specific number of appointments from each administration because it was presumed that the process used for selecting appointees at the beginning of any one administration would differ considerably from the process used for those nominated later on. Methods of recruitment were also expected to vary from department to department and from agency to agency. Appointments were therefore divided into cells and random selections were made from each cell. No discrimination was made between under secretary and assistant secretary appointments. The Eisenhower administration was divided by taking the first round of appointments in 1953 as one cell within each department and placing in a second cell all appointments made from the latter part of 1953 through March 1960, when the sample was taken (thus excluding Eisenhower appointments from March through December 1960). For the Truman administration no such time division was made because it would not have been meaningful, since he inherited a group of officials already in office. Later a sample of Kennedy appointments was also chosen from those made through 1961.

The 108 appointments thus selected were distributed as follows: 37 from the Truman administration, 21 from the first Eisenhower year, 26 from the remainder of the Eisenhower administration, and 24 from the Kennedy administration. The distribution by department and agency was: 17, Defense; 12, State; 9 each, Agriculture and Commerce; 8 each,

Treasury, Justice, Post Office, and Interior; 7, Health, Education, and Welfare; 6, Labor; 3 each, Bureau of the Budget and General Services Administration; 2 each, Office of Civil and Defense Mobilization, International Cooperation Administration, United States Information Agency, and Veterans Administration; 1 each, Housing and Home Finance Agency and Economic Stabilization Agency. The sample included 32 under secretaries, 60 assistant secretaries, and 16 deputy administrators.

Conduct of the Study

The personal interview was the chief means used to elicit information on the recruitment process for second-level positions between 1945 and 1961. Interviews were conducted with some 350 individuals over a period of two years with three specific objectives in mind.

The first objective was to obtain information on the 108 appointments selected for detailed investigation. Both the appointees and those involved in the appointments were interviewed. With the case study individuals themselves, questions were directed primarily toward the manner in which they were invited to join the government (occasionally their own attempts to obtain the position), their initial reactions to the offer, their efforts to obtain advice, the weighing of advantages and disadvantages of a political executive appointment, their later views of the job, reasons for leaving, and the effect of the position on their subsequent careers. Those involved in their selection were asked who was chiefly responsible for recruitment, whom the recruiter consulted to find candidates, what qualifications he was looking for and who evaluated them, what obstacles had been encountered, what kinds of clearance procedures had been required, and how well the political executives had filled the roles expected of them.

The second objective was to gain a broader perspective of the whole recruitment process as it operated during this period and to check the conclusions drawn from the case studies. In this instance, a much larger group of individuals were consulted who had been participants in making or influencing appointments during the Roosevelt, Truman, Eisenhower, and Kennedy administrations. They included members of the White House staff, department heads and their staffs, national party committee officials, senators and representatives, congressional staff members, interest group representatives, business leaders, and others who played informal roles in the identification and selection of candidates. Questions were designed to obtain information concerning the influence exerted on the recruitment process in general by the various institutions and individuals, their attitudes toward political executive appointments as distinguished from other political appointments, the environment in which they operated, and what they thought ought to be done to improve the recruitment process.

The third objective was to obtain additional appraisals on the general level of political executive performance. A group of forty-three raters, comprising department heads (occasionally under secretaries when the secretary was unavailable), career officers, and one congressional staff member, assessed the overall performance of 317 political executives and identified characteristics which they associated with success on the job. Usually individuals were rated by both career and noncareer officers within their departments. Assessments from two or more raters were procured for about 60 percent of these 317 political executives.

Sources of Recruitment, 1933-61

Since the focus of this study is a detailed examination of the recruitment process between 1945 and 1961, the 108 instances of appointment were carefully selected, as described above, to give as broad and comprehensive a picture as possible of the variations and differing procedures operating in each administration and in each department and agency. It was originally planned to include case studies of selected Roosevelt appointees, but it soon became apparent that reliable information was unobtainable because of the lapse of time. Nevertheless, to place the material from the 108 completed case studies in broader perspective, the analysis of recruitment patterns is prefaced by a general review of the education, social background, and experience of a larger group of federal political executives, expanded both by including more positions (not only the approximately 650 under secretaries, deputies, and assistant secretaries, but also some 150 cabinet secretaries, general counsels, and their equivalents in the major agencies, for a total of about 800), and by covering a longer span of time (from the earliest Roosevelt appointments in 1933 through the first round of Kennedy appointments to the end of 1961).[9] Following this review a brief comparison is made, department by department, of the actual sources of recruitment and how the appointees came to be chosen.

Reviewing the System

The concluding chapter reviews the testimony of recruiters and appointees on the selection process as it operated between 1945 and 1961, and attempts to draw the threads together into a fairly comprehensive picture of the existing system. It considers, within the context of this study's findings, various suggestions that have been put forward on how to improve the capacity of the federal government to attract the most highly qualified and experienced men and women into its ranks.

No revolutionary change in the system is envisaged. Modest adjustments to the existing selection process and to conditions of service are suggested which, it is hoped, will lead to a larger reservoir of potential executive talent from both the public and private sectors than at present exists. With certain modifications in current practices, such men who demonstrate superior ability may be able to remain longer without suffering either financially or professionally. And the selection system will be more adequately geared to relate interested and available men to positions for which they are qualified. The rewards of political executive office are great and interest in service is generally higher than is often assumed. The reduction in the imbalance between rewards and dissatisfactions will materially improve the federal government's drawing power.

[9] These generalizations and others used throughout this book are derived from the preliminary findings (for the years 1933-61) of a Brookings study by David T. Stanley, Dean E. Mann, and Jameson W. Doig, *Federal Political Executives, 1933-1965: A Biographical Profile*. The findings (and the generalizations used in the present book) cover cabinet secretaries, agency heads, general counsels, and commissioners in addition to under secretaries, assistant secretaries, and deputy administrators.

2

Sources of Recruitment, 1933-61

IN THEORY at least recruiters have stipulated fairly stringent requirements as to ability and related experience when reviewing the
field of potential candidates for assistant and under secretary posts.
And, indeed, the average second-echelon man has conformed more
closely to recruiters' criteria than he has generally been given credit
for during the past three decades. Despite their familiar and none too
complimentary labeling by political commentators and social histori-
ans over the years in the popular press, political executives have on
the whole had a better than average education, a higher than average
income, and displayed considerable executive initiative and professional ability in their various presecretarial careers. They have also,
more often than not, had a very fair working knowledge of government procedures through close if intermittent association with a variety of federal departments and agencies.

Nevertheless, popular political witticisms and somewhat unkind
character summaries have generally—but certainly not always—a grain
of truth behind them. It may be somewhat frivolous to categorize the
difference between a Roosevelt New Dealer and a Truman Fair
Dealer as about thirty pounds, and the difference between appointees
in the Eisenhower and Kennedy administrations as about thirty years
and a shift from "gentlemen's 'C' boys" to Phi Beta Kappas.[1] But certain characteristics do tend to occur more frequently among Truman
executives than among those chosen by Roosevelt, Eisenhower, or
Kennedy; and certain departments throughout all four administrations

[1] William V. Shannon, "The Kennedy Administration: The Early Months," *The
American Scholar* (Fall 1961), pp. 484-85.

have been fairly consistent in their choice of certain types of individuals as assistant secretaries from specific professional groups or occupations.

Many analyses of the backgrounds of political executives have been confined to relatively few examples, designed to establish the reality of an "elite" or an "establishment" permeating all important institutions of American society and effectively controlling the direction in which it moves. C. Wright Mills, for example, characterized the "second team" of the political directorate in his power elite in terms of a brief period in the Eisenhower administration:

> . . . These men usually have had fathers who were big businessmen; twelve attended Ivy League colleges; and they themselves have often been businessmen or bankers or the salaried lawyers of large corporations or members of the big law firms. Unlike professional politicians, they do not belong to the local jamboree of Elk and Legion; they are more often members of quiet social clubs and exclusive country clubs. Their origins, their careers, and their associations make them representative of the corporate rich.[2]

Because of these origins, these careers, and these associations, political executives become, in Mills' view, members of an informal conspiracy among economic, political, and military leaders which seeks to realize their coincidental interests.[3] With even less evidence, Floyd Hunter also saw an integrated power structure revolving around the corporate rich who "control the political machinery at all levels of government, when control is necessary to their functioning."[4]

With tongue in cheek, Richard Rovere describes an "establishment" in the United States as an amorphous grouping of men ranging in ideology from Walter Reuther on the left to President Eisenhower on the right that "fixes major goals and constitutes itself a ready pool of manpower for the more exacting labors of leadership." Its alleged influence is greatest in the executive and judicial branches of government, in education, organization, religion, and science, and in the new world of philanthropic foundations.[5] In contrast, Charles S. Hyneman observed in relation to the federal "establishment" that executive recruitment tended to operate outside the arena of party politics be-

[2] *The Power Elite* (Oxford University Press, 1956), p. 233.
[3] *Ibid.*, pp. 292-93.
[4] *Top Leadership, U.S.A.* (University of North Carolina Press, 1959), p. 252.
[5] "Notes on the Establishment in America," *The American Scholar* (Fall 1961), p. 490.

cause of the inadequacy of the party machinery to supply men qualified to run complex administrative machines, however loyal to the President and his program they might be, and because of the lack of public confidence in party leaders as government officials.[6]

Background and Experience

How do the facts bear out these and other common generalizations current in political circles today? How do they tie in with the recruitment pattern for the 800 executives during the years 1933-61? The pull and tug of widely differing political and pressure groups during the four administrations from Roosevelt through Kennedy has led to the appointment of men with a variety of personal attributes, backgrounds, and experience for more or less similar positions. A somewhat shadowy and often erroneous image of the actual men and women who held office during this period has been evoked—an image that has lent itself to caricature and to summary definition and that the Brookings study on which the generalizations throughout this section are based seeks either to authenticate or to correct.[7]

Personal Characteristics

Between 1933 and 1961, political executives were as a rule slightly older than their counterparts in the business and professional worlds. Many of them had, of course, already found their niche in private life and had achieved considerable prestige in their own occupational and social communities. Age is, therefore, an inadequate measure of success compared with other professions and occupations. In any event, a fairly large number came from the federal career ranks and these were slightly older than men bearing similar responsibilities outside the government, presumably because a long apprenticeship is indispensable for promotion from the civil service to federal political positions.

The typical appointee holding office during this twenty-nine-year period was about forty-eight years of age at the time of his first political executive appointment, compared with an age range of between forty-two and forty-seven years for business executives on their first

[6] *Bureaucracy in a Democracy* (Harper & Brothers, 1950), pp. 286-87.
[7] See note 9, p. 13.

senior appointment in private enterprises.[8] Cabinet secretaries coming directly from the private sector (whose appointments to the secretaryship had not resulted from step-by-step promotion) tended to be slightly older than their subordinates. Few at any secretarial level were below the age of thirty-five or over sixty-five on their first appointment. There was relatively little difference in median age among the four administrations. The span was only about five years (from forty-seven to fifty-two), Truman's executives as a group being the youngest and Eisenhower's the oldest. The most notable contrast appeared at the extremes of the age ranges, with Roosevelt tending to appoint more younger men (under thirty-five) and Eisenhower more older men (over sixty) than the other Presidents. The Kennedy administration, on the other hand, was remarkable not for its low average age but for its reluctance to appoint men over the age of fifty-five.

Each administration had its female representation at the second echleon. There were seldom more than one or two women serving as under secretaries, assistant secretaries, or deputy administrators in any one administration. The names of those who were appointed are consequently fairly well known. Ellen Woodward, for example, served Roosevelt as an assistant administrator of the Works Progress Administration before moving to the Social Security Board. Anna Rosenberg was the Assistant Secretary of Defense for manpower during Truman's term of office, and Bertha Adkins was Eisenhower's last Under Secretary of Health, Education, and Welfare. There was a marked increase in the total number of assistant secretary positions during the latter administration so there was a slightly larger female representation at that time than in earlier years. Katherine Howard was appointed by Eisenhower as Deputy Administrator of the Federal Civil Defense Administration. Esther Peterson was Kennedy's choice as head of the Women's Bureau and later she was also appointed an Assistant Secretary of Labor. All in all, however, the number of women serving during this twenty-nine-year period is singularly unimpressive.

Even less prevalent than women in top-level government posts were members of nonwhite races. J. Ernest Wilkins, appointed an Assistant Secretary of Labor during the Eisenhower administration, was actually the first Negro ever to be nominated for a secretarial position. When Kennedy chose Robert Weaver as Administrator of the Housing and

[8] W. Lloyd Warner and James C. Abegglen, *Occupational Mobility in American Business and Industry* (University of Minnesota Press, 1955), p. 137.

Home Finance Agency, there was a strong possibility that he would become the first Negro cabinet member. However, this did not materialize when Kennedy's plan to transform the HHFA into the Department of Urban Affairs failed in 1962. Another Negro, George L. P. Weaver (no relation), was given an assistant secretaryship in the Department of Labor during the same administration.

Geographic Associations

Both the general public and the practicing politician have always been in agreement that all sections of the country should be represented in an administration, and recruiters have been rightfully concerned if their choices, for political or other reasons, should lead to the domination of certain agencies by men from specific geographic regions. Nevertheless, appointments during these four administrations continued as in the past to mirror the major interests of certain parts of the country and the skills developed there that related to the needs of specific departments or agencies. They also continued to reflect relative party strength in different localities, with those areas that had consistently provided electoral majorities for a successful presidential candidate being rewarded by a higher proportional representation in his administration. This political influence was discernible in the relatively few nominees who came from the Midwest when the Democrats were in power (twenty-one of the twenty-nine years covered by the study) and the larger number appointed from that region by the Republicans. Understandably, the Democrats also tended to give greater favor than the Republicans to executives from the South, although not to the degree that might be expected from their historically unchallenged position in that area.

The geographic pattern of the birthplaces of these political executives tended to follow closely the population distribution in the year 1900, the census year nearest to their average birth date. But by the time they were called to public office, quite a few of them had moved away from the communities where they were born to establish legal residences, locate their places of business, and practice their professions elsewhere, the most marked movement being in the direction of the Middle and South Atlantic states.

These shifts in location can be explained by the strong tendency for men who later become political executives to attend the better known universities, particularly in the East, and to move into national organizations (including the federal government) whose headquarters pre-dominate in that area, notably in the District of Columbia. The latter alone provided twelve times the number of executives in proportion to its population size (1950 census), mainly at the expense of the Central and Southern states.

Although they displayed considerable geographic mobility in later years, tending to move from the country to the town, about half of these top-level government men were actually born in metropolitan areas at a time when about three-fourths of the population were still living in the country or in small-town communities of less than 25,000 (1900 census). A steady increase of city-born executives (from 45 per-cent to 55 percent) from the Roosevelt to the Kennedy administrations reflects a major population trend toward the towns apparent through-out the United States during the twentieth century. But, because the average political executive born about 1900 was more likely than a member of the general public to have spent his first few years in an urban setting, he presumably had a far greater awareness and appre-ciation of the problems of the city dweller than of the farmer and the rural worker. In this respect, he shared a similar background with the majority of business executives and stood in sharp contrast to United States senators who have had through the years a decidedly rural background.[9]

Education

The political executives who served between 1933 and 1961 were extraordinarily well educated when compared with the general popula-tion. They reflected, as might be expected, the educational standards of the elite groups of occupations from which they were primarily re-cruited. Nearly three out of four (as opposed to one out of twenty of the general public) had obtained college degrees. In each succeeding administration the percentage rose; two out of three Roosevelt ap-pointees had degrees, compared with nine out of ten under Kennedy. This steady rise in academic experience is largely due, of course, to

---

[9] Donald R. Matthews, in his *U.S. Senators and Their World* (University of North Carolina Press, 1960), pp. 16-17, found that a majority of the senators serving between the years 1947 and 1957 were born in rural areas. He concluded that senators were typically from smaller towns and cities which were both grossly overrepresented when compared with the population residing in those towns and cities in 1900. Only 13 percent of the senators were born in cities of 100,000 or more, as opposed to about one-third of the political executives.

rising educational standards throughout the United States and to the ever-increasing need for college degrees in a variety of occupations, especially for the men in leadership positions.

Over half of these 800 political executives had also obtained graduate degrees of some sort, the majority in law. The larger number of Ph.D.'s in the Kennedy administration and the slightly lesser number of those with only master's degrees was probably due to a general change in educational fashion. It might also indicate greater emphasis in later years on more advanced training for management positions, especially those involving complex technical problems. (The latter assumption was borne out by the material in the case studies.) Despite this tendency, nonetheless, those with law degrees were prominent in every type of position in all four administrations.

Since political executives were fairly representative of the United States population in distribution throughout the country, they attended a variety of educational institutions. But the overall picture that emerges, nevertheless, is one of a group of people which, besides having higher academic attainments, had also had a more exclusive and socially oriented education than is the rule for the general public. A much higher proportion attended private secondary schools, for instance, at least one-fifth compared to one-tenth of the total population. At the undergraduate level, appointees represented well over a hundred different colleges scattered throughout the United States, but there was a definite concentration in the Ivy League institutions. The "Big Three"—Yale, Harvard and Princeton—alone supplied the undergraduate education of nearly a quarter of the executives, as against only 4 percent of the total 1921 college graduate population. This emphasis was even more pronounced at the graduate level. About two-thirds of these public officials with postgraduate experience attended a group of seven schools. Harvard was clearly in the lead, primarily because of the Harvard Law School which trained one in ten of all the political executives who served during this period.

Religious Affiliations

Only the religious preferences of political executives at cabinet rank appear to be of concern to recruiters. A test of balance is usually applied at that policy level to maintain the representative character of the administration. This balance is of less importance for their subordinates whose private lives are not subjected to such critical public appraisal.

When the religious preferences of political executives are compared with those of congressmen, military leaders, business executives, and the United States population (1950 census), it appears that the Protestant domination typical of most leadership positions in American society extends into the ranks of political executives. Because of the sizable concentration of Catholics in urban centers, there is a larger Catholic representation among political executives than in the House of Representatives. But, compared to the percentage who have reached leadership positions in elective politics or in the professional military service, Jews have fared somewhat better in the executive branch although they are still far fewer in number than in the business world.

Assumptions of this nature, however, are based on data for relatively few of the appointees who served between 1933 and 1961. Generalizations for those appointed by the Roosevelt, Truman, and Eisenhower administrations, for example, are based on information for approximately 60 percent of the executives, and those for the Kennedy administration on slightly over 40 percent. From examination of their biographies, it appears that many members of certain religious faiths, notably Catholic and Jewish, failed to report their religious preference, and that another significant proportion of those not reporting undoubtedly had no religious affiliation at all.

Catholics numbered about a fifth of the political executives who declared their religious affiliation. In view of their traditional penchant for the Democratic ticket, it is not surprising that Catholics are more adequately represented in Democratic administrations, although in no administration did they achieve a proportion comparable to the national percentage of 34 percent of the population. It is possible, of course, that if all the Catholic appointees had reported their religious affiliation, the proportion would have been greater.

Catholics had larger representation in the Departments of Justice, Labor, and Post Office than elsewhere; and the relative infrequency of either Catholics or Jews in the Departments of Agriculture and Commerce undoubtedly reflects both geographic and occupational factors. Catholics, for instance, are poorly represented in the farm population of the West, Midwest, and South; and these regions form the Department of Agriculture's main recruiting ground.

Protestant churches of relatively high socioeconomic status—notably the Episcopal and Presbyterian—were much better represented among political executives than in the general population. For example, although Episcopalians numbered only 3 percent of the total United States population, they comprised approximately a quarter of the political executives. Presbyterians were also overrepresented among the appointees compared with the general public.

There is a clear tendency for those in religious faiths of high social status to be drawn toward the agencies of high prestige, which operate primarily in the area of national security and the Treasury Department. Other Protestant churches with less prestige (Methodists in particular) are much more prominent in the Departments of Agriculture and Health, Education, and Welfare, and in some of the independent agencies.

Organizational Ties

At least one out of every two political executives at this level was a member of one or more professional associations. The single most significant professional tie was with associations connected with the law; but a slightly larger proportion (just over one-third) belonged to either an educational or a research organization such as the National Education Association, the American Association for the Advancement of Science, or other similar societies. Few of these appointees obtained leadership positions in any of these associations. It was evidently important to recruiters only in connection with agricultural societies and trade unions. Over one-third of the nominees belonging to the latter two types of organizations had at some time or other held leadership posts, indicating that it might have been a factor in their nomination to a political executive position. This was particularly true of those belonging to agricultural societies in the Eisenhower administration.

Perhaps more than any other form of membership, affiliation with such groups as the Community Chest, Catholic welfare organizations, boys' clubs, and hospital boards indicates the degree to which men and women who later became political executives were already engaged in public life prior to appointment. Furthermore, such participation suggests a measure of concern for community affairs and social problems not commonly exhibited by members of the general public outside government circles. One in four of these appointees assisted in this type of welfare organization, the percentages running fairly even among the administrations but with Eisenhower's executives slightly in the lead and Kennedy appointees slightly behind. This type of community tie appeared to be particularly important for cabinet heads and those holding similar politically oriented positions, such as agency administrators and military secretaries, where public exposure is often of greater consequence than professional expertise.

Although the case studies illustrate the increasing emphasis given to ability and experience in the choice of government appointees during the last three decades, there is no doubt that, in the first place, personal contact between recruiters and those who know possible sources of potential executive talent still plays a very large role in the search for suitable candidates. Membership in social clubs, fraternal organizations, and civic groups provides a most effective liaison with potential executives. And an overwhelming majority of the political executives in every administration, except Kennedy's, had this type of personal contact as members of private associations that were fraternal, civic, or social in character. The most distinguishing feature about these memberships is the relatively low percentage who were Elks, Lions, or Eagles as compared with men who aspire to elective office. Belonging to such organizations as the Masons or Kiwanis or Rotary Club is almost a *sine qua non* for the legislative branch of government, for example, for United States senators.[10]

Prior Political Experience

Recruiters in every administration have emphasized their continuing concern for quality and experience in their recruitment practices, but it is inevitable that one of the most important standards in determining acceptability is party affiliation. None of the four administrations failed to appoint some members of the opposition party, but frequently these were "showcase" appointments or they were appointments involving individuals who were only nominal members of the opposing party. In some instances, particularly in the field of foreign affairs and defense, such appointments gave the government an aura of bipartisanship during crises. Nevertheless, the party machinery of both parties is geared to promote the candidacies of men and women who have pledged their political support in the past, and their appointments are often used to reduce the ideological conflict likely to

---

[10] Matthews, *op. cit.,* p. 43.

exist within a party by giving representation to all points of view. There is resistance, too, among opposition party members to participation in the rival administration.

At the second-echelon level, the Roosevelt administration was the least bipartisan and the Truman administration the most, while the Eisenhower administration appointed the largest number of men who had no professed party affiliation. Party support is generally taken for granted in most of the domestic departments, although two Republicans were appointed during both the Roosevelt and Truman administrations to the Departments of Commerce and Treasury. In the Department of Agriculture, however, not a single Republican was appointed during a Democratic administration and only one nominal Democrat was appointed when the Republicans were in office. As one would expect, no members of the opposition were appointed to the Post Office.

During the three Democratic terms of office, bipartisanship was most common in the military departments. The appointments of Frank Knox and Henry Stimson as civilian military chiefs just prior to World War II, and the appointment of Robert Lovett as Secretary of Defense in 1951, illustrate Democratic willingness to select members of the opposition party both for their ability and demonstrated competence and as symbols of national unity. Their selection at cabinet level frequently resulted in a series of appointments at subordinate levels which were relatively nonpolitical. Stimson, for example, brought John J. McCloy and Robert Lovett to Washington as his assistants. Robert Lovett later appointed as his deputy William C. Foster, a Republican who had served the Truman administration for a considerable period.

Traditional party activities, such as acting as delegate to national party conventions and making sizable contributions to political campaign funds, are not characteristic of those holding political executive office, except perhaps at cabinet level. About an eighth of the appointees served as delegates to either of the two conventions prior to their appointment. Other forms of party activity, such as active participation in the campaign, appear to be a much more significant consideration. The highest convention attendance per administration—nearly a quarter of the Kennedy appointees—probably reflects the tendency to reward men who had undoubtedly engaged in other important electoral activities with appointments at the beginning of a presidential term.

The importance of this form of political participation also varied from department to department. For example, about one out of four in both the Post Office and the Department of the Interior had been a convention delegate as against less than one in ten in the security agencies. The only exception in the latter was the Department of the Navy, in which a fifth of the appointees had attended conventions prior to appointment.

Limited information is available on contributions to campaign funds. During the Eisenhower and Kennedy administrations, department and agency heads were much more likely than their subordinates to have helped finance the presidential campaign with contributions of $500 or more. This was particularly true of executives appointed to the Departments of Commerce, Treasury, HEW, Defense, and Air Force; there were a large number of appointees in these departments with business backgrounds. Although political activity is always an important factor in appointments to the Post Office, few nominees during these two administrations appear to have had sufficient financial means to make sizable contributions to the campaign coffers.

Previous Career Patterns

One of the most striking facts about the 800 men appointed to political executive positions between 1933 and 1961 is their mobility. Few entered an occupation at an early age and remained in that occupation without exploring new avenues of activity and new careers. Many entered public service and interspersed periods of government work with their lifelong private pursuits. Quite a few, like Elmer Bennett and Charles Brannan (referred to later in the chapter), gave up their private professions or enterprises to devote themselves exclusively to the federal service. Others switched from legal practice to commerce, from engineering to management, from teaching to journalism, before accepting appointment as political executives.

If versatility, then, is one of the most distinguishing features of this group of appointees, what are the characteristics of this occupational mobility? What occupations—or combination of occupations—supplied the American political system with its largest potential sources of executive talent and to what extent did the supply from each source vary from administration to administration and from agency to agency? The complexity of the previous work histories of this group of exceptionally mobile individuals makes it impossible to define with accuracy specific career lines or trends in occupations characteristic of an administration or department. Some men branched out into so many areas of activity that they could with equal truth be identified as businessmen, bankers, lawyers, or public servants. Within the limitations that a few arbitrary definitions impose in this connection, however, certain key career characteristics are apparent at different periods and places.

Although the private sector as opposed to the public sector provided the majority of executives during these twenty-nine years, the government service was the single most important occupational background. Next came the business world which was the most prominent career source in the private sector, with the legal profession running a close second; the latter has occupied a strategic position in every form of politics for many years. Far behind as potential sources of executive recruitment are the other professions: educators, journalists, engineers, and scientists.

The representation and influence of the different occupational groups (with the possible exception of law) varied considerably with each administration and with the steadily growing expansion of federal activities. Businessmen, for example, were more prominent both in recruiting and in the political executive ranks between 1933 and 1961 than in earlier decades.[11] They were much more active in the administration of government than in its legislation, probably because of their extensive management experience. The converse was generally true of lawyers. Although their representation ran fairly steadily in all four administrations at about one-quarter of the total group, after 1938 they comprised a slightly smaller percentage than before—and considerably smaller than in pre-Roosevelt days. They never dominated administrative policies to the same extent as elective politics but competed on an equal basis with businessmen and public servants.

Attempts to balance representation of major occupational interests were apparent in all four administrations, especially when both primary and secondary career interests were taken into account. Nevertheless, the image of an administration is generally projected by its most senior officials. President Eisenhower's cabinet, for instance, was popularly termed the cabinet of "nine millionaires and a plumber" and, although the President continued to rely most heavily on businessmen to fill subordinate positions, he recruited a higher proportion of his lesser executives from other occupational groups. It is not sur-

[11] Arthur W. Macmahon and John D. Millett, *Federal Administrators* (Columbia University Press, 1939), pp. 290-94.

prising either that cabinet officers and administrators had more diversified career patterns than their subordinates. This accords with the tendency to recruit men for the top posts with liberal educational and professional backgrounds. In the specialized assignments at subcabinet level, on the other hand, focus on fewer areas of interest was more common.

The overall pattern of occupational backgrounds did not change significantly during the course of each administration. Each President —intentionally or unintentionally—retained the same type of representation to implement his political program in approximately the same proportions throughout his term of office. There were certain exceptions, notably the number of lawyers who left the Roosevelt administration prior to World War II, the gap in the political executive complement being more or less filled by government careerists. Lawyers, comprising about 40 percent of the group at the beginning of Roosevelt's term, had been reduced to under 20 percent by the war period. Career federal servants correspondingly increased from about one-fifth to two-fifths of the full complement. Truman's recruitment from government sources declined slightly during the course of his administration, despite acknowledged difficulties in recruiting from outside government sources. Eisenhower's appointees from the government ranks went up, on the other hand, from one-fifth to one-fourth of the appointees at these levels. The number of businessmen serving under Roosevelt and Truman changed very little throughout their administrations, but during Eisenhower's term of office there was a slight decline.

Variations from department to department in occupational backgrounds were generally indicative of the functions which these agencies were called upon to perform. In every administration, businessmen were naturally fairly prominent in the Departments of Commerce and Treasury, lawyers in the Department of Justice, and former government officials in many of the other domestic agencies. There was no predictable pattern for the security agencies except insofar as each administration relied on Foreign Service officers to fill numerous political posts in the State Department.

Public Service Background

The most likely primary or secondary career experience of political executives is the federal service. In fact, the commonly held view that these men came to their jobs without experience in public affairs is mistaken. Between 1933 and 1961, four out of every five of the first- and second-echelon appointees had had some form of prior government service at the national level, virtually all of them in full-time jobs. The few who had not worked full time were men and women with careers in private business and the universities who had a history of steadily growing participation in federal activities through part-time work on national advisory boards and as government consultants. The length of time and the degree of involvement varied materially, but even Eisenhower's executives, who were subjected to the most severe criticism for their alleged naïveté about public affairs and their absorption with business or professional interests, had had at least limited participation in government activities in three instances out of every four.

Approximately one-third of this group of about 800 executives had been public servants for the major part of their working lives and a quarter had chosen the federal service as a full-time occupation at some time or other in mid-career. In many instances, furthermore, this public experience was extremely diversified, involving more than one agency and a variety of activities.

For the most part, these executives had had employment in nonelective positions before their advancement to political executive office. Two good examples are Elmer Bennett, Under Secretary of the Interior in the Eisenhower administration, and Charles Brannan, appointed an Assistant Secretary of Agriculture at the end of the Roosevelt administration, later becoming Secretary of Agriculture under President Truman. Beginning his public career as an employee of the War Department in 1942, Elmer Bennett served successively as a trial attorney for the Federal Trade Commission, as an assistant to Senator Eugene Milliken of Colorado, and in the Department of the Interior as legislative counsel, assistant to the Secretary, and Solicitor, before becoming Under Secretary. Charles Brannan started with a Denver law practice in 1929, became an attorney for the Resettlement Administration in the Department of Agriculture in 1935, later served as an attorney in the Solicitor's office, then as regional director and assistant administrator of the Farm Security Administration until, in 1944, he was appointed an Assistant Secretary of Agriculture.

The mobility within the government that these two appointments from the Eisenhower and Roosevelt administrations illustrate was apparent also in both the Truman and Kennedy administrations, when about 40 percent of the political appointments were filled by executives who had had previous experience in another government agency prior to their secretarial appointment. Whether in the federal service on short- or long-term assignments, their qualifications and ability were readily visible to recruiters.

The overall pattern that emerges for every type of political executive position, therefore, is one where the most common route for advancement is from one subordinate executive position outside the career service to a presidentially appointive position. This has often meant the promotion of an assistant to the secretary to an assistant secretaryship or of a politically appointed bureau chief to a position at secretarial level. Another frequent form of appointment was promotion from the career ranks and shifts within the political executive ranks themselves—from an assistant secretaryship to an undersecretaryship or from an undersecretarial position to a cabinet post. Such shifts, however, were less frequent in the domestic departments and agencies than in the security agencies (State and Defense). One has only to recall the careers of such men as James Douglas, Thomas Gates, Donald Quarles, William Foster, and Robert Lovett, all of whom served as Deputy Secretary of Defense, to recognize the extent of these transfers in the military establishment. Such transfers make the figures for tenure in individual positions appear extremely short but presumably these were promotions in recognition of proven merit.[12] Only rarely did such changes involve diminution in rank.

The executive branch supplied the recruiters with its most promising government source for candidates. Few men with prior experience in other branches of the public service became senior appointees. The separation of powers custom prevented easy transference from the legislative to the executive branch, and most men tended to choose either one or the other form of public employment. Those few who had had elective experience tended to have extended terms of service after switching to the administrative side. There were also cases of "deserving" legislators who lost out in current elections and looked to the executive branch for suitable positions commensurate with their importance to their parties.

[12] The Subcommittee on National Policy Machinery of the Senate held up the Deputy Secretary of Defense position as an example of excessive turnover, failing to give any weight to the fact that the occupants of this position had had an average of 4.5 years of government service prior to appointment as Deputy. *Resolution Expressing Concern of Senate over Turnover in Administrative and Policymaking Posts*, S. Rept. 1753, 86 Cong. 2 sess. (1960). See also Chap. 7, p. 229.

The focus of attention of potential political executives has always been primarily on national affairs rather than on local affairs; and the extent to which participation in the latter prepares an individual for national service is at best uncertain. It is reasonable, however, to assume that a state or local official becomes familiar with the interplay of forces involved in policymaking and administration common to all levels of government. Nearly 40 percent of these federal political appointees had had some form of state or local service, the majority in nonelective positions that most closely corresponded to later federal assignments. The relatively small number who had had prior experience in state elective politics adds further weight to the conclusion that men seldom mix elective and administrative politics.

Chief Business and Professional Interests

Background information on the private careers of the 800 political executives was broken down into some 20 categories according to type of business, profession, or vocation. Many of these, such as farmers, union executives, and blue-collar workers, formed such a very small proportion of the total number of executives in each administration as to be of little use in any statistical evaluation of career patterns. Others, however, particularly in relation to business interests, have a distinct bearing on the types and personalities chosen for office during this period and merit further study as to the general pattern of recruitment and variations among agencies.

FIELDS OF BUSINESS. Nearly half of some 250 political executives formerly engaged in private business pursuits had been executives in manufacturing companies. Their familiarity with large-scale management and personnel problems appeared to make them eminently suitable candidates for political appointments.

One important aspect of the recruitment from the ranks of big business relates to the firms with large defense contracts. Since World War II, and particularly at the beginning of the Eisenhower administration, questions have been raised about the relationships between large government contractors and the agencies with which they do business. Allegations that companies seek to place their men in strategic government positions in order to protect their interests were raised in clear-cut form on the occasion of Charles E. Wilson's appointment as Secretary of Defense.[13] Nevertheless, representatives of government con-

[13] See Chap. 5, pp. 134-52, on Senate confirmation of appointments.

tractors comprised a very small proportion of the total number of persons appointed to high policy-making posts during this period. They tended to be concentrated in the defense-related agencies, though they included only about 4 percent of such appointees during the Roosevelt, Truman, Eisenhower, and Kennedy administrations.

Second to manufacturing concerns in importance to recruiters were the financial institutions—the commercial and investment banks and the investment companies. Consistently prominent in the Treasury Department, former bankers also constituted about one-fifth of all political executives appointed during this period by the Army and Navy Departments. Slightly fewer bankers were among the first appointees during Kennedy's term of office than during the other three administrations, but their specialist knowledge was obviously in demand by all four Presidents. The preponderance of investment bankers was perhaps occasioned by the relative ease with which such bankers could temporarily divorce themselves from their private interests—and their partners—without sacrificing advancement opportunities. It was perhaps also due to the nature of the investment bankers' training in analyzing complex business and industrial situations.

Even more remarkable than the preponderance of corporation executives and bankers among these ex-businessmen is the very small representation of the marketing and distribution industries. Except for agriculture, forestry, and fisheries, the largest number of separate enterprises in any field of private economic activity lies in the wholesale and retail trades. This lack of representation may be because the problems likely to confront the manager of a private retail sales company appear to bear little relationship to those facing an executive managing public enterprises which, in effect, produce a product, regulate, or provide some kind of service. It is also possible that the competitive conditions under which these retail sales managers have to operate preclude long-term absences on public service without serious injury to individual career prospects.

TYPES OF PROFESSIONS. Lawyers predominated among the professions in all four administrations, numbering about a quarter of all the federal political executives. Nearly all were in private practice, the majority associated with well-established partnerships, few with the nation's leading law firms. Only four of the group under review were practicing corporate lawyers, although it is more than possible that there were quite a number of other executives who had begun as corporate lawyers or been retained by corporations and later become businessmen in their own right before accepting public appointment.

Of the other professions, educators were the best represented, but with considerable variation from administration to administration, ranging from 3 to 10 percent of the total. The majority had been college professors, a few had been administrators; but there was only one whose major career had formerly been in teaching at the high school level. Five percent of Kennedy's executives were in engineering or science, as opposed to less than 3 percent for the other three administrations. There were only two representatives of the medical and dental professions altogether, and they were appointed by Eisenhower.

Although the proportional representation of the other professions is very small as against the preponderance of former government employees, businessmen, and lawyers, both Kennedy and Eisenhower showed greater inclination than their predecessors to appoint a diversified group of professional people.

Variations Among Agencies

The above brief review of the most common personal and career characteristics of the 800 men who held office from 1933 to 1961 has revealed marked differences among departments and agencies. These differences have been observed both in regard to the type of individuals recruited and in the policies and pressures that have exerted an influence on Presidents and department heads in their choice of subordinates. Before analyzing recruitment patterns, processes of selection, and the conflicting pressures influencing appointments, here is a brief survey of the backgrounds and experience of many of the people who actually held office during these four administrations.

State and Defense: Professionals and Professional Amateurs

In the Departments of State and Defense, the emphasis on previous government service and relevant experience is more pronounced than in other agencies. Many of the executives who served in these departments during this period may be characterized as "professional amateurs" in that they had spent a considerable portion of their mature lives within the government or closely associated with its activities.

While not government careerists, they were nevertheless remarkably well versed in the duties of their office—in fact, the Bureau of the Budget is probably the only other government agency with a higher percentage of executives with previous service at the political executive level. The proportion was very high in the Department of State. In the Department of Defense, too, there were a considerable number who had held responsible positions in uniform during World War II that had a direct bearing on their later recruitment to political executive office. Membership in the party controlling the administration was certainly a factor in most of these appointments, but there was a much higher representation of the opposition party in these security agencies than in the domestic agencies, particularly during the Democratic administrations. The testimony of department heads concerning the freedom they had to select their appointees regardless of political party corroborates the statistical evidence based on biographical data.

The following examples illustrate the relevance of previous experience for recruitment within these two departments:

Charles S. Thomas: Under Secretary of the Navy, Assistant Secretary of Defense, Secretary of the Navy, 1953-1957. Primary occupation: president of a large retail clothing company on the Pacific coast. Relevant experience: naval aviation, 1918-19; special assistant to the Assistant Secretary and the Secretary of the Navy, 1942-45. Republican.

Dean Rusk: Assistant Secretary of State, Deputy Under Secretary of State, 1949-51, Secretary of State, 1961-. Former college professor; army officer, 1940-46; special assistant to the Secretary of the Army, 1946-47; Director of the Office of United Nations Affairs, Department of State, 1947-49. Democrat.

Carlisle H. Humelsine: Deputy Under Secretary of State, 1950-53. Previously associated with the University of Maryland and Colonial Williamsburg; member of military secretariat, United States Army, attending Quebec, Yalta, Malta, and Potsdam conferences, 1941-45; Director of Office of Departmental Administration and Executive Secretary of the Department of State, 1946-50. Democrat.

Frank Nash: Assistant to the Secretary and Assistant Secretary of Defense, 1951-54. Lawyer, Washington, D.C.; Naval officer, 1941-46; special assistant to the Secretary of the Navy, 1946; special assistant to the Secretary of Defense, 1948-49; deputy United States representative to the Commission on Armaments, United Nations, 1949-51. Democrat.

Francis O. Wilcox: Assistant Secretary of State, 1955-61. Former college professor; chief international relations analyst, Library of

Congress, 1945-47; Chief of Staff, United States Senate Foreign Relations Committee, 1947-55. Republican.

Such emphasis on previous experience did not, of course, preclude politically oriented appointments, but it often made it harder for the administration to gain acceptance for its nominees from the department heads. President Truman may have made life difficult for Secretary of the Navy James V. Forrestal, but only in exceptional cases was he successful in overcoming the resistance of the top Navy executives to highly political appointments. Most of the positions were filled, in any event, by political appointees who had also had considerable experience that related to their executive duties. John L. Sullivan was a "deserving Democrat," but he had had four years' experience as Assistant Secretary of the Treasury before entering the Navy Department. Edwin Pauley was also a politically active Democrat, with an excellent record in handling reparations matters for the federal government, but his nomination was withdrawn because of senatorial opposition to his being an oil corporation executive.[14]

Donold Lourie, Under Secretary of State for Administration, and Fred Seaton, an Assistant Secretary of Defense, were "deserving Republicans" appointed at the beginning of the Eisenhower administration. Lourie was an executive of the Quaker Oats Company, with no government experience. He was the son-in-law of the treasurer of the Republican National Committee, and had taken an active part in the 1952 campaign. Ostensibly, he was recruited because of his managerial experience to bring order to the Department of State which, according to its Republican critics, was much in need of reorganization. Fred Seaton's Defense appointment was in the main due to his 1952 political service, but he was given a public affairs post which was directly related to his broadcasting and publishing experience in Nebraska.

Testimony of top officials in the Defense establishment during the Truman, Eisenhower, and Kennedy administrations confirmed the fact that recruiters tended to consider business experience as highly relevant to political executive service in military agencies and relied on the business community both for recruits and as contacts in the recruitment process. Nearly half of the Defense appointees in the four administrations under review had such a background as opposed to a quarter of the domestic executives.

[14] See Chap. 5, p. 149; also Robert G. Albion and Robert H. Connery, *Forrestal and the Navy* (Columbia University Press, 1962), pp. 211-16.

One under secretary who acted as the chief recruiter for his military agency in the Eisenhower administration declared he had assembled the "finest team you ever saw." He traveled all over the country chiefly to interview businessmen and to evaluate the qualifications of an original list of 100 men. His choices reflected the general Eisenhower approach to recruitment for a military establishment. One appointee, who supervised the agency's aviation responsibilities, had been a pilot during World War II and a high-ranking officer in an airline since the war. Another, who took on the management of materiel and supply, had recently retired from a large merchandising company. A third, who was appointed to the financial post in the agency, had had an extensive background in business and finance and had served as special assistant to the Secretary of Defense. Two others who were appointed had been investment bankers with distinguished records in the uniformed service during World War II. All were "qualified Republicans," but brought to their positions considerably more than partisan affiliations. Their performance on the job is indicated by the fact that three of them became agency heads later in the Eisenhower administration.

In the Department of State, a practice developed of balancing political executive appointments between Foreign Service officers and noncareer appointees. Most frequently, the former were appointed to regional desks and took on responsibility for policy development and coordination in certain parts of the world, or they were appointed to administrative positions at the secretarial level. There was a somewhat greater tendency to elevate Foreign Service officers to political executive positions under Eisenhower than in the Democratic administrations. But Kennedy again preferred noncareer appointees, possibly because of the identification of Foreign Service officers with the previous administration. The case studies suggest, however, that once an administration has worked with and relied upon its career officers, both in the field and within the department, it gains a far greater respect for their abilities and is more willing to appoint them to political positions.

There is no real evidence to support the assumption that senior Foreign Service officers relish assignments as assistant secretaries, although in fact those who occupy such positions are almost always given important ambassadorial assignments after their secretarial service. In effect, they tend to take these assignments as obligations to the Foreign Service, not as a form of promotion. Trained chiefly in diplomacy and in conducting the government's business abroad, such officers are often reluctant to take on the chores of as highly structured a bureaucracy as the State Department, and to support a much lower standard of living than that to which they are accustomed abroad.

Ambassadors are to a certain extent exceptions to the general rule. Many today are career Foreign Service officers, but there are still some who are appointed for political reasons. Posts such as London and Paris are often given to those who have made significant political contributions. The appointment of Winthrop Aldrich as ambassador to Great Britain during the Eisenhower administration was a case in point.

Recruitment for the Department of State has been largely restricted to the foreign policy community and has included those already in the department; other government officials with experience in foreign policy matters, such as those in the legislative committees on Capitol Hill; major eastern universities; banking and legal circles, particularly those involved in international law and finance; and other private organizations dealing with foreign policy, such as the Council on Foreign Relations. Occasionally, recruitment efforts were made beyond this somewhat restricted circle of specialists, particularly in the realm of business, but these were seldom satisfactory. In a very few instances, appointees were accepted by State Department officials at the request of members of Congress or the President.

One interesting side issue of the emphasis on experience in the security agencies is that, at the beginning of both the Eisenhower and Kennedy administrations, executives from the former administrations remained in office during the transition periods. In 1953, Secretary of Defense Charles Wilson retained the services of Frank Nash and Wilfred McNeil. Secretary of the Navy Robert B. Anderson kept on John F. Floberg and Secretary of the Army Robert T. Stevens kept Earl Johnson. John Foster Dulles continued to use John D. Hickerson, H. Freeman Matthews, and Henry A. Byroade, who were all officers in the Foreign Service. In the Kennedy administration, no political executives were held over in the Department of Defense, but Richard S. Morse in the Department of the Army, James H. Wakelin, Jr., in the Department of the Navy, and Joseph Charyk and Lyle S. Garlock in the Department of the Air Force were all retained. In the Department of State, the Kennedy administration kept on Foy D. Kohler and Edwin

M. Martin who were both originally appointed in the Eisenhower administration. In no other agencies in the Eisenhower or the Kennedy administrations was the practice of retaining appointees of the previous administrations so prominent.

Because of the relatively small number of appointees involved in the independent agencies operating in the defense and foreign affairs field, no clear recruitment pattern can be perceived. Nevertheless, as in other independent agencies, party service appears to play a very large role in the selection of executives. Indications of this are found in the appointment of Abbott Washburn as Deputy Director of the United States Information Agency in 1954, as a result of his service in the Citizens for Eisenhower organization during the 1952 campaign. Similarly, Donald Wilson was appointed to the deputy post in USIA after the 1960 Kennedy campaign. In each case, however, the appointees had had some experience in the communications field: Washburn as an official for General Mills dealing with public services and as the executive vice-chairman of Crusade for Freedom, and Wilson as a correspondent for *Life* magazine. In the foreign aid agency there is no clear pattern. Men from a wide variety of backgrounds have held executive positions in the Economic Cooperation Administration and its various successors.

Treasury: The Specialists

Recruitment for the Department of the Treasury has, in recent years, been predominantly a search for men in the banking and legal fields who appear to have the specialized knowledge and experience to perform specific functions within the department. These two professions (finance and law) supplied the Treasury with approximately three-quarters of its executives between 1933 and 1961, whereas the government service contributed only one in six of the total number during this period, the lowest for any department.

This current pattern of Treasury appointments with the emphasis on technical expertise differs markedly from the pattern of earlier periods. Even in the years just before World War II Macmahon and Millett found that three-quarters of the Treasury appointees were politically oriented and that few of them had made a name for themselves either before or after their Treasury service. Except for Roswell Magill and Thomas Jefferson Coolidge who served as Under Secretary in 1937-38 and 1934-36 respectively, few executives had had concrete experience that was relevant to their responsibilities in the department.

Since 1933 when President Roosevelt brought Henry Morgenthau with him from New York, Treasury secretaries have had exceptionally good standing with their respective Presidents and have been given considerable freedom in the choice of their subordinates. With their chief aides to assist in evaluating candidates, secretaries have generally sought out their own recruits. John Snyder, George Humphrey, Robert Anderson, and Douglas Dillon in the Truman, Eisenhower, and Kennedy administrations all had executive experience in the business, banking, and financial worlds and could rely on a wide range of contacts to provide them with a supply of candidates. Organized interest groups, such as the American Bankers Association (ABA), seldom played an important role in the selection process. Individual secretaries would call on particular ABA officials or on one of its member banks for assistance but the organization was seldom used as a formal recruiting organization.

Appointments made by George Humphrey and Douglas Dillon at the beginning of the Eisenhower and Kennedy administrations show clearly the present tendency to recruit men of high technical ability with appropriate financial backgrounds.

George Humphrey, for example, appointed as his Under Secretary one of the leading tax experts in the country, Marion B. Folsom of the Eastman Kodak Company. Folsom had previously served as a member of the President's Advisory Council on Economic Security in 1934-35 and was one of the chief authors of the 1935 Social Security Act. He had been staff director of the House of Representatives Special Committee on Post-War Economic Policy and Planning, had served on both the Social Security Advisory Council of the Senate Finance Committee and the Business Advisory Council of the Department of Commerce, and had also acted as chairman of the Committee for Economic Development. He had a fine reputation with both parties as an intelligent, clearheaded, modest public servant. As a political independent, he would have been acceptable to either the Republican or Democratic party. Secretary Humphrey also appointed W. Randolph Burgess first as his deputy and later to a new post as Under Secretary for Monetary Affairs. Burgess had an established reputation as an expert in debt management through his long service in the Federal Reserve Bank of New York City and, later, the National City Bank of

New York. As a third assistant responsible for international finance, Humphrey retained the services of Andrew N. Overby who had been appointed late in the Truman administration. Overby's background included experience in foreign banking both as special assistant to the secretary dealing with international finance and as a senior official in the International Monetary Fund. The only Humphrey appointee who was not a specialist was H. Chapman Rose, a prominent Cleveland lawyer; his law firm had long advised the M. A. Hanna Company of which Humphrey was chairman of the board.

The Treasury appointees at the beginning of the Kennedy administration presented a similar recruitment picture with emphasis on technical background. When Douglas Dillon moved over from the Department of State, he brought with him John M. Leddy, a specialist in international economic affairs. Leddy had headed—or been a member of —many American delegations to international trade conferences in Europe, Latin America, and the Far East. Typical of the meetings he attended were those on the General Agreement on Tariffs and Trade, and on specific economic and financial assistance programs to individual foreign countries. To deal with tax matters Dillon recruited a professor of law at Harvard University, Stanley Surrey, who had also had extensive experience in the federal government, including the Treasury Department during the war and as special counsel to the House Ways and Means Committee. He had written extensively on federal taxation issues, which brought him a certain amount of criticism as well as fame, and made him a target for barbs from Republican members of the Senate Finance Committee. Robert V. Roosa, an economist and an official of the Federal Reserve Bank of New York, was appointed to deal with debt management. Even Dillon's Under Secretary, Henry H. Fowler, who was more renowned for political party activities and his service in the Truman administration than for his financial know-how, had recently served as a member of the Commission on Money and Credit before his Treasury appointment and had a gift for finding points of agreement and for friendly persuasion—very valuable in minimizing conflicts when transacting public business.

Not all the political positions in the Treasury Department require the type of specialist skills that the above examples indicate. Supervision of activities in the Bureau of Engraving and Printing, the Narcotics Bureau, the Secret Service, and the Customs Service requires broad administrative ability rather than technical knowledge. Very often,

lawyers have been called upon to shoulder responsibility for these bureaus. Moreover, it appears that, even since World War II, political
considerations have still played an important part in some of these
Treasury appointments. In the Eisenhower administration, for example, Elbert P. Tuttle, David Kendall, and Fred Scribner, who were
all appointed as General Counsel of the Treasury, were lawyers who
had held high positions in their respective state party organizations.
Both Kendall and Scribner were later promoted to assistant secretary
and under secretary posts, and Kendall concluded his government service on the White House staff.

Justice: Politics and the Law

As the chief legal agency of the federal government, the Department of Justice has, of necessity, to recruit lawyers for its senior executive posts. This is not as occupationally restrictive as might generally
be supposed, since the legal profession has furnished more men for all
branches of politics than any other professional group. Justice appointees are, therefore, more likely to have a history of political activity than those in State, Defense, or the Treasury. Nine out of ten of
the 125 assistant attorneys general who served from 1859 through 1938
had held some form of political office prior to their Justice appointment.[15]

A large proportion of the deputy and assistant attorneys general
were also former government servants. In fact, during the Roosevelt,
Truman, and Eisenhower administrations, over half were already fed-
erally employed when they were nominated for political office. Their
most typical previous public service was in a subordinate noncareer
capacity in the Justice Department itself, probably in the specialist
area where they had proved their ability and could regard their presidential appointments as a form of promotion.

The Justice appointments made during the Truman administration
that followed this characteristic pattern most closely nevertheless involved appointees who had initially been chosen mainly for political
considerations. These political forces were most apparent in cases
where an individual was appointed as a United States attorney and
later elevated to an assistant attorney general post. Appointments to

---

[15] Macmahon and Millett, op. cit., p. 288.

United States attorney positions are largely under the control of senators and state party organizations and are highly prized as political rewards in most states.

The style of recruiting during these four administrations depended very much on the particular Attorney General in office. Men like Howard McGrath, a Truman appointee who had formerly been a governor and senator from the state of Rhode Island and had also served a two-year term as chairman of the Democratic National Committee, tended to respond strongly to party interest in making appointments. This meant that in looking for candidates, he—and the other Attorneys General like him—tended to rely primarily on members of Congress, governors, and party officials in the states. Those who received appointments, therefore, were generally men who could muster political support or who were on good personal terms with the Attorney General. This did not necessarily preclude the appointment of some very able lawyers; it reflected primarily a willingness to work within the political machinery to find talent and to recognize political acceptability or activity as an important criterion of selection.

In contrast to McGrath, Attorneys General Herbert Brownell and William P. Rogers of the Eisenhower administration tended to search for legal talent from many parts of the nation and from institutions not necessarily involved in party politics. For example, a number of appointees were recruited from the law schools primarily for their legal specialty and not because of any performance in the political arena. Both Brownell and Rogers, his former deputy, had been active in the 1952 Republican campaign and enjoyed the confidence of the President. They were therefore given wide discretion in the selection of their subordinates.

The American Bar Association played a role for the Justice Department similar to that played by the American Bankers Association for the Treasury. Officials or individual members evaluated candidates as a personal favor to the recruiter but no formal procedure was adopted comparable to the one followed when the selection of judges was under consideration.

This emphasis on specialized legal knowledge is apparent in varying degree in all administrations, regardless of the Attorney General in power. It is most notable in certain divisions like the criminal division, where those who take charge have usually had extensive experience in criminal practice prior to their appointment. In the Truman administration, Alexander Campbell, T. Lamar Caudle, and Thomas Quinn had all been United States attorneys and James McInerny had already seen many years' service in the criminal division itself. Tom Clark was the exception, although he had had a considerable legal experience in other branches of the department. In the Eisenhower administration, Warren Olney had long been active as a county and state prosecutor, in state crime studies, and as a teacher of law and criminology in California. His two successors, Malcolm Anderson and Malcolm Wilkey, had both been United States attorneys.

A long history of prior experience is common to the antitrust division also, although not generally in antitrust work. Most Truman appointees had already served many years in the Department of Justice before their political appointments. Both Wendell Berge and Herbert Bergson, for instance, had been in the department more than a decade before being appointed assistant attorneys general in charge of this division. Graham Morrison took over the antitrust post in 1950 after a career that included private practice in Virginia and New York, an assignment with the War Production Board, and following World War II successive positions in the Justice Department, first as special assistant to the Attorney General and then as head of the civil division. In the Eisenhower and Kennedy administrations, the trend ran strongly toward the recruitment of judges for this position. Stanley Barnes, Victor Hansen, and Lee Loevinger were all state court judges prior to their appointments. The reason for this search for candidates from the ranks of the Justice employees and from the bench probably stems from the difficulties encountered by recruiters in obtaining the services of experienced antitrust lawyers. Such lawyers are more often than not already involved in cases which would make it difficult for them to change sides and become the federal government's prosecutor. They probably also recognize that, once having held this office, their freedom of action would probably be limited for a year or two after resuming private practice.

No such clear recruitment pattern is revealed in other divisions. It is generally considered, for example, that the post of Assistant Attorney General in charge of the Office of Legal Counsel requires the talents of an eminent legal scholar; but although both Robert Kramer and Nicholas Katzenbach were former university professors, Wilson White had been a United States attorney and J. Lee Rankin was in private practice in Lincoln, Nebraska. Similar variations are found in the tax, civil, civil rights, public lands, and internal security divisions, and in the office of alien property (which was headed by an assistant attorney general from 1947 to 1961).

Although there was general recognition of the need for specialist legal abilities in certain Justice divisions, Truman and Eisenhower recruiters tackled the problem somewhat differently. Truman's emphasis on prior public experience, usually in a legal capacity, is illustrated below and gives multiple instances of service:

POSITION	NUMBER
Justice Department official (usually as assistant to the attorney general)	14
United States attorney or assistant	9
Legal officer in another federal agency	3
County or state attorney	2
Congressman	1
National party official	1

Perhaps not untypical was the career of Douglas W. MacGregor who served both as an assistant attorney general and as the assistant to Attorney General Tom Clark. A Houston lawyer and a former chairman of the Harris County Young Democrats, MacGregor had also served in the southern district of Texas as an assistant United States attorney from 1927 to 1934 and a United States attorney from 1934 to 1944. In 1946, he was appointed an assistant attorney general and later that year became the Assistant to the Attorney General, then the third ranking post in the department. (The Solicitor General ranked second.) Another example is Herbert A. Bergson, with the Department of Justice from 1934, who was assistant attorney general in charge of the antitrust division from 1948 to 1950. Beginning his government career as a trial attorney, he was promoted consecutively to assistant chief and chief of the legislative division. He then served as a special assistant and legal consultant to the Attorney General until his presidential appointment in 1948. Peyton Ford had also been a public official both in his native state of Oklahoma and in Washington before becoming Deputy Attorney General. After practicing law in Oklahoma City, he served as assistant attorney general of Oklahoma. Military service in World War II was followed by an appointment as a special assistant to the Attorney General, and later promotion to the assistant attorney general post in charge of the claims division. From 1947 to 1951, he was Assistant to the Attorney General and then Deputy Attorney General when the title was changed by Reorganization Plan No. 2 of 1950.

The recruitment pattern in Justice during the Eisenhower administration, on the other hand, can be regarded in part as a reaction to the opprobrium heaped upon the department in the latter days of the Truman administration. Charges involving favoritism and incompetence reaching up to the highest levels had brought the agency into disrepute, and the Eisenhower administration deliberately set a course to guarantee a higher standard of competence and morality in the department. This did not mean that the Eisenhower recruiters ignored political considerations. They were looking for Republicans as avidly as the Truman and Roosevelt recruiters had looked for Democrats, and often they found those who had performed yeoman service during the campaign. But in addition, they tried to recruit men who had distinguished themselves in the legal profession, in order to prevent a recurrence of the conditions for which they had attacked the Truman administration so vigorously. Moreover, they made greater efforts to bring into the agency more men who had specialized in particular fields of law, such as taxation and public lands. The Eisenhower recruiters were much less likely to look for such talent in the highest Justice posts, although appointees were sometimes promoted from the subordinate ranks. There were several instances of United States attorneys being appointed as assistant attorneys general, and there was Robert Bicks who became the assistant attorney general for the antitrust division in 1959, after serving as an assistant to the previous head of that division.

One interesting sidelight that deserves mention is the preponderance of Justice appointees who were already living on the east coast prior to their political assignment. In no other department does residence in the East, particularly in the Washington-Philadelphia-New York-Boston area appear so frequently in the selection of political executives. This was particularly true of the Truman and Eisenhower administrations, as summarized below:

RESIDENCE BEFORE APPOINTMENT	NUMBER	PERCENTAGE
District of Columbia	17	28
New York City	12	20
Other northeast areas	11	18
Other areas of the United States	20	33

Post Office: Politicians and Businessmen

Traditionally, the Post Office Department has been a harbor for deserving party officials and the Postmaster General has usually been a person who has held a high post in the party, often the chairmanship of the national committee. In the twentieth century, four Postmasters General have retained the chairmanship of the national committee while serving in the President's cabinet and six other Postmasters General have served as national party chairman either before or after the cabinet post. Both he and his chief aides have attended to the political needs of the administration, giving only part-time attention to their Post Office responsibilities. Macmahon and Millett concluded in 1939 that the assistant postmasters general "have been prevailingly political."[16]

No detailed study was made of the activities of Post Office political appointees while in office, but there is evidence that they generally used these positions as bases of operation from which they could continue their political duties in support of the President and his party. For this reason, posts in the Post Office Department and on the national committee appeared almost interchangeable. Such was the case with William J. Hartigan who was an assistant postmaster general in the Kennedy administration. Hartigan's appointment was confirmed by the Senate on August 4, 1961. On March 3, 1962, he resigned to return to Massachusetts to help with the Democratic political campaign. After the election, he returned to Washington and was reappointed to his Post Office position, again receiving confirmation by the Senate.[17] Perhaps the only thing exceptional about Mr. Hartigan's record was that he resigned to engage in his political activities.

There is a marked contrast in the recruiting practices of the Democratic and Republican administrations. Both Truman and Kennedy picked the majority of their Post Office appointees from among those members of the Democratic party whom they wished to reward for

[16] Macmahon and Millett, *op. cit.*, p. 36.

[17] Senator Carlson, the ranking minority member on the Senate Post Office and Civil Service Committee, did not formally object to the nomination but recorded his view that the practice of accepting an appointment, leaving to manage a political campaign, and subsequently returning, if carried out extensively "would not lend itself to good government." *Congressional Record*, Vol. 109, Pt. 4, 88 Cong. 1 sess. (1963), p. 4307.

past services or from whom they expected some service in the future. At least four of Truman's executives were associated with the Democratic National Committee, either before or after their appointment; three others had been active in state or national politics. The remaining three were career employees like Jesse Donaldson, who later became the Postmaster General.

Although a career executive like Postmaster General Donaldson might have been expected to resist the importunities of politicians for Post Office positions, such was not the case. Only one of his appointees, Vincent C. Burke, was a career employee of the department. He inherited three political appointees and subsequently appointed four others, three of whom came directly from the Democratic National Committee; the fourth had an established record in local Democratic politics which gained him support in the Democratic National Committee and in the White House. There is no evidence to indicate that any of these individuals had any particular background that would peculiarly qualify him for the position.

The Kennedy administration followed a similar pattern. In its first round of selections, political considerations were paramount. Two of the five assistant postmasters general came directly from the Democratic National Committee, and a third had taken an active role in the 1960 campaign. Another had been staff director of the House Committee on the Post Office and Civil Service. The Deputy Postmaster General had been the staff director of the Senate Post Office and Civil Service Committee and had also taken a leading part in the 1960 campaign. The sixth appointee was a Democratic businessman from New York. These Truman and Kennedy appointments may possibly have reflected weakness in the face of political pressure, or the positions may have been regarded as essentially supernumerary.

In sharp contrast to Democratic practices stands the record of the Republicans during the eight-year period of the Eisenhower administration. Although Postmaster General Arthur E. Summerfield followed the traditional route from the chairmanship of the Republican National Committee to the cabinet, at President Eisenhower's insistence he resigned from the National Committee upon taking office. Summerfield selected only Republicans as his aides, but he defied tradition by filling the subordinate posts in the Post Office with individuals whose primary qualification was managerial experience rather than partisan political service. Some of the initial appointees, such as Charles Hook, had taken part in the presidential campaign but in no sense could they be considered professional politicians. Except for two appointees, one a career official in the department and another a former Civil Service Commissioner with extensive service in the federal government, all of the Summerfield appointees were businessmen. In most instances, they were selected because of some special knowledge or skill gained from their business careers and considered useful in Post Office operations. Albert J. Robertson, for example, was appointed Assistant Postmaster General for Finance in 1953 after a lifelong career in Midwest banking. His successor, Hyde Gillette, had been with a Chicago investment company for most of his working life before accepting a post as Deputy Assistant Secretary for the Air Force at the beginning of the Eisenhower administration. Two businessmen whose primary interests were in real estate, Ormond E. Kieb and Roland D. Barnard, were appointed to supervise the physical facilities of the Post Office Department. Two of the three Assistant Postmasters General who were placed in charge of the Bureau of Transportation had formerly occupied business positions dealing with traffic and transportation. Finally, the three men who headed the Bureau of Operations had formerly occupied important managerial positions in manufacturing and utility companies prior to their government service.

The methods of recruitment used by Postmaster General Summerfield consistently led him to business specialists. He relied heavily on organizations such as the American Management Association, the National Industrial Conference Board, the American Bankers' Association, and other professional groups in the field of business to supply him with the names of eligible candidates. When he was looking for someone to take charge of the financial management of the Post Office Department, for instance, he tended to contact leading ABA officials.

In terms of internal management, reliance on professional politicians in the policy-making positions of the Post Office Department leaves something to be desired. Some, such as Jack Redding, apparently have worked hard at their management responsibilities and turned in superior performances. The President, however, has often found these positions indispensable in maintaining the vitality of his campaign organization and in ensuring the presence near him of men on whom he can rely for political duties. Under these circumstances, the actual management of the bureaus has devolved upon the career officials who presumably have the skills to manage Post Office operations.

Interior and Agriculture: Politics,
Pressure Groups, and Policy

Of all the major domestic departments or agencies in the national government, Interior and Agriculture are probably the most deeply involved in controversy over public policy on almost every aspect of their day-to-day activities. These disputes are in large part related to the interests of private groups whose welfare is inevitably affected by the decisions rendered by the executive branch as well as by the statutes passed by Congress. Decisions about the level of price support for major agricultural commodities directly affect the income of millions of farmers and determine the degree of freedom with which the farming enterprises may operate. Recommendations that the United States government construct hydroelectric installations on the major streams of the West are obviously in conflict with the interests of private power companies that wish to develop water power for profit.

Decisions on subordinate appointments by department heads are strongly influenced by the known views and affiliations of their prospective candidates. Differing interests with strong regional connections result in a concentration of appointees from areas where the recruiters have identified themselves with the local policy makers. Congressional representatives from such areas have exceptional influence.

This impact of policy on the recruitment process has been particularly prominent in the Department of Agriculture since World War II. At the close of the war, the two subcabinet positions were occupied by long-term departmental officials, Norris Dodd and Charles Brannan. The postwar demand for agricultural products in the United States encouraged continued high-level production and relative prosperity for the country's farmers. By the 1948 election, however, the controversy over farm prices had developed into an important issue which President Truman exploited during his campaign in the Midwest.

In May 1948 President Truman had appointed Charles Brannan as his Secretary of Agriculture to replace Clinton Anderson, who had resigned to run for the Senate. Brannan, although a career employee, had long been identified with the National Farmers Union position on farm pricing. He advocated a high level of farm price supports and direct subsidies to the farmers rather than flexible supports and indirect subsidies to guarantee fixed prices. The three appointments he made at the subcabinet level indicated both the policy and the political considerations involved in such appointments. His first Under Secretary, Albert Loveland of Iowa, had long been associated with the Department of Agriculture bureaucracy, serving as chairman of various local and state agricultural committees. He served as a branch chief for seven months before being appointed Under Secretary in 1948; and he had memberships in both the American Farm Bureau Federation and the National Farmers Union. As a Democrat from a Republican state, he represented a happy solution to the Secretary's political problems. Subsequently, Loveland resigned to run for the Senate in Iowa. His successor, Clarence J. McCormick, provided a fairly similar kind of partisan support. While a member of the Farm Bureau Federation in Indiana, he represented its liberal wing rather than the violent opposition which the Farm Bureau had presented to the "Brannan Plan." Brannan's third appointee, Knox Hutchinson, gave representation to the South and to an active Democratic campaigner.

    With the advent of Secretary Ezra Taft Benson's administration in Agriculture in 1953, there was a sharp change in the sources from which political executives were recruited. Great emphasis was placed upon the Benson view of agricultural policy which was generally espoused by the American Farm Bureau Federation, the National Grange, various cooperative organizations, and the agricultural business community—and ardently opposed by the National Farmers Union. Benson had long been a leading figure in agricultural cooperatives, serving for five years as executive secretary of the National Council of Farmer Cooperatives. He had, therefore, a wide range of acquaintances in the field and could work directly through them and his own friends—particularly among Mormons in the agricultural field —to garner names of candidates acceptable to him because they shared his philosophy.

    Benson's actual appointments illustrate the balance of these various interests. The support he received from the relatively conservative farm organizations, such as the Farm Bureau, was indicated by the fact that three of his appointees had been officials of the Farm Bureau, one as a national vice-president and two as state directors. The business side of agriculture was represented by appointees who came directly or after an interval from such organizations as the Spreckels Sugar Company and the Cooperative Grange League Federation Exchange.

Two executives, an assistant secretary and the solicitor, were former associates in the National Council of Farmer Cooperatives. His Under Secretary, True Morse, had been the chief officer in the Doane Agricultural Service, a leading agricultural consulting firm; two other assistant secretaries were former members of the Purdue University Department of Agricultural Economics, one moving up from a position as a special assistant to the Secretary.

The supremacy of policy considerations in the Benson administration did not preclude attention to other factors. At least two appointees had been active in national politics. Morse served as an important member of the committee that wrote the agricultural plank for the Republican platform in both 1948 and 1952, and Ross Rizley was a former Republican congressman from Oklahoma whose acquaintance with agricultural questions derived primarily from his relatively brief experience as a member of the House Agriculture Committee. While their backgrounds were not necessarily political, the fact that Earl Coke and Ervin Peterson had both held high state agricultural positions made their appointments significant in terms of the department's acceptance within the agricultural industry.

The Kennedy victory in 1960 appeared to have again shifted the balance toward the more liberal wing of agricultural politics, with the National Farmers Union regaining ascendant influence although not directly represented in the highest councils of the agency. The one Farm Bureau official to receive an appointment was John Duncan, the former head of the Georgia Farm Bureau, who was reportedly one of the few Farm Bureau officials who openly supported the candidacy of John F. Kennedy. The remaining three appointees in the Department of Agriculture under Orville Freeman had considerable political backing, particularly from members of Congress who were anxious to have their sections of the country represented in the department. The support of the National Farmers Union was important in one appointment that was closely contested. Three of these Democratic appointees had taken an active part in the 1960 campaign.

The search for executives with acceptable policy positions in the Department of Agriculture has tended to lead to special interest groups and to party organizations. For reasons not entirely clear, the same search in the Department of the Interior has led either to the bureaucracy or to members of Congress. In no other agency of the federal government have members of Congress played a more significant role in the selection process—especially those from the West where the department's chief area of activity lay.

At least part of this deep congressional involvement is due to strongly conflicting regional interests that can be resolved only at the national level. Members of Congress champion their state and district interests and become the spokesmen for their community causes. These local vested interests are far-ranging and must necessarily implicate high-level appointees in the Department of the Interior. Water management in the major river basins in the West, for example, is a particularly sensitive issue, and all the states in the vicinity of an interstate river, such as the Colorado, have a direct interest in the individuals who are appointed to positions concerned with water and power allocation. It is significant that to counterbalance the appointment of former congressman Stewart Udall of Arizona as Secretary of the Interior in 1961, California—Arizona's arch-rival across the Colorado River—was given the appointment of James Carr (the former general manager of the Sacramento Municipal Utility District) as Under Secretary, while the Assistant Secretary for Water and Power came from the Missouri River basin. Each region had advanced candidates for both the undersecretaryship and the assistant secretaryship in a desire to occupy the strongest possible position when policy decisions were to be made in the water and power field.

Because of the vital importance of these matters, western congressmen have always had a sense of proprietorship in relation to the Interior appointments. The Great Plains and Rocky Mountain states may lament lack of representation in other major government departments but failure to be represented in the Department of the Interior may mean failure to be represented at all, an indication that a congressman lacks influence in a presidential administration of his own party.

In half of the subcabinet appointments in that department during the period 1945-61 congressional influence played an important role. Powerful senators in at least three cases during the Truman administration made strong representations to the Secretary urging prominent individuals from their own states. Two of these appointments involved men who could contribute little technical ability or experience to the department and its program; instead, one appointee was enabled to increase his stature in order to run for high office in his state, and the other was provided with a base of operation to help in the 1952 election campaign.

Congressional influence in Interior appointments did not necessarily lead to the appointment of executives unfamiliar with resource problems, however. In fact, the relevance of background to appointed positions was probably as high in this Department as in most of the other domestic agencies. Six of the nine Truman administration appointees were long-time Interior officials who had moved up the administrative ranks, either on a career or a noncareer line. And, during the Eisenhower administration, although congressional influence appeared to be preeminent in at least six appointments, all involved support for prominent individuals in legislators' home states who could be recommended on the basis of specialized experience and skills. Some had experience in outside organizations in the resource field, such as the Tennessee Valley Authority. Some had been heads of state resources agencies. Some had been connected with public or private organizations concerned with the management and use of water.

Nevertheless, Interior, like Agriculture, is often caught in the crossfire of conflicting interest groups whose demands on the department are irreconcilable. For this reason, it has often been necessary to avoid identification with specific issues and policies by refusing to appoint individuals whose allegiances are obviously with one interest group or another. One Secretary asserted that, when he first came to office, he considered it appropriate to consult with various interest groups on possible candidates for subordinate positions. He later learned from sad experience that such a practice was out of the question because of the impossibility of getting the candidate of one group accepted by another. One candidate who had long been associated with a faction that normally gave strong support to Democratic administrations was not appointed, at least in part because it was felt that his appointment would create needless opposition among other groups interested in the Department's activities.

Considering the legislators' continuing concern over these resource department appointments, the active participation of clientele groups, and the normal recognition which department heads had to pay to considerations of balance among political, geographic, and group interests, Interior's succession of department heads more closely approximated political brokers than did the heads of the other major departments.

Commerce and Labor: Clientele Politics

In sharp contrast to the resource agencies, organizational representation rather than policy consideration is the crucial factor in the selection of political executives in the Departments of Labor and Commerce. Particularly in the Department of Labor and especially during
Democratic administrations, recruitment has reflected interest group
conflicts which have their roots in the history of American trade union-
ism. While policy issues may occasionally be at stake, the primary concern among recruiters has been that each of the union factions receive
adequate representation in the department, "adequate" being more
often than not interpreted as "equal."

As the chief clientele groups for the Department of Labor, the
American Federation of Labor (AFL) and the Congress of Industrial
Organizations (CIO) strove to receive equal departmental representation in recognition of their equal status in the union movement. Prior
to the merger in late 1955, the AFL tended to be highly suspicious of
the intrusion of CIO representatives in the department, resisting any
situation in which a CIO representative might possibly have supervi-
sory authority over an AFL representative, such as would have occurred, for instance, if an under secretary had been chosen who was
supported by the CIO unions.

Recruitment during the two Democratic administrations followed a
fairly similar tack. Of the ten Truman subcabinet appointees, six came
from organized labor—three from AFL unions, two from CIO unions,
and one from an independent. Two of the remaining four were career
employees with brilliant reputations in the national government. The
others were appointed primarily for political reasons, having little to
do with the labor movement. The initial selections in the Kennedy administration appeared to follow this practice. One appointee came
from an AFL background, although he had served just previously as
the state executive for the combined AFL-CIO. A second appointee,
George L. P. Weaver, had been an official of the Electrical Workers
Union-CIO. As in the Truman administration, no labor appointee became under secretary. That post went to W. Willard Wirtz, a lawyer
and former professor of law whose major activity was in labor law and
who had been active during the 1960 presidential campaign.

Eisenhower's recruiters, on the other hand, adopted entirely different procedures, largely because of the relative estrangement of the Republican party from labor interests. To compensate for these strained relationships, President Eisenhower selected Martin Durkin, the president of an AFL international union and a Democrat, as his first Secretary of Labor. As his Under Secretary Durkin chose Lloyd Mashburn, who had been a California labor leader and commissioner of labor under Governor Earl Warren. Mashburn, a Republican, balanced Durkin politically, although they both came from the building trades. The other three appointees consisted of another AFL union official from the railroad unions, a Negro lawyer from Chicago, and a New York University professor with strong political connections in New Jersey. There was no representation for the CIO, undoubtedly because of the general antipathy of the CIO officials to a Republican administration.

The tension between unions and the Republican administration soon resulted in the resignation of Durkin and Mashburn because of the alleged failure of the Eisenhower administration to keep its promises with regard to modifications of the Taft-Hartley Act. These tensions also infiltrated the lower echelons, creating difficult procedural problems. Following traditional practice, the next Secretary of Labor, James P. Mitchell, tried to find at least one suitable candidate with a trade union background but he was unable to locate any who was acceptable both to him and to the White House. The impasse over one union prospect resulted in mutual agreement that there would be no attempt to provide direct union representation in the high ranks of the Labor Department. As a result, from 1954 on, Eisenhower appointees in the Department of Labor were men with professional or business backgrounds, some of whom had strong political connections. Several had been appointed on a political basis to subordinate positions within the department and later moved up into secretarial posts. Such were the appointments of John Gilhooley, George Lodge, and Newell Brown. In spite of party difficulties and the agreement to disagree on the appointment of labor candidates, the unions and Secretary Mitchell were on good terms and the unions generally approved the Republican selections.

Recruitment for the Department of Commerce also has leaned to balanced representation of the various interest groups involved. Quite naturally, too, Commerce selections have, since the beginning of the Eisenhower administration, relied almost exclusively on businessmen, and an occasional lawyer, to fill their subordinate political positions. Thirteen of the fifteen men appointed to under secretary and assistant secretary posts during Eisenhower's Presidency were businessmen in private life, one was a lawyer, and the fifteenth was a former lawyer turned congressman. Throughout the administration there was a heavy reliance on men who had had no previous government experience. Except for those who had been appointed at a subordinate level and advanced to a political executive position later, nearly all had had careers exclusively in private business or the professions. This circumstance is understandable in view of the fact that this was the first Republican administration in twenty years. Nevertheless, the relative lack of public experience stands in sharp contrast to many other agencies during Eisenhower's administration whose political executives had had rather extensive service during World War II or the Korean War, in state government or in career positions in the federal service.

Since Commerce is mainly a service department for the business community, emphasis on filling these positions with businessmen is understandable. Recruitment during the Eisenhower administration was dominated by the figure of Sinclair Weeks who depended on his contacts in the formal business organizations, particularly the National Association of Manufacturers. As the former treasurer of the Republican National Committee, Weeks was of course not unsympathetic to political considerations. A number of his appointees had had a fair amount of political experience, particularly during the 1952 campaign. His Under Secretary had been chairman of the Republican State Central Committee of Washington (state) and later national chairman of Citizens for Eisenhower. His Under Secretary for Transportation had been on the Republican National Finance Committee in 1952 and had previously engaged in fund-raising activities in the state of New York. Assistant Secretary James Worthy, a Sears Roebuck official, was co-chairman of the Illinois Citizens for Eisenhower-Nixon in 1952.

The only appointments made by Frederick Mueller who became Secretary in 1959 were advancements of men already in the department serving at deputy assistant secretary levels, and the appointment as Under Secretary of Philip Ray who had previously served as the department's General Counsel under Secretary Weeks.

The two Democratic administrations differed somewhat from each other. Kennedy followed a pattern of recruitment similar to Eisenhower's; and the Truman administration laid less stress on a business background and followed a more variegated system of selection. Averell Harriman chose men with whom he had served in government during World War II. His appointments of William C. Foster, David K. E. Bruce, and John Alison were all based on his own knowledge of their capabilities. In fact, these close personal ties led both Foster and Bruce to leave Commerce with Harriman in 1948, in order to work with him in the Economic Cooperation Administration. While Foster and Bruce were both businessmen, they also had previous federal service and were recruited as much for demonstrated competence in a governmental setting as for business acumen. Alison, on the other hand, had had a long career in the Army Air Force which served him in good stead as Assistant Secretary of Commerce for Aeronautics.

Charles Sawyer, Harriman's successor, relied a great deal more on career officials in making his selections. But no official of the Truman administration was more responsive to the needs of the White House in finding positions for candidates with political connections. Considering these subcabinet positions as relatively unimportant and not likely to attract experienced and successful businessmen, Sawyer was willing to rely on the Democratic National Committee and the White House personnel office to search out appropriate candidates. He made little or no effort to find his own "team" but tended to ratify the selections made by other interested parties. These political appointments were most typical of the latter part of the second Truman administration.

On the other hand, just as Eisenhower had done before him, Kennedy relied almost exclusively on the business community in making his first appointments and paid no heed to lack of government experience. All four of the original appointees were businessmen, some of whom had impeccable political connections—in particular Hickman Price, Jr., whose wife, Margaret Price, was vice-chairman of the Democratic National Committee. A change may have been inaugurated, however, with the creation in 1962 of a new assistant secretary post which was assigned to science and technology, and a later consolidation of two assistant secretaryships into one (for domestic and international business), with the other being converted into an assistant secretaryship for economic affairs. The three men appointed to these posts were all specialists, one in metallurgy and engineering, two in economics and business administration.

Health, Education, and Welfare:
Politics and Expertise

This is the newest of the executive departments.[18] Actually created in 1953, its components had been grouped together in the predecessor Federal Security Agency for a dozen years. The elements were disparate and specialized, the major branches being the Public Health Service, the Office of Education, the Social Security Administration, the Office of Vocational Rehabilitation, and the Food and Drug Administration. Each necessarily has operated with a good deal of autonomy. Furthermore, each has been supported by different types of interest groups, competing with each other before Congress for authorizations and funds. The secretary has, therefore, special need for assistants with a talent for administration and coordination. He also needs able personnel for the direction of field services and grants-in-aid, and for liaison with Congress and many external organizations.

The search for people to perform these functions during the years 1953-61 led to the appointment of persons from a diversity of backgrounds but with one thing in common: nearly all had experience in government or politics. Only two of the thirteen under secretaries and assistant secretaries were completely without some public service although a few others had just local or state experience.

The first Under Secretary in the Eisenhower administration, Nelson Rockefeller, had participated actively in the affairs of his family's Rockefeller Center but had also seen government service in several capacities, including Co-ordinator of Inter-American Affairs 1940-44 and Assistant Secretary of State in 1945; he had also helped to plan the creation of HEW as a department. The next two Under Secretaries were educational administrators, one of them with no government experience, the other with varied experience in the state of Michigan but on leave from the presidency of the University of Delaware while he served a year in HEW. Another Under Secretary, Bertha Adkins, had been dean of women at one institution and dean of residence at another before becoming active in politics as Republican National Committeewoman for Maryland in 1948, director of the women's divi-

[18] On Sept. 9, 1965, President Lyndon Johnson signed a bill creating the Department of Housing and Urban Development.

sion of the Republican National Committee in 1950, and assistant chairman of the committee in 1953.

The assistant secretaries under Eisenhower came chiefly from law and business; two of the lawyers had served as assistants to United States senators and one as a consultant on social security in HEW prior to his secretarial appointment. Another lawyer came from the business world; he was vice-president and general counsel of a large flour milling company, with service along the way in helping to write the Food and Drug Law in the thirties, assisting in the setting up of HEW in 1953, organizing Minnesotans for Eisenhower and pushing for the latter's nomination in 1951-52. Another businessman had spent his entire career in his family's meat packing firm, with no time previously in public service.

The Kennedy appointees to the department were all experienced in government service of some kind. Ivan Nestingen, the Under Secretary, was a lawyer who had been a member of the Wisconsin legislature and then mayor of Madison; he also served as chairman of Citizens for Kennedy-Johnson in 1960. Assistant Secretary James Quigley of Pennsylvania, another lawyer, had served two nonconsecutive terms in the House of Representatives. After he was defeated for reelection in 1956 he became administrative assistant to Senator Joseph S. Clark of Pennsylvania for the ensuing two years. He was defeated for reelection again in 1960, so was available for appointment as a "deserving Democrat." The other assistant secretary, Wilbur Cohen, was an expert on welfare legislation and a long time federal employee; he had worked on the drafting of the original Social Security Act of 1935 and remained with the organization set up under it until 1956 as technical adviser and later as director of the research and statistics division. In 1956 he went to the University of Michigan as professor of public welfare administration; in 1960 he was chairman of the Task Force on Health and Social Security set up by President-elect Kennedy.

All in all, the careers of HEW's appointees reflected the hodge-podge of assorted functions that fall under the one umbrella. Specific duties have varied with individual capabilities, but the lower the grade of political position the more specialized the qualifications of its incumbents are likely to be. The real specialists, of course, are the career (or appointive) officials who administer its various branches.

The Independent Agencies: A Mixed Bag

Recruiters in the Truman, Eisenhower, and Kennedy administrations followed no clearly identifiable pattern when choosing executives to run the independent agencies. In some, there was a certain tendency to use rather more career men in deputy director positions; in others, party obligations were obviously paramount. In all agencies, there were so many exceptions to the general rule that no fixed criteria were discernible. During all four administrations, however, the President and his aides appeared to have taken the stand that political debts could more readily be paid off in these independent agencies than in the major departments. Except in one or two instances, they were less strategically placed and therefore less likely to be in the public eye. The characteristic recruitment approach in four of these independent organizations deserves mention.

As a rule, appointments in the General Services Administration and the Office of Civil and Defense Mobilization tended to take on a more political character than in the other agencies. Many of the appointees had had important political careers before their appointment but little relevant experience. Appointments were in the main rewards for service or palliatives to demanding party workers; and at least two were made because of the appointees' close personal relationship with the President in office. The agency heads tended to be passive figures in the appointment process in these agencies and to accept recommendations made by the President or White House officials.

Reliance on the career service for prospective candidates is typical of the Veterans Administration, where four of the six deputy administrators appointed since 1945 were promoted from subordinate positions in the agency. The two exceptions occurred in the Eisenhower administration, and one was the appointment of F. Bradford Morse, which was clearly the result of the close political connection between Morse, Veterans Administrator Sumner Whittier, and Senator Leverett Saltonstall, all of whom had been active in Massachusetts politics.[19] In view of the great congressional interest in the Veterans Administra-

---

[19] Morse resigned his post in the Veterans Administration in 1960 to run successfully for Congress.

tion, it is significant that congressmen have themselves promoted the appointment of career officials for leading positions in the agency, apparently preferring good performance on the job to political advantage.

Appointments in the Bureau of the Budget follow no distinctive pattern but are a combination of professional, career, and political appointments which appear to depend on the individual Director of the Bureau more than anything else. The advancement of Fred Lawton, Elmer Staats, and Roger Jones to the deputy directorship are clear instances of appointments based on demonstrated competence as career officials in the agency over a long period of years. In spite of the sensitivity of the Bureau of the Budget operations to presidential interest, Elmer Staats was able to survive the 1960-61 transition. Staats had been the Deputy Director of the Budget at the end of the Truman administration as well, and was therefore acquainted with many of the incoming Democratic officials, particularly with David Bell, Kennedy's new Budget Director. A significant number of these appointees followed a political route to the deputy directorship, although in most instances their backgrounds included a wealth of public service in executive capacities. Paul Appleby, for eleven years prior to his appointment in the bureau had been in the Department of Agriculture, first as assistant to the Secretary and later as Under Secretary. Frank Pace had served as an assistant both to the Attorney General and to the Postmaster General before moving over to the Budget Bureau under James Webb. Robert Merriam had had both administrative and elective political careers, having served in Chicago first in local public agencies, then as an alderman.

Summary

As far as personal characteristics were concerned, federal political executives who served in the government during the twenty-nine-year period from 1933 to 1961 were, on the whole, a knowledgeable, versatile, articulate, and experienced group of people. Aged about fifty on appointment, most of them had achieved success—and a certain amount of public recognition—in their private lives, whether they were in a government or private career. They showed social responsibility, went to the best known schools (especially at the graduate level), joined the important clubs, and generally preferred town life to the country. These executives did not constitute an elite in the sense that entry into their ranks was closed to those who lacked these precise qualifications; but they did reflect the characteristics of many other leadership groups throughout the country.

Geographically, political executives represented all regions of the country, but with a penchant for the Northeast urban areas. They were extremely well educated, far beyond the general population and to a higher level than the business executive. They were the product of a large number of schools, preferring the more prominent northeastern universities for their graduate education. These executives belonged to a bewildering variety of professional organizations, social clubs, and civic societies; but generally did not play a leadership role in them. Most were Protestants belonging to the more socially prominent churches, although the Catholic Church was better represented within their ranks than in business and military circles. Because of two world wars, the majority were veterans; nevertheless, military experience appeared to be a consideration in recruitment only for the military departments.

The majority of these appointees were recruited from primary occupations in the private sector, but the largest single source consisted of men with established careers in the government. In fact, the commonly held view that political executives at these levels are relative neophytes in government and politics must be revised. A very large percentage in all four administrations had had experience in public office, many for extended periods of time. For the most part, this experience was administrative in character rather than elective, and primarily at subordinate political and career levels in the national administration. A percentage larger than might be expected had had experience in more than one agency.

Varied occupational resources supplied the necessary manpower for political executive office from the private sector. Practicing lawyers were prominent in every administration, as they were in elective politics. The number of businessmen, however, depended on the character of the administration and the nature of the times, as indicated, for example, by the relatively high percentage of businessmen in the Eisenhower administration. Other professions and occupations contributed only limited numbers of executives in all administrations, but there appeared to be greater professional diversity during Kennedy's term of office.

These appointees tended to be highly mobile, moving from firm to firm and even from occupation to occupation. They had strong leanings toward the presidential wing of their party and their urban background gave them a sympathetic understanding of the social and political problems of city life. Few had had experience in legislative bodies.

Marked differences were found among agencies, both in the processes of recruitment and in the sources relied on for prospective candidates. In the departments and agencies concerned with national security and foreign policy there was a strong tendency to rely on the business and professional world. Far from being inexperienced in public affairs, however, the men appointed often had had previous public service or had engaged in private activities directly related to the work of the agencies in which they served. Presidential interest tended to be high in these agencies and the intrusion of outside groups—whether political or interest group—was minimal.

The processes and sources for selecting political executives in domestic agencies tended to follow a pattern more closely associated with what is commonly called "political." Members of Congress and interest groups exercised considerably more influence, particularly in setting up standards and boundaries within which those directly involved in recruiting had to operate. Moreover, when the President intervened in the selection process in these agencies, he did so in order to repay a political obligation. Party membership or political loyalty to the President was everywhere an important requirement, but active party participation loomed larger as a factor in selection in domestic agencies as opposed to the security agencies. Nevertheless, even in these domestic agencies, subject-matter competence and previous administrative experience weighed heavily in the final choice.

In large part, the explanation for divergencies in recruitment practices for the different agencies stems from the American propensity for specialization. Recruiting executives for the Department of the Interior and the Department of Agriculture naturally led department heads to agricultural institutions of the Midwest, South and West—to the colleges of agriculture, to state resource agencies, to interest groups, and to private businesses and companies operating in the resource field. Moreover, with their strong tendency to promote subordinates, whether in the career or noncareer service, to political executive positions, the department heads were taking advantage of the training which men who may have come from many sections of the country received while actually on the job. In contrast, recruitment for the Departments of State, Treasury, and the Defense establishment emphasized the business and professional world of the eastern seaboard. In Treasury, this appeared to reflect the demand for men with certain technical skills and experience, dealing with such matters as taxation, debt management, and international finance. In the State Department, recruiters relied strongly on a community of men, both in and out of the government—in universities, foreign policy associations, law firms, and banking institutions—who had had a broad and active interest in international affairs. In somewhat similar fashion, but to a lesser extent, the Defense Department became the center of a community which relied more heavily on the business world than was the case in the Department of State.

In all, the background data reveal that the most commonly held view of political executives as part of a unified "political directorate" cannot be validated in fact. While tendencies exist in certain departments to recruit from an eastern, industrial, financial class, they appear chiefly to reflect the interest such groups have taken in the issues of national security and the special qualifications they are thought to possess. However, despite the current emphasis on specific experience and knowledge of a particular area of public policy, political executives viewed as an entity represent a fairly broad spectrum of the American political scene.

3

The Appointment Process

THE FIRST HIGH-RANKING OFFICERS chosen for the new federal government in 1789 were characteristically well-educated, wellborn, and "respectable" men of the community. One step removed from colonial America in their social conventions, the natural inclination of a George Washington, a John Adams, or a Thomas Jefferson was to call upon men from his own social class to occupy the high-level posts. They were generally wealthy landowners, merchants, or men of letters, many of whom had played leading roles in the Revolution. Washington set the standard of "fitness of character" as his chief criterion for eligibility, which implied a certain personal integrity and standing in the community. Jefferson drew from essentially the same classes departing from his predecessors only in seeking "due participation" for his fellow partisans in a government which was thoroughly dominated by Federalists. During this period, control of the processes of selection remained substantially in the hands of the President and his department heads. Recommendations of legislators and party leaders were considered important but were seldom decisive, even with respect to positions within their own constituencies.[1]

Throughout this era, party interests and geographical representation were important factors in the mind of the Chief Executive when making selections—always, of course, within the confines of the upper classes. But the social and political revolution which brought Andrew Jackson to power in 1828, and which had long been brewing in the states, was a portent of momentous changes both in the selection process and in the standards of fitness for high office. The New De-

[1] See Leonard D. White, *The Federalists* (Macmillan Company, 1948), Chap. 21; *The Jeffersonians* (Macmillan Company, 1951).

mocracy, as represented by the western farmers, workers, and other formerly disenfranchised elements, demanded government participation. In his first annual message Jackson made the well-known statement defending the practice of rotation, arguing that "the duties of all public officers are, or at least admit of being made, so plain and simple that men of intelligence may readily qualify themselves for their performance."[2] Education, social standing, and integrity were replaced as criteria for selection by party activity, political and personal influence, and persistence. As an antidote to class control of the administrative machinery, the medicine proved as bad as the malady.

The process of selection gradually changed also. No longer did the President and his department heads judiciously select their nominees from among the best families. Instead, they were swamped with comparatively uneducated and inexperienced men whose thirst for office was unquenchable. Moreover, their quest for jobs was often supported, if not promoted, by members of Congress and party officials who importuned the President and his aides without cessation. By the end of the Jacksonian era, congressmen had won substantial control of local appointments and principal field offices. The President retained his independence over Washington appointments, but in practical terms congressional and party influence over these appointments was augmented, particularly when the chief executives were less stubborn than Jackson and James K. Polk.[3]

Party influence over political appointments grew stronger and more widespread throughout the period of Republican domination that began with the Civil War. Presidential control of the selection process almost completely collapsed with the impeachment and near conviction of President Andrew Johnson over his appointments policy. Members of Congress became brokers of patronage. This was particularly true of local offices, although members' control also extended to the highest administrative ranks. Occasionally, Presidents proved strong enough to resist these intrusions; such a President was Rutherford B. Hayes who vanquished the Senate in its attempt to control his selection of department heads and federal field officers.[4]

[2] James D. Richardson, A Compilation of the Messages and Papers of the Presidents 1789-1897, Vol. 3, (Bureau of National Literature, 1897), p. 1012 (Dec. 8, 1829).
[3] Leonard D. White, The Jacksonians (Macmillan Company, 1956), Chap. 6.
[4] Leonard D. White, The Republican Era, 1869-1901 (Macmillan Company, 1958), Chap. 2.

Patronage excesses led to demands for reform. There was, too, general recognition that, with growing government influence in a technological society, public office required men of ability and experience. The main objective of personnel administrators during the first half of the twentieth century was the reform of the civil service, which is now normally protected from partisan job raids and interference in personnel policies. Emphasis is on merit in recruitment and promotion practices, and strenuous efforts have been made to improve professional skills. The classified service at many points reaches high levels of administration, although partisan influence has hardly been eliminated in the upper echelons.

The positions of assistant secretary and under secretary with which this study is principally concerned are a relatively recent addition to the government's organizational machinery. In times past, similar duties were performed by chief clerks and assistants to the secretaries, but assistant secretaries as such were almost unknown until the last half of the nineteenth century, and the first under secretary position was created in 1919. There were four under secretaries and twenty-five assistant secretaries in 1933; in early 1961 there were seventeen and sixty-four, respectively. The scope and variety of duties performed by these second-level political executives have fluctuated with the shifting emphases of federal commitments at home and abroad; and their proportion in relation to the career service has been considerably reduced during the last half century. The enormous growth of federal activities, however, has led to a complicated presidential recruitment operation, particularly at the beginning of an administration.

In his cabinet selections the President has continued to be the central figure, weighing and assessing the qualifications of each candidate, and there is a consistent element of presidential control over all appointments. But even at this level, there has been no uniformity from administration to administration in the degree of presidential interest or the extent to which the Chief Executive has controlled the criteria used in selection. Woodrow Wilson, for example, disliked the job of appointing people and therefore gave to Joseph Tumulty and Colonel Edward M. House the primary responsibility for sorting out the candidates. Warren Harding leaned heavily on his campaign manager Harry Daugherty; and Herbert Hoover was primarily interested in questions of integrity and administrative ability, disregarding for the most part questions of political advantage. Franklin D. Roosevelt virtually ignored his chief associates in selecting his cabinet, taking a markedly personal and unmethodical approach in choosing his aides.[5] Harry S. Truman, because he took office in mid-term with a clearly defined political program to which he had been committed as Vice President, tended to recruit from those already in government service. Although important personnel changes occurred very quickly in the Truman administration, they were not comparable in number to appointments at the beginning of an administration subsequent to a party overturn.

Presidential Recruitment Policies, 1952 and 1960

Presidents-elect Dwight D. Eisenhower and John F. Kennedy differed considerably in their approach to cabinet recruitment, and their selection procedures for the second echelon diverged even further. A more detailed look at their individual methods of handling political executive personnel problems as their administrations began will pinpoint some of the major factors affecting recruitment at the under secretary and assistant secretary level.

The Eisenhower Approach, 1952

Reliance upon a staff operation came easily to the former general, Dwight D. Eisenhower. He was used to and preferred a situation in which his subordinates presented to him a solution or a limited number of alternatives among which he could choose. A relative newcomer to the political scene, the President-elect also lacked information about potential candidates possessed by others who had had longer experience in the political wars. Therefore, when he installed his entourage during the pre-inaugural period at the Commodore Hotel in New York City, he immediately established a small group of trusted veterans of both politics and war to assist him.

The central figures in this recruitment operation were Herbert Brownell and Lucius Clay. Brownell was an experienced political figure whose efforts in behalf of the Republican Party reached back over a decade. He was a former national party chairman and campaign manager for Thomas E. Dewey and constituted one of the prin-

[5] Richard F. Fenno, Jr., *The President's Cabinet* (Harvard University Press, 1959), pp. 56-58.

cipal links between the Eisenhower people and those who had long been loyal to Dewey. He had served as Eisenhower's principal strategist in the 1952 presidential campaign and Eisenhower had great faith in his judgment. General Clay was a lifelong military associate and personal friend who was then serving as chairman of the board of the Continental Can Company. He also had played an active part in the 1952 campaign. Of these two men, Sherman Adams reported: "I think Eisenhower at that time had more confidence in Brownell's political advice than he had in anyone else's and in General Clay he had a close friend and counselor, a tough-fibered and keen observer who had taken hold of many a difficult situation for the President-elect."[6]

In their personnel search these two made limited use of lists that had been prepared by McKinsey & Company of some 5,000 names of possible candidates for positions at various levels in the administration. This management consulting firm had been hired soon after the Republican convention by New York businessman Harold E. Talbott, acting for an informal group of Eisenhower supporters and fundraisers. Others prominently associated with the recruitment effort were Sherman Adams himself and businessmen like Sidney Weinberg and Harold Boeschenstein.

At the outset, Brownell, Clay, and their assistants were primarily concerned with helping the President select his cabinet officers. Adams reported that at the time of the election Eisenhower had probably made up his mind definitely about only two positions—John Foster Dulles as Secretary of State and Joseph M. Dodge as Budget Director.[7] But he was remarkably quick in making up his mind about other appointments. By the beginning of December, his cabinet had reached full complement with the appointments of Sinclair Weeks as Secretary of Commerce and Martin Durkin as Secretary of Labor.

Eisenhower's choice of cabinet officers at the beginning of his administration indicated an approach to the appointment process which was partly traditional but partly at variance with some established norms of American political life. From the selections, it was clear that the President-elect and his aides had followed the time-honored practice of balancing various factions and interests. The cabinet included two New York lawyers, several prominent businessmen, several active political figures, a woman, a labor leader, and two westerners. But the

[6] *Firsthand Report* (Harper & Brothers, 1961), p. 45.
[7] *Ibid.*

pattern of these appointments was the source of considerable disquiet among the members of the Taft wing of the Republican party who were strongly represented in Congress but who felt that their wing of the party was inadequately represented in the executive. In terms of personal loyalties the appointees had been, with the exception of Ezra Taft Benson and Martin Durkin, for Eisenhower before the convention. Benson was the only identifiable "Taft man." To the Taft people these appointments suggested a violation of the spirit, if not the letter, of the "Morningside Agreement" of September 1952 in which General Eisenhower approved a statement drawn up by Senator Robert A. Taft of Ohio, which stated in part:

> . . . In the making of appointments at high levels or low levels there will be no discrimination against anyone because he or she has supported me [Taft], and that he [Eisenhower] is determined to maintain the unity of the entire party by taking counsel with all factions and points of view.[8]

These appointments further suggested a tendency to ignore the patronage needs of the party by an administration and a President that had tried hard to convince the public of its "above" party orientation.[9]

Once a cabinet officer or agency head had been selected, President-elect Eisenhower delegated to him the authority to select his subordinates. Sherman Adams reports that "Eisenhower gave each Cabinet member and agency director complete responsibility for his department and almost never intervened in the selection of their assistants and other key personnel."[10] Each cabinet secretary could establish his own criteria for selection, search out his own candidates, and present his preferred candidate to the White House for the President's approval. This degree of independence in selecting subordinates was entirely consistent with President Eisenhower's propensity for delegating authority and even accepting views and actions which deviated from his own policy preferences. Such a delegation of authority indicated an unwillingness on his part to exercise his prerogatives in order to blunt the criticism from congressional sources that the legislators were being short-circuited in the appointment process.

[8] Quoted in Robert J. Donovan, *Eisenhower: The Inside Story* (Harper & Brothers, 1956), p. 104.
[9] Sherman Adams, *op. cit.*, p. 58.
[10] *Ibid.*, p. 59. He reportedly assured one cabinet officer, "I will not appoint anyone to serve under you who is not fully acceptable to you."

The Commodore recruitment group continued to look for candidates and evaluate those in their files. Several were located in this way and ultimately appointed; and only in three instances did the Commodore group put "pressure" on a department head to make a specific appointment. Presidential assistants in the Commodore urged "political" considerations but, lacking the influential support of the President, there was little they could do to enforce their views.

Appointments to subcabinet positions began with the nomination of William P. Rogers as the Deputy Attorney General in late November. On December 15, Marion Folsom, Randolph Burgess, and H. Chapman Rose were selected for Under Secretary, Deputy to the Secretary, and Assistant Secretary of the Treasury, respectively. Four days later, Roger Kyes was designated Deputy Secretary of Defense; Robert T. Stevens, Secretary of the Army; Robert B. Anderson, Secretary of the Navy; and Harold E. Talbott, Secretary of the Air Force. The appointments of Walter Williams as Under Secretary and Samuel W. Anderson as an Assistant Secretary of Commerce were announced on the same day, and on December 25, True Morse was named Under Secretary of Agriculture. On January 8, Walter Bedell Smith, a close friend of the President who had served also in the Truman administration, was appointed Under Secretary of State.

Announcements of other appointments continued at irregular intervals throughout this pre-inaugural period. Many nominees were personal friends of cabinet members; others, such as Walter Williams who had been national chairman of Citizens for Eisenhower, were prominent Eisenhower supporters. Few had important ties with Congress or the Taft wing of the party. One appointee was said to have met with a more enthusiastic response from the Democrats in his home county than from his local Republican organization.

During late December and early January, Republican members of Congress continued to criticize the Eisenhower appointments. In an effort to resolve the differences between the administration and the Senate, three Senate leaders—Taft, William F. Knowland of California, and Eugene Millikin of Colorado—met with Eisenhower at the Commodore Hotel on January 12, 1953. They complained that suggestions made by senators had largely been disregarded and that even clearances had at times been forgotten. Eisenhower took the position that he and his cabinet officials had the right to select their own subordinates but that he would not object to the senators taking their suggestions for all positions directly to the department concerned, rather than sending them to the White House or to the Republican National Committee.[11]

This "Commodore Agreement" had some effect. The Taft wing and members of Congress generally, appeared to have a greater role in subcabinet appointments made during the winter and spring in certain departments, such as Interior and Labor, and in appointments to commissions and other independent agencies. Even so, several cabinet members continued to disregard congressional and party recommendations.

Meanwhile, in early January 1953 primary responsibility for locating and screening candidates had shifted from Brownell and Clay to Sherman Adams. The latter, who had become Eisenhower's chief assistant in the White House, now took on the major responsibility for recruiting and clearing candidates. In this effort he was assisted by the former vice-chairman of the Citizens for Eisenhower, Charles F. Willis, Jr., who was a special assistant in the White House Office. A considerable number of positions remained to be filled, and Adams and Willis attempted a systematic compilation of these positions and candidates for each post. This later formed the nucleus for a continuous personnel operation in the White House. But, by the end of January, the special recruitment effort begun in the Commodore Hotel had substantially ended.

The Kennedy Approach, 1960

Senator John F. Kennedy pledged during the 1960 campaign that the key positions in his administration would be filled by "the best talent in both parties."[12] As in 1952, however, little effort was made before the election to prepare for the difficult job of recruitment. In August 1960, Mr. Kennedy assigned to Clark Clifford, a former aide to President Truman, the task of determining what priority decisions should be made by a President-elect. Among the responsibilities Clifford listed was a series of important appointments. Studies of the

[11] The committee had little influence in appointments during this period. Arthur Summerfield resigned from the chairmanship shortly after being appointed Postmaster General; his successor Wesley Roberts was not well known nationally and exerted little influence on appointments during these early months.

[12] Speech at Wittenberg College, Springfield, Ohio. Reported in the *New York Times*, Oct. 18, 1960.

transition problem by the Brookings Institution also recommended immediate attention to staffing the administration as a means of facilitating the transition. In the turmoil of a political campaign, however, no staff member could be spared to consider matters that would be contingent upon the one major necessity: winning the election. One Kennedy staff member observed retrospectively that if anyone had diverted his attention to such secondary matters, "Kennedy wouldn't have won."

Like Eisenhower, as soon as victory was assured, Kennedy and his staff turned their attention to the selection of cabinet officers, agency heads, and their subordinates. While he vacationed in Palm Beach, and later when he returned to his home in Georgetown, the President-elect spent the major part of his time talking with prospective candidates and evaluating the qualifications of those who had been recommended or who were recommending themselves. Kennedy was extremely active in these early recruitment efforts, consulting with the elders of the Democratic Party and with his chief political aides, but he delayed his decisions much longer than President Eisenhower, making his first appointment to a cabinet position on December 1, the same date on which President Eisenhower in 1952 announced his last cabinet appointment.

Kennedy and his advisers had two important criteria when making high-level presidential appointments: recognition of service to the party, and recognition of the need to obtain the "best talent." To make these criteria operative, the recruitment task was divided between two groups of Kennedy aides, one focusing primarily upon finding "deserving people," hoping that they "were bright enough;" and the other reversing this order of priority. Together, these two groups became known popularly as the "Talent Hunt."

Heading these two operations were the President-elect's brother, Robert, and his brother-in-law, R. Sargent Shriver. Robert Kennedy restricted his efforts to the nationwide network of contacts he had made during the 1960 campaign, while Shriver relied on his contacts in the business, professional, and university worlds. The operation under brother Robert was staffed by the President-elect's campaign and senatorial aides: Lawrence O'Brien, Richard Donahue, and Ralph Dungan. The Shriver operation was primarily in the hands of young lawyers who had also been active in the campaign, such as Adam Yarmolinsky and Harris Wofford. In spite of this informal division of labor between the two recruiting operations, the allocation of responsibilities was hardly distinct. In time, in fact, "everyone got into everyone else's business," as one staff member expressed it. When it was necessary to make final evaluations and decisions on specific appointments, members of both groups exercised their judgment on both political and capability standards.

Of particular interest were the criteria the recruiters reportedly used in appraising their candidates' qualifications. A prospect's colleagues, professional associates, and other contacts were asked by a Kennedy staff member to assess him in terms of his "judgment," "toughness," "integrity," "ability to work with others," "industry," and "devotion to the principles of the President-elect." The evaluators were also asked to state whether they considered the candidate had a wide or limited acquaintance with qualified people in his specialized field or "only local contacts"; and to estimate whether the candidate's appointment to a high-level government position would enhance the administration "nationally," "in his professional group," "in his state," or "in his community."[13] As things worked out, however, interviewers found it difficult to find time for more than the simple question, "What do you know about this guy?" In fact, according to one Talent Hunt member, these evaluations were often not particularly useful because of the hurried manner in which they had to be conducted and also because a candidate was seldom being rated in terms of a specific type of job. The summary evaluations were in such general terms as "highly qualified," "qualified," and "some qualifications" on the competence side; and "good Democrat," "political neutral," "Republican," or "politically disqualified," on the political side. They were then sent to the President-elect or to his cabinet officer or agency chief for consideration.

The Eisenhower administration had offered a precedent for allowing independence to the cabinet member to select his own subordinates, giving some consideration to the roster of names that had been put together from the diverse sources available to those at the Commodore Hotel. In some instances Kennedy and his chief aides followed the same route when they felt themselves lacking in competence; but where the appointments required a sensitive balancing, as in those agencies attempting to promote a bipartisan approach and where the

[13] See Adam Yarmolinsky, "The Kennedy Talent Hunt," *The Reporter*, Vol. 24 (June 8, 1961), pp. 22-25.

President-elect had a strong commitment to particular policies or political values, he was unwilling to delegate his authority. For example, he took a much greater interest in the Department of State and the Department of Defense than he did in appointments in the Departments of Labor, Agriculture, and Interior.

Kennedy was relatively slow to announce his first cabinet and sub-cabinet appointments. In fact, the first nomination on December 1 was Governor G. Mennen Williams of Michigan as Assistant Secretary of State for African Affairs. It was followed a few hours later by the announcement of Abraham Ribicoff as Secretary of Health, Education, and Welfare. On December 12, after protracted discussions, Dean Rusk became the new Secretary of State, with Chester Bowles as his Under Secretary. By that time it was also known that Kennedy had offered the post of ambassador to the United Nations to Adlai Stevenson—a position of great consequence for any Secretary of State.

These actions made it clear that the President-elect was not going to give his cabinet officers carte blanche in selecting their subordinates. Indeed, in those agencies in which he had a direct and compelling interest, the President appeared to make his selections independently; his secretary had to acquiesce. The simultaneous announcements of Edward Day as Postmaster General and William Brawley as Deputy Postmaster General tended to confirm this pattern of presidential and White House interest.

Each department was, in any event, assigned a Talent Hunt recruiter, who reviewed with the newly appointed cabinet member the list of possible candidates available. In certain domestic agencies the recruiter then ceased to take an active part, since these department heads were generally assumed to be acutely aware of political considerations and could be relied upon to make appropriate selections. In other departments and agencies, however, the Talent Hunt members continued to assist the chief in the screening of available candidates until the end of January 1961.

In the middle of December, Sargent Shriver had left the Talent Hunt group and Ralph Dungan took charge during the weeks remaining before inauguration. Recruitment and screening activities continued, along with specific assignments for certain department heads. But by January, political pressures were mounting rapidly and the Talent Hunt members responsible for canvassing relatively nonpolitical candidates found it increasingly difficult to gain sympathetic hearing from Kennedy's closest advisers. The longer high-level positions remained vacant, the greater was the pressure to fill them, thereby reducing the discretion of the President-elect and his appointees. This situation was accentuated upon the return of Congress in early January. As the legislative session approached, Kennedy's aides began to think about the President's legislative program and its reception by Congress and saw advantages in using some appointments to build congressional support for the program.

During December and early January, neither the Democratic party organization nor members of Congress had an important role in the recruitment process. The two groups operating the President-elect's recruitment program had essentially supplanted the national party organization, operating as they did out of the headquarters of the Democratic National Committee. The President's brother and his former senatorial staff were concerned with the strength of the national party, but they were now operating as presidential assistants and this institutional base tended to give them a somewhat different perspective than that of the National Committee or members of Congress.

During this pre-inaugural period congressmen followed two divergent policies. Some maintained a lively interest in the positions being filled, forwarding to the President and to the Talent Hunt group the names of candidates whom they were sponsoring. At times, these were political figures in their own states, but often they were individuals to whom the members of Congress owed no commitment but whom they considered excellent prospects. Other congressmen refused to take any part in recruitment at all, particularly for positions in departments or agencies which would be subject to their jurisdiction as chairmen and members of legislative committees; they did not want to restrict their freedom of action in holding administrative officers accountable through having responsibility for their appointment. Although some congressmen and senators privately expressed disquiet over the manner in which the selection process was handled by Kennedy and his assistants, there was no public display of dissatisfaction. In part this relatively favorable reaction resulted from the care which Kennedy's department heads took always to consult with members of Congress on appointments and to give serious consideration to their suggestions. Clearance procedures were not particularly systematic, but usually an attempt was made to check before appointments were announced with home state senators and occasionally with chairmen of Senate committees. By mid-January, however, clearance procedures had been more carefully worked out and these were followed in subsequent months.

By the end of January, the Talent Hunt group had ceased to operate as an entity. Fewer positions remained to be filled and the functions were performed by various White House staff members who continued to play an important role in recruitment, in the clearance of recommendations with the President, and with the political participants.

Participants in the Selection Process for Second-Level Positions

Although the recruitment process in each administration reflects the personality and political orientation of its Chief Executive, practice and expediency dictate that presidential control over appointments has to be shared with others who also have a stake in the administrative branch of the government. In some instances, even for appointments only two echelons below the President, his responsibility has been delegated to such a degree that he has often been able only to ratify (and with rarity, to veto) choices made by others.

Many groups and individuals participate in the selection of under secretaries and assistant secretaries, but not all of them involve themselves in every appointment. Before undertaking a more detailed analysis of the 108 specific appointments in the last three administrations that have provided data for the present study, it will be helpful to review here in general terms the role that each of these participants is likely to play in the appointment of high-ranking political executives.

The initial impetus for an appointment to executive office may begin anywhere in the political system. Several candidates are usually suggested for each position; some are the prime movers in their own nominations. Each group or individual having a stake in a specific appointment must compete with all the others until the final selection is made that leads to presidential nomination. Bargaining, rallying support in the party or elsewhere, secret negotiations, and even threats, all have their place in the selection process.

Each administration, each agency, and even each specific vacant position, may impose special curbs on the recruiters' freedom of choice, and there are also some more general limitations. Statistically, there is little likelihood, for example, that a woman, a Negro, or someone under thirty-five will be appointed (though President Johnson has pushed appointments of Negroes and women). Democrats are unlikely to appoint Republicans, and Republicans appoint very few Democrats. Democrats appear to select men with extended periods of higher governmental service for political executive positions. Those responsible for recruiting political executives in the Department of Agriculture nearly always select men who are identified with agriculture or the food industry and who fairly represent the major farm-producing areas. In the Treasury and Defense Departments there is an obvious tendency to draw heavily upon the business and financial communities in the Northeast, although it is not explicit and it is doubtful that there is any deliberate exclusion of men with other occupational and regional backgrounds.

Presidential Interest

Presidential control and interest in second-rank appointments are greatest at the beginning of a new administration. As he puts together his new political team the President-elect is less encumbered by policy and administrative responsibilities than he will be after inauguration day. In starting from scratch in each agency, he is not only filling slots with adequately qualified appointees but integrating the personnel requirements of an entire administration, with some awareness of the need for complementary skills both within the agencies themselves and in the executive establishment as a whole. The President may even make the appointment of a department or agency head contingent upon the latter's acceptance of certain candidates already chosen for subordinate positions.

The interest of the President in controlling the selection process and in making a positive contribution toward the selection of those with the right mixture of abilities and political qualifications has led to the establishment of a presidential personnel office. In earlier administrations, the function of political recruitment lay primarily in the hands of party officials. During the Roosevelt administration, for example, James Farley had a leading role in the selection of executives, clearing appointments with party officials, and receiving recommendations from members of Congress. Beginning with the Truman administration, however, a personnel office was located in the White House itself, distinct and separate from the party organization. In the beginning, its primary function was to collect the names of those recommended (or who recommended themselves), to negotiate among contending parties, and to advise the President. In the Eisenhower administration, this office developed more systematic, if no more effective, procedures through the use of card files and cross-indexing. The Kennedy administration attempted to strengthen the office by giving it positive recruiting functions and forcing it to operate within manageable limits in filling only the highest level posts.

Department and Agency Heads

Department and agency heads have little independent political authority in the appointment process. As presidential appointees they enjoy whatever discretionary powers the President is willing to delegate to them. Nevertheless, these men of the first echelon play a vital part in the selection of their own immediate subordinates and, by and large, a more active role than the President himself, who is generally interested in only a few of the departments and agencies.[14] The President may, in fact, like other participants, become a point of clearance rather than an active agent in the process. Indeed, negotiations often take place only with the White House staff—not the Chief Executive—and the initiative clearly remains with the department heads.

In every administration there have been certain top-level executives held in such high esteem by their President that they were given wide discretion in selecting their staff. John Snyder as the Secretary of the Treasury clearly had this kind of relationship with President Truman. George Humphrey and Herbert Brownell were held in special regard by President Eisenhower; and, unquestionably, the preferences of Robert Kennedy were respected by President Kennedy and his aides.

The perspective of a department head nevertheless tends to conform to that of the Chief Executive. As the operating chief of an executive agency he, like the President, needs skilled assistance in the development of his programs and policies. He needs help in coordinating operating bureaus which often resist integrated management, in carrying out the somewhat delicate negotiations with other units that have an

[14] "Department" and "agency" are used interchangeably throughout this book.

interest in his agency's activities, in bargaining with Congress for funds, in settling disputes between opposing interest groups, and in winning popular support for the department's programs.

Although this delegation of authority to a department head to select his own appointees is a delegation of presidential power, there is considerable logic in the practice. The head may be more strategically located for making the required political judgments than the President, in view of his more frequent and intimate relationships with members of Congress and interest groups who are affected by, and therefore concerned with, these appointments. He may have greater awareness of the need for rapport between deputies, assistant secretaries, under secretaries and their legislative overseers on the Hill; and he may know what type of person will prove acceptable to a congressional committee, particularly to its chairman. He is often in a better position to assess the reactions of interest groups to specific candidates and to use them more effectively in finding and evaluating potential nominees. The department head is also strongly motivated to make good choices, for he has to work closely with his under secretary and assistant secretaries. He must be able to depend on them.

Party Organizations

Political interests in recruitment are most clearly identified with the national party organizations and the state organizations. Skills and experience are conceded to be important in any assessment of executive abilities, but the committees are primarily interested in "patronage" and the dispensing of jobs and other emoluments as rewards for party service. Many men who take part in political campaigns want a more tangible reward for their efforts than the satisfaction of seeing their candidates elected. Party officials have also to maintain solidarity within their ranks by balancing appointments among the various factions within their organizations. Moreover, they are determined to prevent the appointment of men of the opposite party.

Political parties usually make their most significant contribution in the selection process at the beginning of a new administration, primarily because party officials are then in close touch with the President and are frequently destined themselves for important executive posts. Seldom do they become part of a continuing campaign organization;

instead they find positions either in the White House or in the administrative agencies. The Democratic Advisory Council was exceptionally useful in that it contributed a significant number of candidates for political executive positions at the beginning of the Kennedy administration, although the men suggested were usually distinguished individuals who could hardly be regarded as traditional party workhorses. Prominent members of auxiliary party organizations that played a major part in election campaigns, such as the Citizens for Eisenhower and Citizens for Kennedy, have figured significantly in the early appointments.

Some party officials recognize a wide gap between positions that have been subject to what has been termed "executive recruitment," and those that are within the realm of "patronage." One Republican party official recalled that, during the Eisenhower administration, the Republican National Committee was given an opportunity to make recommendations to fill large numbers of posts in a new agency. The committee recommended a number of individuals for the positions but few were appointed. The primary reason given for their lack of success was that the persons suggested were not qualified for the positions to be filled. On the other hand, party organizations have always been useful in filling lower-level positions both in Washington and in the field. Party officials are particularly interested in claiming jobs that can be given to party workers to use as bases of operation for future campaigns. One national chairman stated that the committee would rather have "twenty-five labor jobs at a naval ordnance plant than three assistant secretaries."

Members of Congress

Every administration recognizes that it must depend on legislative goodwill to implement its party program. The interchange of favors is an extremely subtle bargaining process and seldom if ever is there a *quid pro quo;* but failure to recognize congressional interest in executive appointments may adversely affect reception of the President's program on Capitol Hill.

Like their state party officials, members of Congress are anxious to reward their able and deserving party members back home. Winning assignments shows a congressman's constituents that he can "get things done in Washington," and this, of course, consolidates his political support. Nor is this all. The influence that a congressman can exercise through his appointee is perhaps of greater practical consequence when the appointment is in a department or agency having important installations or operations in his home state, or in an area where he has a special policy interest.

Nevertheless, congressmen recognize that they are dealing with an essentially executive prerogative. They are free to nominate and even to threaten reprisals if not listened to, but the degree to which they are given heed will depend on the quality of the product they try to market. Consistent failure to propose men of adequate ability or consistent effort to promote the candidacies of men with too obvious attachments to particular interests may reduce executive responsiveness.

Special Interest Groups

The concern of many special interest groups is less to control the selection of any one person for a particular post than to prevent the selection of someone unacceptable to them. In this fashion, these groups establish limits for the recruiters without appearing to dictate to the responsible executives. It does not appear that the American Bar Association or the American Bankers' Association is active in proposing candidates for political executive positions or in helping to make a specific decision. But in exceptional cases, where a candidate appears entirely contrary to their interests or professional standards, they may use their influence to defeat him.

The interest of other groups is not so passive, and their activity may range from passing on the candidates proposed by the executive branch, supporting the candidate favored by a congressman, to active advocacy of one of their own membership. The success of such advocacy depends largely on the group's access to the highest political levels in the particular department or in the White House. Organized labor had much easier access to the top officials in the Department of Labor and to the White House during Democratic administrations than during the Eisenhower administration, when business management interests predominated. A result has been more frequent appointment of labor executives in the department when the Democrats have been in power and of business executives during the Republican regime.

The character of these special groups varies widely. Some are interested primarily in program content with little direct economic stake in the department's affairs. The Foreign Policy Association and the many groups interested in American Indian policy in the United States are typical examples of this type of organization. At the other extreme are those groups which have direct economic benefits at stake, such as the commodity groups in agriculture or the building industry in the housing field; the pressure behind the support or opposition they give particular candidates generally reflects the degree of economic involvement.

Finally, a specific situation may cause powerful economic groups to eschew participation in the selection process entirely. In the Defense Department and the military agencies, with billions of dollars of contracts to award, the industrial giants find active promotion of candidates a perilous venture, in view of the possibility of attack for attempting to influence the course of government contracting through their former personnel.

The Candidates

Individuals who are being considered for political executive appointments are sometimes pawns in the hands of those making appointments but not infrequently they are active in their own behalf. The techniques of self-nomination are as numerous as the candidates themselves. One may notify the recruiters that he is available; another may undertake an out-and-out campaign, enlisting every form of political and professional support he can.

Men seek public office for a variety of reasons.[15] Some are already in the federal establishment and see in a political executive position the logical sequence to a long government career. Preferring government to other occupational settings, they look to public office for professional advancement. Many men in private life (particularly men who have operated at the periphery of elective politics, who have served on advisory boards, or who have already held public positions) find a fascination in public affairs which lures them into political job-hunting. They often have strong policy commitments which they hope to promote while in office. The prestige of high-ranking office is an impor-

[15] The question of motivation is dealt with in more detail in Chap. 6.

tant attraction. So too, for some, are career opportunities in later life to which public service opens the door.

The campaign for nomination is a tricky business, however, because the traditions of American politics demand that offices appear to seek men rather than the reverse. Department heads, White House officials, and even members of Congress are suspicious of the office seeker who cannot demonstrate those skills or experience that make him particularly suitable for appointment. These recruiters tend to regard such office seekers as men who have failed in their own jobs and who want top-level government positions to enhance their own personal advantage. For many recruiters, the highly successful man who is happy in his present employment and has little interest in the government appears to have much more potential as a political executive.

Other Interested Parties

Many individuals participate in the recruitment process on an informal and personal basis that has little or no apparent relation with political interest or institutional affiliation. Often, these private individuals provide the largest number of potential candidates. Department heads, for example, are inclined to call upon their former associates for assistance in finding men with executive talent. They, or the President, may also resort to other individuals who have become almost an institution in their own right in recommending potential executives, regardless of the party in power.

Bernard Baruch, the financier, has occupied a position of this kind. So did investment banker Sidney Weinberg in recruiting during World War II and the Korean War, and at the beginning of the Eisenhower administration. The contacts of Weinberg and Baruch are naturally much greater in the world of business than in other fields, but their recruiting efforts were less related to the control of positions in the government than to helping their friends fill demanding posts. Even when these friendships have been based on common membership in organizations such as the Business Advisory Council of the Department of Commerce, the Committee for Economic Development, or the Foreign Policy Association, personal relationships have often been more important than institutional interest.

The news media—newspapers, newsmagazines, journals of opinion, syndicated columnists, television, and radio—all play a part in the appointment process. Editorial opinion, and the public opinion it influences, may be an important consideration in the minds of those involved in appointments. The planted story and the trial balloon are favorite recruitment techniques for assessing readiness to accept particular nominees. Misreading public opinion can lead to stormy sailing for appointees between the time of their nomination and the end of confirmation hearings. Speculation on the overall pattern of political appointments is a much easier proposition for the news commentators at the beginning of an administration than later. Their precise influence on appointments is difficult to determine but cannot be overlooked in the case of such organs as the *New York Times* and journalists like Walter Lippmann.

Changes in Recruitment Practices During an Administration

The role of the various participants in the selection process for second-level positions in the executive establishment tends to change as the administration ages. Concern with appointments at the beginning of a new administration persists for several months after Inauguration Day. The new Chief Executive, his cabinet officers, and administrators continue to seek assistant secretaries and deputies long after they have formally taken over the reins of government. The pressure to fill the remaining posts, and particularly to remove any holdovers, grows acute and less and less careful judgment is apparent in the appointments made. Campaigns for favored candidates become more intense and expectations are higher as decisions are delayed. In addition, there are many other less prominent positions to fill, for which competition is keen from many different sources. Toward the end of the first year, however, the major initial recruitment effort is over. A few obvious misfits have to be replaced and shifts resulting from reorganization put into effect. Unfortunately, this does not put a stop to the large-scale necessary recruitment efforts of the President and his department and agency heads. The personnel situation of the political executive is never settled for long. Some appointees have committed themselves only for a limited period of time and therefore prepare for departure.

Others, finding attractive and what may appear to be once-in-a-life-time opportunities resulting from their new visibility, feel compelled to move on. Still others achieve success in public life and are lured into alternative positions in the national government or are encouraged to run for elective office. And a few, at least, find their jobs unduly difficult or unpleasant. As the departures begin, the President and his department heads again must devote a share of their valuable time to canvassing potential appointees. But the President himself is by now heavily involved in the other responsibilities of his office and usually can concern himself only with the selection of the highest level officers directly responsible to him. Consequently, the decentralization of personnel decisions which is apparent even at the beginning of an administration becomes still more pronounced as an administration ages.

At the beginning of an administration, the recently won political campaign sparks the enthusiasm of many eligible candidates who want to see those promised platform programs translated into action. The large majority do not actively promote themselves for political executive positions, but their responsibility for the success of the new administration predisposes them to consider favorably the prospect of an appointment. But as each succeeding week passes without noticeable change, enthusiasm wanes. It soon becomes perfectly clear that radical reform either is not possible or can be accomplished only with persistent, strenuous effort. Potential political executives may therefore make a more realistic assessment of the constraints of the situation; and disillusionment further reduces the number actively seeking public service or who are "available" when opportunities arise.

Uncertainty over the political fate of the new administration grows greater, too, as the months go by. There is always the possibility that the President will not be reelected, and the prospect of coming to Washington for what may turn out to be only a few months or at the most a year or two is not too alluring, especially when it is accompanied by financial losses. This situation was most apparent in the Truman administration when it was almost universally concluded that President Truman would not be reelected in 1948. Truman's executives were actively engaged in finding berths for themselves outside the government, and qualified replacements from private life were almost impossible to find for many agencies. A similar situation exists at the end of a President's eight years in office. The incoming President may be of the same political persuasion as his predecessor but, even so, there is no assurance that cabinet or subcabinet officers will be retained. At the end of the Eisenhower administration, it became apparent that this was an important factor in the minds of those who were being considered for political executive positions.

Besides the difficulty of finding appropriate candidates outside the government, a high rate of turnover in the senior political echelons of the major departments also leads subordinate officials to expect that successful performance will be rewarded by advancement to more senior office when vacancies occur. Failure to promote or even to give such men serious consideration has been a critical factor in the decisions of some executives to leave the government.

The result of these circumstances is that, having less time to devote to recruitment than they did at the beginning, and wishing more and more for experienced staff to aid them, department and agency heads have a stronger tendency than before to take the easier solution of selecting replacements from among those who are already closely associated with them in the government.

4

Recruitment Patterns, 1945-61

THE PRECEDING SURVEY of recruitment procedures for second-level executives has necessarily been somewhat oversimplified and couched in general terms. A description in terms of types and patterns can give no idea of the diversity and complexity of the actual appointment process. This can best be illustrated by giving details of the 108 instances of appointment and of the men selected to fill them during the Truman, Eisenhower, and Kennedy administrations.

The appointments chosen for special study are classified below according to the various groupings that exerted the most influence on the decision to appoint in each instance. In only eight of the 108 cases was the President's participation in the selection considered dominant. In general, the department head[1] was the central figure in the selection process for his own immediate subordinates although there was considerable variation in the precise role that he played from appointment to appointment. On most occasions he, or someone acting for him, was active in searching for candidates and assessing their qualifications. In others, he accepted a candidate put forward by a member of the President's staff, a member of Congress, an interest group, or by party officials. Seventeen of the total sample involved candidates who brought their own pressure to bear on the selecting officers; of these, seven submitted their names for office in the Kennedy administration, five in the Truman administration, and five in the Eisenhower administration. The seventeen cases are assigned to the various categories according to the actual role played in the appointment by the partici-

---

[1] "Department head" and "department" are terms used throughout this book to refer to both department and agency heads, and to both departments and agencies.

87

pants, not according to the source responsible for the appointee's original candidacy.

CHIEF PARTICIPANTS	TRUMAN	EISENHOWER		KENNEDY	TOTAL
	(1945-52)	(1953)	(1954-60)	(1961)	(1945-61)
President—White House staff	3	1	1	3	8
Secretary—Friends and associates	26	14	13	7	60
Secretary—White House staff	5	3	6	10	24
Secretary—Congress	—	2	3	3	8
Secretary—Interest groups	2	1	0	1	4
Secretary—Party officials	1	0	3	—	4
Total	37	21	26	24	108

Presidential Interest

In those instances when the President intervenes to make a nomination for a subcabinet position he is generally concerned with political interests and the balancing of the various factions within the party. Some of these appointments concern presidential nominees who have previously been considered for cabinet level positions but failed to survive the competition. The appointment of Adlai Stevenson as ambassador to the United Nations appeared to involve considerations of this kind. Others involve the President's personal friends and long-time supporters whom he wishes to appoint to positions in noncabinet agencies. Sometimes these assignments are rewards for faithful service, sometimes they reflect the President's confidence that these associates will protect his interests. Occasionally, they appear to provide a way out for a hard-pressed President who must recognize the persistent job-seeker but is unwilling to give him a position which carries with it major responsibilities of direct concern to the administration.

Three examples among the cases studied illustrate these various types of action by the President. The first involved *John Smith*,[2] a businessman who had worked long and hard in the 1952 Eisenhower campaign. Prominent in his locality, he had been chairman of his state committee. With the election won, *Smith* had strong support from the liberal wing of his party for a cabinet post and was obviously "available" if a suitable offer were made, even discussing the possibility in public, although he denied he was seeking a position. President-elect

[2] To protect the confidential nature of interview material, fictitious names are used for the men who were objects of the case studies. They have been italicized in each instance.

Eisenhower appeared at one point to favor his candidacy, but eventually the cabinet post went to another man who had an even longer record of top-level party service and who came from a wing of the party that lacked representation in the highest councils of the new administration. At least one member of the Commodore group had serious doubts about Smith's ability to fill the cabinet post. However, immediate efforts were made to find a suitable spot for him, and "four or five" possibilities were suggested, including the post as deputy head of the department for which he was originally proposed as head. Smith was "not intrigued with the idea" of the latter appointment—or any of the others—so he returned home. At this point the President-elect reportedly told his newly designated cabinet officer, "I don't want to shove anybody down your throat, but I'd like you to make [Smith] your deputy." Somewhat reluctantly the department head acceded to the president's request. Eisenhower then telephoned Smith, who finally accepted "with good grace," although it "did take some convincing on the part of the President."

The second example describes more direct action taken by President Kennedy early in his administration to persuade Thomas Jones, a reluctant candidate, to take the deputy post in an agency which the President considered of key significance to the administration and which he wished to strengthen. Jones had first met Kennedy when the latter was a candidate for the Senate in 1952, they had developed a "casual personal relationship," and Jones had gradually become identified with Kennedy's presidential endeavor. He had been chairman of his midwestern state's Citizens for Kennedy before the 1960 convention, but played no official role during the campaign; he did, however, act as host at meetings for the Democratic candidate when Kennedy appeared in the area. After the election the President-elect asked whether there was any position in the federal government that Jones wanted. Jones replied that he was not interested in a federal job and had worked in the election with no anticipation of reward. He was fully satisfied in his professional life, was at the prime level of earning potential, had children in school, and everything was going perfectly. He had only wanted to see Kennedy elected. Some months later Jones had a telephone call from a White House staff member inviting him to meet with the President. Jones was obviously impressed at such personal attention and felt bound to go to Washington. The President wished to talk to him about the vacant deputy position in the key agency where the head had not been appointed until some time after Inauguration Day and who, even at that relatively late date, was still encountering considerable difficulty in finding the type of man he wanted to serve under him. He "had turned down many people who were seeking the job." During the course of their talk Kennedy indicated to *Jones* his keen concern with the effective operation of the agency and expressed confidence that *Jones* would contribute much as deputy director. He suggested that *Jones* find out about the agency's prospects himself by talking with various presidential advisers. *Jones* was taken by surprise at the offer, but he nevertheless consulted with the top people mentioned by the President and met the newly appointed agency head who, it was apparent, would defer to Kennedy on the matter. Both *Jones* and the director decided they could work well enough together and the former accepted the deputy position. *Jones* accepted because he felt that he had an obligation to serve, since the President had made a direct appeal to him; but he was fully aware of the personal disadvantages of a Washington assignment.

The third example of presidential involvement concerns the effort to find a sinecure for *James Doe*, a deserving but not-too-well-qualified party worker, a very active Republican who did everything he could to obtain a cabinet post at the beginning of the Eisenhower administration. *Doe* had been both a member and an official of the Republican National Committee and promoted Eisenhower's candidacy before, during, and after the Republican convention. When Eisenhower was elected, *Doe* informed both the President and the senator from his state of his desire for a cabinet appointment. But the Eisenhower staff took a negative view of the idea and eagerly sought another post for him that would give him sufficient prestige and yet where he would exert little or no influence on administration policy. *Doe's* senator supported his political colleague's claim for recognition, but it was evident that he did not want to undertake to campaign for him. *Doe* was offered two lesser posts which he refused; and a White House aide finally went to a friendly agency head of noncabinet rank and asked him to take the persistent candidate off his hands as deputy. The agency head was not enthusiastic but, since he expected to use his executive assistant as his primary aide, his formal deputy would have very little to do. The President then offered the deputy position to *Doe* who accepted, even though he had previously learned from his prospective agency head that his duties would be relatively minor. He was bitterly disappointed at this meagre recognition of his past loyal party services.

The Department Head as Chief Recruiter

Presidents in office have generally conceded department heads as much freedom as possible in the selection of their subordinates. This was amply borne out by the case studies since 100 of the 108 instances of appointment directly involved the department heads. The willingness or unwillingness of these men to acknowledge pressures from the White House, Congress, political parties, and special interest groups has determined the pattern of recruitment for posts in the executive branch during the three administrations here under review. Over two thirds of the secretaries and administrators whose recruiting methods were examined took primary responsibility for finding suitable candidates, either through personal contacts or by a broader search. The remainder allowed or were expected to accept leadership from some other source, although usually reserving the right to object and even veto individuals who were not acceptable to them. The one notable departure from this pattern was at the beginning of the Kennedy administration when the tendency was to rely on candidates supplied by the Talent Hunt, or by the President himself, who directly intervened to find positions for men in whom he had personal confidence or to whom he owed a political debt.

The type of search conducted did not necessarily dictate the type of candidate finally selected, although there was clearly some relationship. The instances where the department head relinquished control of the process were usually those in which party and interest group considerations became paramount in the selection. The criteria for selection tended to be related to geographical representation, party service, or access to some other power-holder in the political system. When the department head retained control, there was often—although not always—an emphasis on past administrative experience, policy objectives, or substantive knowledge of operations. Furthermore, he operated under certain restraints in many departments. Where the clientele groups were powerful, his scope of search was narrowed and he had less discretion in choosing among candidates. Where the clientele groups were more numerous, disunited, or had interests which did not entirely parallel department activities, the discretion of the department head increased.

Department Head's Criteria of Selection

Party membership was almost invariably required of political executives appointed between 1945 and 1961, although within that general framework more professional standards were also applied. There was generally an implicit assumption that only the candidacies of those who had a policy orientation similar to the President's were ever seriously considered. In this context, self-promoters and the individuals who appeared on the lists of the Talent Hunt during the Kennedy administration were, of course, almost automatically qualified on policy grounds since they were usually individuals who supported the incoming administration. Obviously, sympathy with the new administration did not necessarily mean conformity in policy views on specific issues arising in any particular agency.

The web of personal relationships that develops around each department head in his recruitment efforts clouds the selection procedures followed and the criteria used in deciding upon appropriate candidates to fill the various positions. Even those appointments termed "political" by the appointees themselves and others involved in their nominations are seldom purely "political." They are generally at least partially justified by the candidates' talents and experience.

Based on the considered judgments of the 108 appointees and some 200 other individuals having a stake in their appointments, certain criteria were discovered during the course of this study that showed, even if only approximately, the guiding factors behind the department heads' selection of their subordinates in each instance:

CRITERIA FOR SELECTION	TRUMAN (1945-52)	EISENHOWER (1953) (1954-60)		KENNEDY (1961)	TOTAL (1945-61)
Expertise in a specific area of responsibility	3	7	5	8	23
Expertise plus political factors	2	1	3	1	7
General experience in the area of responsibility	20	3	12	4	39
General experience plus political factors	9	8	3	9	29
Service to the party	3	2	3	2	10
Total	37	21	26	24	108

The distribution of cases according to these rather broad criteria illustrates another interesting feature about recruitment during this period—the inclination of department heads and other participants in the selection process to stress general experience and capacity rather than narrower criteria related to specific agency activities. Very often, they expressed this preference by saying they were looking for men with "administrative experience" or of "good character." This was particularly true of businessmen-recruiters who regarded general business acumen and success as indicators of competence for a variety of tasks in all agencies. It is significant, however, that political considerations seemed to play a much larger part in appointments made on this basis. The combination of political and general ability appeared to be particularly crucial in the selection of under secretaries and deputies. Whether the Secretary was looking for an alter ego or for an internal administrator, he was generally searching for someone with a broader perspective than he would expect from the head of one of his operating units. If he hired a specialist as a deputy, he was likely to lose the deputy to his specialty.

General experience also appeared to be more important in appointments made later in an administration than in those made at the beginning, perhaps because of the greater tendency to check the government personnel lists before resorting to outside recruitment sources. Twenty-nine of the thirty-seven Truman cases studied (which could all be regarded as appointments made during an administration) and fifteen of Eisenhower's twenty-six later appointments involved choices based on the appointees' general background.

A typical case among those studied involved the undersecretaryship in a department that had recently been extensively reorganized. Prominent in this reorganization was a well-known political figure (a close friend of the President) who considerably impressed the chief with his keen interest in the department's activities and his patience and energy in working out the reorganization plan. Surrounded by specialists, the secretary recognized the need for someone with such general administrative experience to coordinate the activities of these experts and saw in this individual the precise qualifications he was looking for in an under secretary.

Sometimes the quest for individuals having certain kinds of administrative experience takes a curious turn, with the agency head selecting someone who lacks most of the qualifications originally thought indispensable to the job: someone who has, nevertheless, a record which suggests a strong probability of success in government work. Such an instance occurred at the beginning of the Kennedy administration. One agency head had a strong preference for delegating responsibility to his chief assistants, so that he himself could act as a kind of chairman of the board—making policy decisions and fashioning the agency's image both at home and abroad. Logically, he preferred a deputy who would act as his administrator, responsible for detailed agency operations. In his search, however, he came across a man who had strong political recommendations and a brilliant record as an administrator in private industry but limited active political experience. This individual would obviously not be content to act solely as an organization man; but the agency head chose him, nonetheless, and the businessman became, in effect, his alter ego, sharing responsibility for policy decisions, working with outside interest groups, as well as coordinating the work of the agency.

Personal Selection by Department Head

The recruiting effort takes on a personal character when the department head relies on his own circle of acquaintances and his professional and business associates as the most fruitful source for candidates, or for contacts with other prospects. Many political executive appointments have been made on this personal basis. Shortly after Frank Knox was appointed Secretary of the Navy, for example, he enlisted Ralph Bard, a Chicago investment banker and a Republican friend, as an assistant secretary.[3] At about the same time, James Forrestal brought to the attention of Secretary Knox his personal friend and fellow New York banker, Artemus L. Gates.[4] When John Foster Dulles became Secretary of State, he immediately selected as his Assistant Secretary of State for Public Affairs Carl W. McCardle, his best friend in the Washington press corps.[5] James Byrnes appointed his friend and fellow South Carolinian, Donald Russell, to positions in the various agencies which the former headed in the executive branch— the Office of Economic Stabilization, the Office of War Mobilization

---

[3] Robert Greenhalgh Albion and Robert Howe Connery, *Forrestal and the Navy* (Columbia University Press, 1962), pp. 7-8.
[4] *Ibid.*, pp. 9-10.
[5] John Robinson Beal, *John Foster Dulles* (Harper & Brothers, 1957), p. 165.

and Reconversion and the Department of State. In the latter department, Russell became the Assistant Secretary of State for Administration.[6]

Among the appointments studied *Frank Adams* was a case in point.[7] He had served with one of the Kennedy cabinet appointees during previous tours of duty in the Truman administration, and they had remained close friends during the Eisenhower years. Both had played roles in the Kennedy 1960 campaign, though relatively minor. The cabinet head's appointment was announced at the same time as that of his under secretary, a prominent party leader whose appointment clearly bore the stamp of presidential selection. The new cabinet member almost immediately telephoned and asked *Frank Adams* to come to Washington to help him. No specific position was discussed, but *Adams* had already expressed a desire for a political appointment and he expected an offer of some kind to be made to him at a later date. Both *Adams* and his cabinet head worked closely together during the pre-inaugural period, although it was not until after some rearrangement of functions had been effected that a top policy-making position was created to *Adams'* liking and he was given an appointment.

Another cabinet secretary made a personal choice of *George Edwards* as an assistant secretary at the beginning of the Eisenhower administration. The secretary had already made known his decision to retain two Truman appointees and to select a business associate as his chief assistant; the latter nomination encountered the vigorous opposition of some Commodore Hotel aides who felt that a more broadly representative team should be formed. When *Edwards* first came to his attention as a possible candidate, the secretary was considering prospects for another assistant secretary post still vacant and wondering if any of them had sufficient background to cope with the complicated substantive problems involved in that division. *Edwards*, a prominent public official in the secretary's home state, had written regarding a problem of mutual interest and the secretary was instantly struck with his suitability for the vacant position. He said to himself, "This is the man I want," and immediately called *Edwards*. *Edwards* had already been considered for other important positions in the ad-

---

[6] James F. Byrnes, *All in One Lifetime* (Harper & Brothers, 1958), pp. 161-62, 186, 310.

[7] *Frank Adams* and the subsequent names in italics are fictitious names used to protect the confidential nature of the interview material.

ministration, so there was no problem about his acceptance with the Commodore Hotel group; but *Edwards'* superiors in his home state were much disturbed at the prospect of losing him and with what would happen to his job. They realized that the assistant secretaryship was a "step up" for *Edwards,* however, and so they consented to his departure after the secretary had talked to each of them individually on the importance of making this particular appointment.

A somewhat broader approach, but still dependent upon personal contacts, was found in another early Kennedy appointment. A secretary was considering several men for the post of under secretary. He had stipulated that he wanted to appoint someone who would be loyal to him and, at the same time, have broad knowledge of the department's activities and of the specific duties to be assigned to the under secretary. An important presidential aide had also advised him to find someone who could replace him as head on a day's notice. Prospective candidates for the position were drawn from many different sources— the White House, the Senate, the Democratic National Committee— although there was no pressure to appoint any particular individual. But the secretary was dissatisfied with all of them; most of their qualifications, it seemed to him, were more appropriate for an assistant secretaryship than for an undersecretaryship. At least two of the candidates alienated him with their overeagerness. Inauguration Day came and, still without an under secretary, the department head mentioned his problem to two former political executives with whom he had maintained contact since their earlier association during the Truman administration. They both suggested a mutual acquaintance, *Paul King,* a Washington lawyer whom the secretary had also known fairly well for nearly a decade. The secretary thought this was an excellent suggestion and immediately began to make preliminary checks on reactions to the appointment with the under secretary's possible associates in the government. After he had won their approval of his choice, he invited *King* to come and see him. The subject of an appointment was first broached in this vein: The secretary began discussing the various specialists he needed as assistant secretaries, then commented that what he would require of his under secretary would be more general abilities and much broader experience. He came abruptly to the point with "that man is you!" *King* was "stunned." He had been in private law practice since his government assignment under President Truman. After the 1960 election he had felt, to be sure, an interest in returning to the government, but one of his partners had suggested that he wait until things "shook down." With his legal background he had thought vaguely about the Justice Department rather than the specialized agency for which he was now being sought. However, as the secretary wanted a man of general competence and as one of their mutual friends who knew both of them very well thought *King* could do the job, the latter accepted.

Extended Search Initiated by Department Head

Some department heads are not satisfied with a limited recruiting effort, but use the resources of many interest groups and public organizations to provide them with candidates. In certain instances, this has indicated a relatively sophisticated approach to the problem of putting together a politically balanced administrative team—and a recognition that many interests and many areas should be represented in a national agency. In others, only a desire to find men specifically qualified for particular positions has been apparent.

One secretary placed great emphasis upon close personal relationships and consistency in policy views in the selection of his first round of subordinates, largely discounting prior political activity. Although the President-elect's recruiting staff found him responsive to their suggestions, they recognized that they had little to offer in a field far removed from their own areas of competence. Well-known in his own field, the secretary was able to make extensive contacts among public and private organizations active in the substantive work of his department. One technique he used was to wire the heads of all state agencies dealing with his department asking them for recommendations. He then embarked on a nationwide tour to interview suggested candidates. At the last stop of the tour he interviewed *Harold Parker*; an immediate rapport was established, and the secretary asked *Parker* to take one of his top appointments without specifying which one. *Parker* had been politically active and was undoubtedly familiar to the President's recruiters through the recommendation of his state party organization. He had participated in the work of the previous two national conventions and had worked in his own locality for the President during the last campaign. The secretary returned to Washington and on the following day telephoned *Parker* and offered him the undersecretaryship, saying, "the President and I want you to come." On his tour the secretary had also met *Richard Clark*, a man with no political experience, but named as one of the three top men in his field by the state agency heads whom the secretary had asked for recommendations. The secretary interviewed *Clark* a second time at more length before he offered him an assistant secretaryship. *Clark* accepted on the condition that he would stay no longer than two years, since he did not wish to resign his permanent position. The secretary was unhappy at this but said they would cross that bridge when they came to it.

Several Republican businessmen who became department heads in the Eisenhower administration made extended searches for their political executives, using business contacts to develop lists of candidates. One used his contacts in organizations like the National Industrial Conference Board, the American Management Association, and management consultant firms. He also contacted such organized interest groups as the American Bankers' Association. Another executive relied primarily on his contacts in industry, particularly making use of his ties with the National Association of Manufacturers. Still another relied to a considerable extent on names presented to him by a management consultant company. Organizations representing these special interests seldom operated as formal recruiting agencies. The department head merely asked individual members well-known to him through organization affairs to suggest the names of candidates qualified along specified lines. For example, one agency chief contacted the president of the American Bankers' Association who was also a personal friend. He was looking for someone to fill a position requiring some knowledge of financial affairs. The ABA president recommended a banking associate in his own locality who was later appointed to the position.

Supporting testimony for the crucial part played by department and agency heads in the selection of their subordinates can be found in studies of the appointees' occupational backgrounds. Even at the beginning of an administration when competition for control over appointments is greatest, the department head still plays the dominant role. In the Eisenhower administration, for example, the Secretary of Defense and the chiefs of the three military services all had business backgrounds. So also did eleven of the seventeen men recruited to subcabinet posts in those departments in the early days of the administration; another two were New York lawyers who had important business connections. Similarly, in the Department of Commerce with Secretary Weeks as its head, all five men recruited were from business. Postmaster General Summerfield during his first year in office appointed six subcabinet officers: five businessmen like himself and one banker. Secretary Dulles in the Department of State, having had extensive experience in the government in addition to his New York law practice, drew much more from men already in the government. Of the thirteen men he recruited during the first year, seven were from the government—primarily Foreign Service officers for whom he had developed a very high regard.

The foregoing cases present variations of the quite large number of instances where the role of a secretary has been extremely prominent in the selection of his own subordinates. Very often, of course, he has been subjected to pressures from many different sources both inside and outside the government; and candidates have been variously assessed by the White House, members of Congress, party officials, and interest groups according to their own specific requirements. In cases of this nature, however, the part played by the agency head has been crucial in making the final selection.

White House Influence in Appointments

These examples blend almost imperceptibly into a class of cases in which the department head continued to exercise his prerogative to choose his own subordinates subject to presidential approval, but in which the White House influence on his decisions was much more keenly felt. This pressure took many forms. Often, the candidates were first suggested to the department heads by the White House or those put forward by department heads were subjected to close scrutiny by the White House aides and some rejected as unqualified. At other times, presidential aides resisted recommendations made by the department and agency heads, going so far as to carry their objections to the President. It was essentially a bargaining process, but with the head generally making the final decision, subject only to the approval of the President. The case material indicates that, where secretary and White House staff conflicted over an appointment, the secretary generally won. The same was true to a lesser degree for the agency administrators.

The White House may exert pressure on department heads to consider other possible candidates, however; and the President or his staff may request additional evaluations of the abilities of the candidates presented. They may even force a department head into a *quid pro quo* situation where he gets his way on one appointment while agreeing to a White House nominee for another. This type of barter is more likely to occur at the beginning of an administration, when the President is more personally interested in the balance and unity of his team.

The White House is also the central mechanism through which candidates are cleared with other important groups. More often than not, if selections are to be reviewed by members of Congress, the clearance will be conducted by a White House aide. It is at this point also that the Federal Bureau of Investigation undertakes its full field check of all presidential nominees, a time-consuming process which, at the beginning of an administration, can hold up appointments for weeks at a time and cause considerable embarrassment to a candidate whose nomination has become public knowledge. Appointments referred to the White House are also cleared with the party national committee at this stage, the latter conducting whatever checks are necessary with state and local party organizations.

The degree of pressure brought to bear on the department head by the President and his aides has varied from administration to administration. The influence of the recruiting operation centralized at the White House was greater at the beginning of Kennedy's term in office, for example, than at the beginning of Eisenhower's.

A case in point involved the selection of a deputy in one of the major domestic agencies. The department chief, appointed by Kennedy, had encountered much party opposition to his own candidacy because of his political deficiencies. Wishing to gain the confidence of the new administration's top officials and members of Congress, he deliberately sought as deputy a person with a strong national party identification who was also a lawyer with broad experience. The Talent Hunt group gave him a list of prospects. On this list he found the name of *William Hall*, a prominent Democrat who had held important posts in the Truman administration. He knew *Hall* only casually but they had a close mutual friend. Checking first with the latter and then making other inquiries in both Washington and New York, the secretary was convinced that Hall would be eminently suitable. He "sold" his prospective candidate to President Kennedy and his assistants, who made their own independent evaluation and agreed that *Hall* would be a fine choice. At this point, however, the nominee ran into potent congressional opposition because he had once run for Congress against a powerful congressman identified with the conservative wing of the party. The department head allayed the suspicions and fears of the congressman by obtaining testimonials from influential conservatives as to the nominee's integrity and ability; and *Hall* was later appointed.

Similar sensitivity to political considerations was found in another early Kennedy case. The department head came from a background of elective public service and hoped to obtain a deputy with a perspective similar to his own who could serve in his stead if necessary. After a rather extensive search, he finally decided upon a man with strong professional qualifications and government experience. He was out of luck, however, because, while he was making up his mind, Kennedy had found greater need for this particular candidate in another prominent position. The secretary's next two choices for under secretary were the presidents of two important professional institutions, but both turned the offer down. Other possibilities that did not work out included a former governor and a prominent member of the Kennedy entourage. The secretary was by this time beginning to feel very keenly the pressure of time (particularly since his assistant secretaries had already been appointed), and so he was particularly receptive to the suggestion of a White House aide that *Ernest Miller* would be a good prospect. *Miller* was a local elected official who had been very prominent in the 1960 campaign, and had worked closely with Kennedy at one point. He had had the responsibility for a major segment of his state's presidential campaign. Although the secretary did not know *Miller* personally, he had confidence in the good judgment of the presidential aide and therefore accepted the suggestion; *Miller* had already answered a White House query by saying that he had a general interest in accepting a position but it would depend on the job that was offered him. The proffered undersecretaryship appeared quite an honor to him and he accepted without even talking to the secretary.

An early Eisenhower appointment also illustrates the role of presidential staff in introducing candidates for executive posts. Several businessmen with an interest in the public service, closely associated with the Clay-Brownell effort in the Commodore Hotel, identified various personal friends and associates as potential high-level public servants. One of the businessmen approached *Lawrence Scott*, a New York investment banker who had spent much of his recent life in the federal government and in international agencies. The businessman told *Scott:* "Now look, you're a Republican and you've had experience in government service. Several of us are sort of an informal recruiting committee for the Eisenhower administration; and I think you should consider serving in the new administration." *Scott* thought it over and consulted with a former business partner, who was also a member of the recruiting group, considering possible positions. Some days later *Scott* called his former partner and said he would be interested in either of two positions that would make use of his experience in international affairs. One of them was already filled, but the recruiter recommended *Scott* to the man appointed to head the department where the other was located. The appointee and *Scott* had a slight acquaintance dating from an earlier campaign. In a long interview they explored various phases of the job, particularly in relation to foreign policy, and realized that their views differed markedly in some important respects. Several days later, however, after some further checks, the Secretary called *Scott*, said he did not want to surround himself with a lot of "yes men," and was recommending *Scott* to the President for an assistant secretaryship, where he would have wide latitude in carrying out his job.

Another appointment initiated by presidential staff, this time by aides in the White House office and based on political considerations, was that of *James Black* to a domestic department early in the Kennedy administration. The cabinet officer had accepted his own appointment with the knowledge that the White House would play an important role in the selection of his assistant secretaries, though he would have the right of final decision. *Black's* primary qualifications were his years of party service and an active role in the 1960 campaign, though he had at one time intended to go into teaching. Immediately after the election he happened to meet a close friend, one of the President-elect's aides, who suggested that *Black* file an application for a federal post. *Black* did so, expressing a primary interest in international affairs, but heard nothing until shortly before inauguration, when at another chance meeting the White House aide mentioned casually that there were some problems in one agency where

Black would be useful. However, there was no definite word for several more weeks, when he was finally interviewed by both the deputy and secretary. They were favorably disposed toward his nomination, but *Black* himself felt that it was imperative that he obtain prior approval from the Senate committee passing on his appointment because of one personal characteristic that might be regarded as objectionable. The Senate committee, however, approved him unanimously.

Relations between department head and White House are not always quite so cordial, however. One appointment in the latter part of the Eisenhower administration caused a certain amount of irritation to both sides. Owing to an abrupt change in personal circumstances, a highly respected and experienced assistant secretary in the Defense establishment decided he had to leave the government for an attractive offer in industry. The departing executive, the deputy (his immediate superior), and the department head discussed his possible replacement from among those already employed in the organization. Two likely candidates whom they were considering were finally discarded, the first because they were unwilling for the man to leave his extremely responsible job in another division, and the second because they concluded that the officer's ability was inadequate for such a gruelling assignment. A third was sounded out, but he was quite uninterested in undertaking anything so much more demanding than his current position; and a fourth, the deputy to the departing political executive, was actually offered the job and would have accepted if the company for whom he had worked prior to his government service had not vigorously objected on the grounds that it would create serious conflict of interest problems. While these four prospects from within the organization were being scrutinized by the department head and his staff, the White House had also busied itself in the search for appropriate candidates, and a professional association tried unsuccessfully to have someone from its ranks appointed through its contacts in Congress and the Republican National Committee.

All along, however, the man who was leaving had had a special applicant at the back of his mind whom he now put forward and supported. He was *Walter Lewis*, a lawyer and a former aide during World War II whom the departing assistant secretary had several times urged to return to the government. *Lewis* had already been considered for several other positions and he was obviously interested in a post "at the minimum level where I could make a contribution at this stage of my life." There was opposition to his selection at the White House because the staff there felt that a lawyer was not qualified to handle certain aspects of the work. But time was becoming an important consideration and so many prospects had either fallen short of the requirements or turned down the job that, when approval was finally obtained for *Lewis* from a prominent White House officer, the other White House aides also grudgingly gave their consent to the appointment.

There is no invariable rule that men who come from a relatively nonpolitical background are suspicious of recommendations of candidates that come through political channels. The fact that General Eisenhower's executives took this approach in this instance in no way indicated the approach which other secretaries in that administration or secretaries in the Kennedy administration would take. For example, one Kennedy executive came to Washington with relatively few political contacts and little political experience. He worked closely with the Talent Hunt, particularly with those who specialized in appointments in his agency. He demanded extensive evaluations and other explanations for additional candidates but nonetheless gave serious attention to the individuals suggested by the Talent Hunt, and appointed several of their candidates.

Self-Initiated Appointments

Although the literature on political executive recruitment tends to emphasize the problems of obtaining the services of qualified men in public life, it is clear that few successful men behave like shrinking violets, answering the call to service only with great reservations and with obvious distaste for the publicity entailed. Many men in private life eagerly seek appointments and use their political skills to great advantage in making themselves known to the right people at the right time. Such self-promotion is a delicate procedure and requires a nice balance between humility and self-confidence.

Most potential executives of this type initiate their own candidacies without campaigning for office. They are simply available for a call to service, doing political chores (legwork in the campaign, helping on task forces, giving advice on policy) to keep their names in the party eye. When the lists of prospects are compiled, it is only natural that their names should appear and that the party's debt to them be recognized.

A particularly interesting case involved *Joseph Gray*, a lawyer who had spent a number of years in government service during the Truman administration, maintaining an active interest in Democratic politics during the eight-year Republican interim. He attended the 1960 convention and took part in the Democratic campaign although he was not an original Kennedy supporter. When the Democrats won, *Gray* began to speculate on the possibility of another government position. On the whole, he thought he would be well advised to remain outside the administration, except that one cabinet post particularly intrigued him. He mentioned his interest to a few friends but, recognizing that his background gave him little hope of serious consideration, did no active campaigning. *Gray* was later invited to talk with two presidential aides about his experience under President Truman; this gave an opportunity to mention his interest in this position to them. Although the aides agreed that he could not hope for the top-level job, one of them called *Gray* that evening and said that he had spoken of the conversation to Kennedy, and had been asked to find out if by any chance *Gray* would be interested in the undersecretaryship. No definite commitment was made on either side; but, when a well-known political figure was named to the cabinet post, *Gray's* name was suggested to him. In the latter's view, *Gray's* only drawback was that he lacked specific qualifications for the duties entailed in the position. He agreed, however, that, if *Gray* could obtain congressional endorsement and support from other influential sources, he might be seriously considered. Strong congressional backing was necessary in this instance because the President had made certain commitments on appointments in this department and there were a number of other candidates with active congressional campaigns behind them. *Gray* had been only moderately interested in the deputy post until competition piqued him to action. Working often through intermediaries, he was able to obtain congressional support because of his long government experience and his own circle of friends on Capitol Hill. He was also able to generate support from important clientele groups that played a crucial role in the agency's operations. The department head took his time about coming to a final decision but he eventually recommended *Gray's* appointment to the President, concluding that the lawyer would make the most effective deputy in spite of his deficiencies in substantive knowledge of the agency's program. The congressional candidates were placed in positions at somewhat lower levels.

Louis Robinson also promoted his own candidacy during the Kennedy administration. He had taken an active part in the 1960 general election campaign and had long been a well-known party figure in his own state. In addition, he had served as a consultant in the defense area for both his state and federal governments. When the Democrats won, Robinson considered the possibility of trying for a post in the defense establishment. He recognized, however, that he would have to do a great deal of legwork in his own behalf if he wanted to be considered for any position because he lacked the prominence or the leverage otherwise to bring his name before recruiting officials. He deliberately restricted his contacts to personal acquaintances, keeping them as informal as possible since, in his words, "it would be presumptuous to be an obvious office-seeker." Robinson spoke to his state chairman, governor, and congressman, each of whom was a personal acquaintance and supported his candidacy. He also communicated with several Washington friends whom he knew to be active in Democratic politics and concerned with defense policy and personnel. The first choice of defense recruiters for one of the positions—a college president—had declined, and Robinson learned through one of his Washington contacts that he was being seriously considered for the appointment. He decided to promote his own nomination more openly, and discussed his prospects with a well-known defense appointee whom he knew slightly. Shortly thereafter, he received a call from Washington. After meeting with the secretary and his deputy, Robinson was offered the position and accepted it.

Men who have spent long periods of time in the national government, including the career service, are also interested in advancement. While many are reluctant to take the risk of political exposure, some have felt confidence that they could establish a new career if forced to leave the government with the advent of a new administration. Harry Young, a career official, had served his department for sixteen years, rising to the post of assistant to the assistant secretary, a position he occupied for five years. When his chief (the fourth assistant secretary to hold that office in five years) resigned to run for the Senate, Young asked the secretary's personal assistant to consider him for the post. Nothing happened for several months while other applicants were being reviewed, including one lawyer who was favored by the President and the White House staff. *Young* had the feeling that his candidacy, although not actually opposed, was certainly not supported by a powerful bureau chief under whom he had previously worked and who was himself under the nominal jurisdiction of the assistant secretaryship for which *Young* was applying. When he heard nothing for several months, he went to the personal assistant again and was told to "sit tight" and avoid making any appearance of promoting his own appointment. His only political support was his slight acquaintanceship with the secretary; this proved crucial. The secretary placed great trust in *Young* because of his past accomplishments and therefore convinced the President that he should be offered the post. An interesting sidelight was supplied by a presidential assistant who observed when *Young* went to see the President that he had not been particularly active in the previous presidential campaign. The aide implied that a more active political role was expected of presidential appointees.

The Role of Congress

To a surprising extent members of Congress have been willing to recognize selection of political executives as primarily an executive prerogative and they have allowed the President as wide discretion in the choice of his subcabinet officers as they have in the composition of his cabinet. This has not meant, of course, that they have not suggested their own candidates, and occasionally resisted or outspokenly opposed presidential nominees whom they have found undesirable. But for the most part they do not attempt to dictate to the President or to the department and agency heads in matters where executive responsibility is so clear-cut and the imposition of unwanted personnel may be so damaging.

In some departments and agencies, such as the Department of the Interior, members of Congress have greater influence on executive appointments because of strong sectional interests and the importance of policy and representational considerations. Some members of Congress are also acknowledged experts in certain subject areas and the executive has sought their advice in the filling of certain key positions. In one appointment in the early Eisenhower administration, for example, the newly appointed secretary sought out a prominent Republican member of the House of Representatives for advice on filling a highly sensitive assistant secretaryship in the field of national security. The congressman suggested a man long active in that field who was later approved by the secretary and the President.

There are two sides to the coin, of course. Members of Congress are also subjected to considerable pressure from their constituents and others who are interested in obtaining appointments. Although somewhat skeptical about the qualifications of many of these individuals, congressmen are obliged to submit their names even if they do not, in fact, support the candidacies. Frequently this is a pro forma action and the very lack of enthusiasm constitutes a major deterrent to the candidate's chances. One leading Republican senator said that he had had to submit the names of many applicants because of pressure from people in his home state, but in general he felt that these individuals were not of a particularly high quality. He cited the case of an active Republican who had been prominent in a veterans organization and in National Guard activities in his state. He had wanted to be an assistant secretary of Defense for many years. The senator felt compelled to send his name to the White House and the department head, but he would do nothing more to promote the candidacy.

The type of constituency the congressman represents also affects his participation in executive recruitment. Senators from Illinois, for example, who are close to the business, financial, and labor communities may provide easy access to many aspiring officeholders and may make a positive effort to have certain individuals appointed. Senators from midwestern or southern agricultural states are likely to know men qualified for positions in the Department of Agriculture. Even so, fewer senators make use of their potential influence than might be expected.

Two Democratic committee chairmen in the House and one in the Senate expressed extreme views in this connection. In spite of their strategic positions, they claimed they deliberately refused to exercise any influence on the grounds that they wished to retain complete freedom of action in dealing with political executives once they were appointed. They would feel responsible, they said, for executives who owed their appointments to them and would no longer feel free to criticize their performance.

A typical congressional attitude was expressed by Representative Clem Miller of California when Assistant Secretary of Agriculture James Ralph was dismissed for his part in the Billie Sol Estes affair.

Congressman Miller stated: "No one wants to dictate to the Secretary of Agriculture. We will merely notice that the greatest agricultural state in the country is no longer represented in the highest councils of the government."[8] Ralph's replacement, however, was Roland R. Renne of Montana.

The restrained and moderate behavior of the majority of senators and congressmen is somewhat qualified by those who are naturally aggressive and enjoy the power they exercise over other men's futures. Their influence is particularly potent if they preside over or sit on powerful congressional committees. A Democratic committee chairman in the Senate, for instance, vigorously sought to control appointments in two government organizations that were subject to the jurisdiction of the two committees on which he served during the Kennedy administration. He strongly urged the appointment of a man from an adjacent state as deputy in one organization because of its importance to the interests of his region. Unsuccessful there, he urged the appointment of another candidate for the position of general counsel but met with a rebuff because the agency head wanted a personal friend in this position. He "raised hell" when the first list of appointees was made known, none of whom came from his region. When the agency head proposed to appoint still another man from outside his area he "really tore up the place." He and the other senator from his state both urged the President-elect to see that the agency head "resolve" the difficulty. This effectively removed the last candidate from the competition for an assistant secretary post. When the senator suggested someone from his own state who had had long experience in the substantive area with which the position dealt and who had actively supported the Kennedy candidacy, his nominee was at last given recognition. The senator emphasized that he would not embarrass the administration once the appointments had been announced but that he felt free to exercise his influence without restraint before an appointment had been made public.

The tendency to assume that candidates supported by congressmen are likely to have chiefly partisan or constituent qualifications to recommend them may, as a general rule, have some validity. But at least one case in the Kennedy administration proved the exception. While President-elect Kennedy was in Florida, he received a letter from a

[8] *New York Times*, Feb. 24, 1962.

congressional committee chairman strongly urging the appointment of a career official, *Donald Davis*, as head of an agency in which he had served for more than ten years. The various clientele groups were also almost unanimous in their support of *Davis*. He had worked with congressmen on many occasions because of their intense interest in the work of his organization and had therefore established excellent rapport with them.

Although *Davis* claimed that he did nothing to engender support for his candidacy, he was aware that some forty congressmen had written letters advocating his appointment and that many senators favored his nomination. Moreover, his family had been active Democrats for years. President-elect Kennedy, however, chose to appoint the head of the special 1960 national campaign group that had concentrated its attention on the principal clientele for this agency. The agency head-designate was a prominent member of the clientele group, so that even those congressmen who had supported *Davis'* candidacy were agreeable to his appointment. The congressmen and the interest groups then focused their attention on the deputy post for *Davis*. On the President-elect's return to Washington, he called the committee chairman who had first put forward *Davis'* name and advised him that he would recommend *Davis* to the new agency head for the deputy position. The new head had already had several candidates suggested to him from outside his organization but he wanted to have a deputy with intimate experience in the organization's affairs. He had known *Davis* for a number of years in official capacities but was not a close associate. He therefore spent several weeks getting to know people within the agency who had worked with *Davis* or who might be likely prospects themselves. He concluded finally that *Davis* had the best qualifications for the deputy post and offered him the job.

Congressmen sometimes fancy themselves as assistant secretaries or under secretaries and occasionally one of their number is appointed, but the majority in both the legislative and executive branches are somewhat dubious of a legislator's ability to adjust to the executive environment. In recent years, congressional interest in political executive positions has been satisfied to a large extent by appointments given to personal or committee staff members. Although few instances of such appointments were found in the sample drawn for this study, a substantial number of such staff officers have received executive appointments, in 1961 for example. Kenneth BeLieu of the Senate Committee on Aeronautical and Space Sciences was given an assistant secretaryship in the Navy Department; John Carver of Senator Frank Church's office was appointed an Assistant Secretary of the Interior. Other examples are Paul Rand Dixon to the chairmanship of the Federal Trade Commission after serving as chief counsel to the Senate Subcommittee on Antitrust and Monopoly; Frank W. McCulloch to the chairmanship of the National Labor Relations Board after service as administrative assistant to Senator Paul Douglas; and Edward Welsh to the secretaryship of the National Aeronautics and Space Council after serving as legislative assistant to Senator Stuart Symington.

Members of Congress, especially members of the Senate, are willing to accord the President and his department heads considerable discretion, but they expect to be consulted on subcabinet appointments in which they might have a legitimate concern and are likely to be disgruntled over failures to observe protocol. Few are willing to object to particular candidates, but they appreciate being advised of their nominations early enough in the selection process so that they *could* object if they wanted to. Frequently, they have been told about an appointment on the day that the nomination papers were being prepared and long after commitments have been made to the appointee. One high-ranking Republican senator reported that he had not been consulted on any personnel assignments during the Eisenhower administration. He had had nothing to do with appointments in the department over which his committee had jurisdiction; the secretary might call regarding a nomination, but only with the expectation of receiving the senator's approval. He observed that he was consulted more on appointments by the secretary's more politically astute predecessor in the Truman administration than he had been by his own party's appointee.

Failure to observe accepted procedures in selecting executives incensed many other Republican senators at the beginning of the Eisenhower administration. Not only were their own candidates ignored but in many instances they were given no opportunity to assess the qualifications of men nominated by other groups. Similarly, at the beginning of the Kennedy administration, a Democratic senator complained that he did not learn of the appointment of a person from his state until the man was in Washington conferring with the department head. By that time, the Republican senator from his state had publicly announced his support of the appointment, and by implication claimed credit for it. But the Democratic senator, nevertheless, insisted on following the regular patronage procedures by having his state's patronage committee approve the nomination before it was sent to the Senate. The senator was certain he could have stopped the nomination, but he was not at all inclined to do so because he had great confidence in the candidate. Failure to obtain clearances on this candidate was laid at the doorstep of a White House aide, causing embarrassment both to the senator and to the department head.

The attitudes of members of Congress regarding political executive appointments at the deputy, under secretary, and assistant secretary levels stand in sharp contrast to their attitudes toward appointments to field offices in their states, to membership on state and local committees, postmasterships, and judgeships. When these types of positions are filled, members of Congress generally dictate who will be appointed. These are the positions that are of vital significance to their political life as they are offered as rewards to faithful party followers and friends and, at the same time, help to build up the party organization at home. The full force of senatorial courtesy is felt with regard to these positions and the more celebrated cases of senatorial opposition to presidential appointments have occurred over them.[9]

Variations in Recruitment During an Administration

With two exceptions, the examples thus far presented from the case studies have illustrated appointments made at the beginning of an administration. As might be expected after an election involving a party overturn, such appointments go primarily to men not currently serving in the federal government, and it has been seen that many individuals are eager to take a part in the new administration. But after the first year there is less enthusiasm among outsiders to join the government; the big changes of policy have been introduced and political executive jobs offer less challenge to men whose success in their own careers marks them as good potential material for the government. The Presi-

[9] Joseph P. Harris, *The Advice and Consent of the Senate* (University of California Press, 1953), Chapter 17; see Chapter 18 for a discussion of senatorial interest in other field officers.

dent, Congress, political parties, and special groups interested in the selection process for second-level executives are all deeply committed to their own ongoing programs and the department and agency heads are likely to be given greater freedom of action in their choice of subordinates. Among the cases studied, in only four of the sixty-three appointments made during the Truman administration (1945-52) and after the first year of the Eisenhower administration (1954-60) did the President play the dominant role. The department head was given a relatively free hand in replacing those of his subordinates who left before the administration was over.

Quite naturally the department heads, busy with their own political and policy commitments, turned to the men about them of whose abilities and experience they had now some knowledge. In several executive agencies, particularly in the military departments, there has been a strong tradition to promote from the ranks. This was especially true of the Navy where men like Struve Hensel, Charles Thomas, John Kenney, John Sullivan, Ralph Bard, James Forrestal, and Thomas Gates were all promoted. For the most part, these men were chosen in the first place because of professional and executive qualifications rather than because of party service.

The case studies confirm this pattern of reliance on men already in government service when recruiting for political executive positions during an administration. Thirty-eight of the sixty-three later appointees were already in the federal service, as is shown in the following tabulation of sources of recruitment after the first year of an administration. Truman's tendency to recruit from the national govern-

	NUMBER	TRUMAN	EISENHOWER	BOTH ADMINIS- TRATIONS
National government sources				
Promotion of political appointees	(16)	22%	31%	25%
Promotion of career officials	(15)	35	8	24
Transfer of political appointees	(7)	8	15	11
Subtotal	(38)	65	54	60
Private and other sources				
Appointment of former federal appointees	(5)	11	4	8
Other appointments	(20)	24	42	32
Subtotal	(25)	35	46	40
Total	(63)	100	100	100

ment throughout his term in office reflected the continuity between his administration and Roosevelt's. Since both shared the same party allegiance and generally the same policy orientations, there was no strong urgency on the part of the Truman recruiters to seek men outside the government who might introduce new policy viewpoints. Moreover, many Truman executives had had long prior experience in the federal service and were acquainted with men in their departments who were considered capable of assuming high-level responsibilities. Younger civil servants who had served their apprenticeship during the New Deal and World War II had strong hopes that they might be considered for leading political positions as rewards for their faithful service. The administration also faced widespread public antipathy toward public office and a keen desire by most men to return to or continue in essentially private pursuits.

There are major differences between the Truman and Eisenhower administrations in the extent to which individuals with varying kinds of government backgrounds moved up into positions at deputy, under secretary, and assistant secretary levels. The case studies verify a generally held view that Truman and his staff were strongly inclined to advance career officials to political executive positions. Often these men had already moved into politically sensitive positions as confidential assistants or personal aides and it was a short step to move into a formally political appointment. The Eisenhower administration, on the other hand, was much more inclined to promote men who had previously entered the federal government as political appointees.

Advancement of Political Appointees

Some promotions of persons within a department have been due to failure to find qualified candidates from private sources. Such an instance was the appointment of *Herbert Price* to an assistant secretaryship during the Eisenhower administration. The post had been vacant for some three years. Traditionally it had been filled by a man from a powerful clientele group; but the appointment was declined by two men from that group to whom the secretary offered the job, and he in turn refused to accept the suggestions put forward by the group leaders. The functions of the vacant position were discharged in the interim by the secretary, with the help of his career officials and his special assistant *Price*, a lawyer whom the secretary had appointed at the time he took office himself. *Price* showed considerable ability, took on major responsibilities for policy development, departmental management, and such ticklish matters as patronage. Eventually *Price* decided that he wished to return to his law practice, but the secretary ignored his wishes and made all the arrangements to promote him to the assistant secretaryship without consulting *Price* and asked him to take the post only when "he had the presidential appointment in hand." This procedure made it impossible for *Price* to refuse, because of his "personal loyalty" to his chief.

Another reason for promotion from within may be familiarity with the overall activities of an agency rather than just those of certain bureaus. One fairly typical example of the operation of this factor was the advancement of *Edward Jackson* from general counsel to under secretary during the Eisenhower administration. *Jackson* had originally been selected by the chairman of the senatorial committee with jurisdiction over the department's functions; he came from the chairman's state and they were friends of long standing. *Jackson* took the post on condition that he have a role in development of high policy and freedom within his own area. The new secretary did not object and the two men got along very well; their philosophies seemed to coincide, and the secretary consulted him across the entire range of department affairs. When the under secretary left after about a year, *Jackson* pretty much assumed that he would be asked to take the job, although some time passed without any direct word from the secretary. Other candidates for the position included two assistant secretaries (one of whom was very much interested in the post) and individuals from outside political sources. Eventually, however, the secretary asked *Jackson* to become his under secretary.

Other promotions of political appointees involve transfer from one government body to another due to personal contacts with the White House staff, party personnel, or individuals in other government agencies. *Robert Nelson*, a Truman appointee in a domestic department, was promoted as the result of just such associations. Immediately after graduation from law school he had taught and practiced law, then served as an attorney in two government agencies during the Roosevelt administration. He was serving as legal counsel for a large business concern when a "big blowup" resulted in a change of management, leaving *Nelson* in an unhappy position. A presidential assistant with whom he had become acquainted during his early government service arranged for *Nelson's* appointment to a regulatory agency; but a Democratic state chairman had already laid claim to a position in that agency for a candidate of his own from the same state as *Nelson,* and it was undesirable to have two men from the same state on the commission. The White House aide then found the lawyer a position in the Defense area. In the latter position he was in frequent communication with an assistant secretary in another department; and after some two years, the latter informed *Nelson* that another assistant secretaryship was open in his own department and wondered if Nelson would be interested. Nelson had encountered certain difficulties in his Defense post and was ready for a change; but when an interview with the assistant secretary's department head was arranged, no mention was made of the job. Two weeks later, however, *Nelson* was invited to see the White House aide, who queried him on his willingness to accept the vacant assistant secretaryship. This interview clinched the matter, for the secretary tended to defer to the White House and the Democratic National Committee on this type of appointment.

One political appointee, *David Harris,* was promoted to an assistant secretaryship in the summer of 1948 when it seemed probable that President Truman would be defeated in the November election. *Harris* had served as an assistant to two successive under secretaries of a domestic department for some two years. When the second of these under secretaries left, an assistant secretary was moved up into the spot. Both of the under secretaries *Harris* had served recommended that he be given the vacant assistant secretaryship. The privilege of filling a post for a presumed six-months-only period was not particularly attractive to prospective candidates; and the secretary looked with favor on the advancement of a man like *Harris* who was familiar with the agency's functions. The secretary had a close personal relationship with the President and wide discretion in the selection of his subordinates, so that all that was necessary was to inform the President once the selection had been made. The secretary also made pro forma contacts with the chairmen of the two legislative committees having responsibility for the agency's activities and the senators from the candidate's home state. *Harris* was delighted with the promotion, feeling that he had "moved into the big leagues."

Promotion of Career Officers

Vacancies in second-level executive positions occurring after the first year of an administration are sometimes filled by promoting career men. In the State Department this is an accepted practice, even at the beginning of an administration, and foreign service officers often find their opportunities for later promotion enhanced by such an appointment, with the prize of a career ambassadorship at the end of it. In other departments, however, advancement to political posts very often leads to the termination of a government career. Examples of State Department appointments are those of Livingston Merchant at the beginning of the Eisenhower administration and of Foy Kohler at the beginning of the Kennedy administration, each to the position of Assistant Secretary for European Affairs. Both later became ambassadors. On the other hand, Vernon Northrop moved up from the career position of administrative assistant secretary to the undersecretaryship of the Department of the Interior for a brief period at the end of the Truman administration, and was promptly turned out when Eisenhower took office.

Two categories of individuals are likely to be interested in moving from career positions to political appointments: those who are nearing the end of their government service and can anticipate retirement at the end of the presidential term; and younger men who fully recognize the risk but are willing to embark on new careers in private life when the administration changes. One fairly typical example from the case studies occurred during the Eisenhower administration when the assistant secretary for one of the State Department regional bureaus was appointed to an ambassadorship because he had "reached his physical limit" in Washington. The political situation in the region for which he had been responsible was unstable, and the stakes in terms of American interests were very high. The top departmental officials concluded that it would be desirable if the replacement were someone with extensive experience in that area. Little or no consideration was given to bringing in an outsider, especially since the administration had less than two years to run. Several of the top officials (not including the secretary) informally canvassed the foreign service officers of sufficient rank who might be available for such a post. The choice quickly narrowed to three men, two of whom were already serving as ambassadors in the region in question. One of the three was ruled out because of the critical importance of his ambassadorial assignment. Another was eliminated because he could not have gained Senate approval owing to certain private business dealings of which one senator had been particularly critical. The third (the second ambassador) was finally selected because he had demonstrated a high degree of imagination, initiative, and ability; he was available; and he had sufficient private income to withstand the costs of Washington life. Furthermore, he had not "made anybody mad . . . nobody would disapprove of his appointment." With all of these considerations in his favor, the ambassador was recommended to the secretary who quickly approved the nomination. He again became an ambassador when the Kennedy administration came to power.

During times of national crisis, career officials are much more likely to consider political assignments. This is particularly true of emergency agencies, where staffs may have to be hurriedly put together and men with broad familiarity with government procedures are at a premium. An example of this situation occurred in the Truman administration during the Korean War. An emergency agency had been in existence approximately seven months when *Charles Taylor*, a career official from one of the established agencies, was induced to join its staff. *Taylor* had been wishing to transfer because of his concern over advancement in the permanent agency, and the new appointment gave him a higher rating for what he thought would be stimulating and exciting work. Soon the director of the emergency agency resigned to return to private industry and took his deputy with him. The new administrator, a man from the business world, found himself without a deputy. He tried to obtain several people from outside the agency and outside the government, but was turned down in every instance. He finally decided that "he didn't need anyone of such high aptitude" and began looking within the agency itself. He had had several weeks to observe *Taylor's* work and offered him the deputy post which was quickly accepted. Approval was easily gained from the "czar" of all the defense programs and from staff officials in the White House.

A career man with decades of service at high levels in a domestic department was *Peter Brown*. Early in 1960 his superior, an assistant secretary, was promoted to the post of deputy. The new deputy strongly recommended *Brown* for the assistant secretaryship he had vacated. Since the short time remaining before the end of the Eisenhower administration seemed to dictate a choice from inside the department, the secretary concluded that "it would be nice" to let *Brown* cap his career with a presidential appointment. *Brown* quickly accepted the offer; he thought that in his department a career man could almost always return to the career ranks. Clearance with the White House and his home state senators presented no difficulty. As he anticipated, he was able to return to a career position at the end of the administration.

Recruitment of Former Associates

The close personal association that develops between men who are engaged in a common enterprise or who have established business or professional relationships over a long period of years often provides the basis for a recruitment effort. These relationships are more than likely to grow up during periods of government service. The tendency to recruit former associates was particularly noteworthy at the beginning of the Kennedy administration when it almost appeared that a shadow government was taking over. But such practices are even more prevalent after the first year of an administration, as men move from position to position and agency to agency, and as they develop relationships which crisscross the government.

A department head generally has greater leeway in selecting personal friends late in an administration because there are fewer pressures of a political character to influence his decisions. Two instances of this kind occurred in the sample of appointments studied, one in the Eisenhower and one in the Truman administration. In the Eisenhower case, a secretary called on *Henry Johnson*, an old personal friend and associate. The secretary had had an unfortunate experience with his deputy, who insisted on operating at the policy level when the secretary was looking for an administrator. Fortunately, the deputy took a leave of absence and subsequently was appointed to a position elsewhere in the government. The secretary immediately thought of *Johnson*, whom he had known since 1940 when they served together in World War II. *Johnson* had been in business since the war; the two men had kept in touch, and *Johnson* had served a few days each year as consultant to the secretary since 1953. *Johnson* was an expert in the agency's area of responsibility and had had a long period of service as an administrator in private industry. Furthermore, the secretary was confident that *Johnson* would agree with him on policy matters. His one liability was political—he came from the secretary's own state, was a member of the same church, and came from a similar industry. Objections were raised on these grounds, but the secretary was able to mollify those who objected by offering his own services for additional political activities. The secretary furthermore told the home state politicians that it was in their interest to take credit for the appointment, since the alternative was to appoint someone from another state. The state's Republican senators did not involve themselves in the discussion, merely ratifying the appointment.

In the Truman case, a secretary promoted one of his assistant secretaries to the position of deputy, and filled the vacant assistant secretaryship by appointing *Fred Thomas*. *Thomas'* appointment came about as a result of his friendship with the deputy, to whom the secretary delegated the responsibility of looking for his own replacement since he "knew more about the job's requirements than anyone else." The secretary and the deputy had both agreed that the new assistant secretary should assume major responsibility for a recently planned crash program involving large-scale construction and that "a man of industrial experience coupled with 'broad concern' was called for." The deputy's first choice was the vice president of a large corporation in the Midwest, who he found could not be seriously considered because his wife was very ill and could not be moved. The vacancy was public information by this time and the agency was deluged with other prospects. The President's advisers thought that the new assistant secretary should be: (1) a Democrat and (2) a person from an area of the country where an appointment might "do some good." None of the White House suggestions was acceptable to the Secretary or his deputy, however.

While all these other possibilities were being considered and turned down, the deputy had been in touch with his former college associate and business partner, *Fred Thomas*. *Thomas* was currently an executive of a large industrial corporation. Although a Republican ("not very far advanced from McKinley in his views"), he was acceptable to the department head because he had a reputation for "pulling things together" on special projects and thorny problems. *Thomas* was not inclined to accept the offer; he was well established in his own organization. But the deputy, who was by this time becoming very anxious to get things settled, proceeded to call the head of the corporation *Thom-*

as worked for, and it was agreed that it would be possible for *Thomas* to take a year's leave of absence from his firm. The choice of *Thomas* as assistant secretary, of course, ran counter to the White House stipulation that only a Democrat should be appointed; and it was President Truman who cast the deciding vote by overruling the objections of a state Democratic party chairman and consenting to the Republican's appointment.

Appointments of former members of Congress to executive office are usually assumed to be based on partisan or "political" considerations, but accommodations to outside pressure may sometimes be involved, or a particular department head may wish to capitalize on the knowledge a congressman has acquired in his own area of specialization. *Albert Lee's* appointment, however, was an instance where political interests were dominant. One of Eisenhower's department heads was being severely criticized both inside and outside Congress, for major changes he had made in organization and policies. He was also accused of leaving too many Democrats in key positions and failing to appoint enough men who were politically acceptable. *Albert Lee* was a former congressman who had served with both Sherman Adams and Leonard Hall in the House of Representatives and who had been on a committee that dealt with the department under attack. He was serving in another agency at that time and he was told by his superior there that the President and others in the White House and on the Republican National Committee believed his most useful service to the administration would be to go to work for the beleaguered department in a liaison capacity with Capitol Hill. He hesitated to accept the appointment, insisting that he could not be effective in such a position without the prestige of secretarial rank. There was, indeed, a vacant assistant secretaryship in this particular agency but it had been earmarked for another purpose.

Although the White House did not exert great pressure on the secretary, it was clear that the latter was under obligation to repair the damage arising from his own failure to create political support for his department. When *Lee's* state congressional delegation and party organization also added their voices in support of the appointment, the department head finally agreed. He felt that he could probably compensate for the ex-legislator's lack of detailed knowledge of the work of the divisions he would nominally supervise by having division chiefs who were expert in their areas. *Lee* himself was reluctant to take on the position but did so because he was a "team player," and he "was anxious to see the first Republican administration in twenty years be popular and make good." He also felt it would enhance his claim to a district judgeship after his period in office.

Summary

Significant differences in the style of recruitment and selection and the sources from which political executives were recruited have been clearly established. An incoming administration tends strongly toward elimination of all vestiges of control likely to be exercised by members of the previous administration. The President organizes his recruiting effort around a nucleus of trusted advisers who have assisted him in innumerable ways during the course of the campaign and throughout his career. These advisers extend his reach into the community and the many groups composing it, suggesting candidates, evaluating their qualifications, sifting the wheat from the chaff. The President's aides are besieged by office-seekers and others who are promoting candidates and must attempt to balance the many conflicting values presented by alternative candidates.

Presidential interest and involvement is relatively high at the beginning of an administration, but the President's participation is limited because of the time and energy he must spend in organizing his team and becoming acquainted with diverse public programs and problems. He is normally the prime mover in the selection of his cabinet members, but their nominations usually lead directly to a decline in his active role. His department heads almost immediately assume a share of the burden, both from a sense of obligation and because of their strong interest in these positions. They undertake their own recruiting efforts and engage in the negotiations with members of Congress, party and interest group officials, and self-promoters as they choose their subordinates. Very often, however, the presidential recruiting group continues to play an active part in contributing the names of possible candidates.

As an administration matures, the tendency toward the department head's independence in the selection of his aides becomes even more pronounced. With somewhat more tarnish on the administration and fewer eager aspirants for office, the department head turns his attention inward, toward men who have demonstrated loyalty and ability on the job. The men in lower political posts seek advancement, indeed demand it as the price of remaining. The primary route for filling these positions in the later years of an administration is therefore through advancement of subordinate personnel, or of men with considerable government service.

In relation to the President, his cabinet officers, and agency heads, other participants in the selection process—members of Congress, interest group officials, party leaders—play a relatively minor role in the recruitment of under secretaries, assistant secretaries, and deputy administrators. Their influence is subject to presidential discretion and the political awareness of the department heads. Yet the government at this level is a political machine run by political appointees, and a cautious President and department head pay careful attention to the legitimate interests of these groups in certain appointments. Generally, however, if their right to such participation in the selection process is recognized in certain crucial instances, congressmen and other interested parties are willing to concede that the President cannot be held accountable for his administrative operations unless he has freedom to put together his own political team. The President himself generally acts with similar discretion toward his immediate subordinates. Although ultimate responsibility for all second-level appointments resides in him, the Chief Executive leaves his department and agency heads as the de facto chief decision-makers in staffing their own part of the executive establishment.

5

Clearance and Confirmation

of Appointments, 1945-61

THE PRESIDENT, the department heads, and their advisers play the central role in the recruitment of deputies, under secretaries, and assistant secretaries, but sometimes other important participants exert more than their usual pressure to have specific candidates, or types of candidates, appointed. Although their influence is usually limited to the safeguarding of political or professional interests, these participants—party national committees, special interest groups, and Senate committees—have, on occasion, discouraged or blocked the choice of candidates, nominated their own, or in some other manner directly affected the appointment procedures. Clearance with these groups is an important factor in every presidential appointment.

After such informal clearance has been obtained, the formal process of Senate confirmation of presidential appointments at this second level in the Executive constitutes primarily a ritual through which the nominees are inducted into government service. Seldom is it a serious hurdle. Nevertheless, the existence of this power to advise and consent to presidential appointments gives the senators one final opportunity to raise objections to candidates not acceptable to them on personal, political, or policy grounds. If a nominee is subjected to a gruelling inquisition, it is generally due to inadequate clearance with the appropriate congressmen and political leaders beforehand, a miscalculation on the President's part, or a desire to put some particular issue involved in the nomination to the test.

124

Role of the National Committee

The primary function of the party national committee in appointments at this level is to ascertain the political acceptability of candidates in the states where they have residence. The staff of the national committee checks with the national committeeman in the state, with the state chairman, and with local party organization officials. Fairly systematic procedures are set up in each state through which such clearances are obtained. The lack of active party opposition to the choices of the recruiting officials at the beginning of the Eisenhower and Kennedy administrations suggests that few party officials are willing to make vigorous protests against a new administration's appointments. Unquestionably there is occasional disgruntlement, particularly when a man is chosen who is a member of the President's party but who has no record of local political activity. The local and state party organizations recognize, however, that outright opposition may lead to the selection of a candidate from another locality or state, and seldom make a last-ditch effort to defeat the nomination.

Like other active political figures, members of the national committees and staff have recommended individuals to the White House and department heads, and also provided points of access for individuals seeking jobs. But there is no evidence to indicate that this source is a particularly reliable means of promoting a candidacy or of ensuring access to those who ultimately make the decisions.

It was clear in the Eisenhower recruitment effort that nominations coming from political sources were considered suspect. Sherman Adams reported that President Eisenhower was time and again indignant over political interference in the selection of his aides and, while sympathetic with the National Committee Chairman's concern for party harmony, did little to make Leonard Hall's job any easier. Adams said that the President "carefully avoided giving the Republican National Committee any responsibility in the selection of government officials, a duty the committee would have been happy to assume."[1] Hall declared in July 1953 that he could not find six members of Congress who were indebted to the administration for ap-

[1] *Firsthand Report* (Harper & Brothers, 1961), p. 58.

pointments sponsored by them.[2] He complained that it was White House policy to make appointments and then later obtain support from others in the party on behalf of the candidates.

Interviews with Republican party officials revealed that they considered themselves almost entirely outside the appointment process. An agreement which permitted members of Congress to go directly to the White House or to the department heads made it impossible for the national committee to exercise any control over appointments or to maintain any kind of geographical or factional balance. One Republican party official pointed out that three of the assistant postmasters general serving at the end of 1953 were from the state of New Jersey— a situation which he considered to be "wrong." The tendency of department and agency heads to make appointments independent of the state and local party organizations resulted in considerable disaffection among these party organizations, since the candidates often were either unknown to the local party organization or had taken little or no active part in the campaign. They were monopolizing positions that should have gone to more "deserving" candidates.

Nevertheless, the party organization does occasionally play an important role in the selection process, both in promoting and in blocking certain candidates. There were only four instances among the appointments studied where party influence was dominant in the decision to appoint a particular individual, but one case in point was that of *Howard Carter*,[3] which occurred toward the end of an administration. *Carter* had been an official of his party national committee for some years, where he had obtained considerable administrative experience, and wanted to move into an executive agency. He talked with the national chairman, and the chairman talked to the President, urging *Carter's* appointment to the first appropriate job. The President agreed, having already been impressed with the party aide's work. When a vacancy occurred in a domestic department because of the departure of an under secretary, the national chairman urged the appointment of *Carter*, arguing that it would give recognition to the party and was a natural position for a person with his professional and

---

[2] Robert J. Donovan, *Eisenhower: The Inside Story* (Harper & Brothers, 1956), p. 99.

[3] *Howard Carter* and the subsequent names in italics are fictitious names used to protect the confidential nature of the interview material.

political background. The appointment looked good also in terms of the oncoming off-year election. The department head, however, who was himself going to leave in a few months, had decided almost immediately to advance one of his assistant secretaries who had done an excellent job and was considered one of the bright young men of the administration. When the national chairman suggested *Carter* to the secretary, the latter objected, stating that he thought this would be the wrong kind of appointment in view of his interest in establishing confidence with the clientele groups of his agency. Moreover, he personally did not want a person with such a political background in his agency.

The chairman stimulated a campaign for his aide, resulting in a deluge of letters from various organizations urging *Carter's* appointment. He also went to the President, who called in the department head and strongly urged the appointment, even expressing a wish to announce it that very day. The secretary reiterated his arguments, stating that "in all of my years in the government, I have made appointments only on the basis of ability and I don't want to make a political appointment now." Although the President was not happy about it, he finally agreed to delay a decision. On his way out, the secretary encountered another member of the administration, who was apparently there to help apply pressure. The department head said he could not agree to the appointment, and if it was insisted on, he himself would just have to leave the Cabinet earlier than intended. One White House aide, however, sympathized with his stand and this helped to prevent a showdown.

Nevertheless, the cabinet officer decided that earlier resignation was desirable and during the following weeks the President sought a replacement. In a conversation with the man who eventually accepted the position, the President spoke of his desire to place *Carter* in an appropriate government post; he also spoke of *Carter's* competence, excellent performance in the party organization, and professional background; and he concluded by asking the prospective department head if he would be willing to consider appointing *Carter*. The new cabinet appointee felt no sense of pressure, but thought the undersecretaryship of the department appeared to be a logical position for the President's choice; he checked with national committee people and White House staff members who were familiar with *Carter's* work. He talked with *Carter* himself and became well acquainted with him, and concluded that the "appointment made good sense." Not bothered by the fact that the name originated with the national committee, the department head noted that this is a political government and declared that a rich political experience should not be a disqualifying factor for political appointment; in his frame of reference such experience was an advantage. He therefore approved the appointment.

A typical political reward occurred in the appointment of *James Morris* in the Truman administration. *Morris,* an active local politician and businessman, had worked diligently with Democratic forces to upset a powerful Republican organization in a municipal election. He had also been a leading figure in his state in the 1948 Truman campaign. As a result, he was strongly recommended for an appointment by his state party chairman, who was eager to obtain representation in the Executive for his section of the country. President Truman suggested to one of his agency heads that if a vacancy occurred in his agency something should be done for *Morris.* When the agency head attended a meeting in *Morris's* state, he met *Morris* and also received favorable recommendations from a number of local people. Support was also forthcoming from his senator and congressman and the state labor leaders. Other candidates of a political character were also being advanced for a position in the agency, including a generous contributor to the Democratic party who had the support of the national chairman. When an appropriate post became vacant, the agency head decided that *Morris* should have the job. *Morris* was reluctant to accept, preferring to keep his business going, but President Truman called him and said, "I want you in there."

Appointments of individuals having party service as their primary qualification normally would be considered rewards, but, paradoxically, in some instances they can be looked upon as punishment, or at least as attempts to undermine their influence. One such case occurred at the end of the Eisenhower administration involving *John Turner,* an influential member of a Republican state party organization. For about a quarter of a century, *Turner* had held party and public office in his state and was recognized as a powerful albeit "maverick" Republican. Having been defeated for re-election to a high executive post in his state, he was interested in obtaining a federal appointment. He was living in wealthy semi-retirement and was curious about the operations of the national government. He approached the Republican senator from his state to get the latter's assistance in obtaining an appointment on one of the regulatory commissions. *Turner's* background, however, did not qualify him for such a position. He maintained his interest in state and national politics at the same time and showed some interest in supporting Governor Nelson Rockefeller of New York if the latter ran for the Republican nomination in 1960. Since *Turner* wanted a Washington job, the Nixon group in his state thought that this would be a good opportunity to remove him from the scene until the nomination was safely wrapped up. Working through a senator, the Nixon group contacted a White House aide, who found a vacant position at the deputy level in one of the agencies. White House observers commented that the agency head probably did not know where *Turner* came from or why, but he did realize that the candidate had strong party support. The agency head had had no deputy for some time because of his reluctance to delegate authority, but he nevertheless told the candidate he could have the position if he wanted it. In spite of a chilly reception and a clear indication that he would operate as a "fifth wheel," the candidate accepted the offer.

While party allegiance is assumed to be or is irrelevant in certain appointments, in others it is the crucial factor that can disqualify a man. One such instance occurred during the Eisenhower administration, when a new agency head encountered unexpected difficulty in securing the appointment of *Paul Stewart* as his deputy and eventually selected *Charles Martin*. The preceding head had served his entire term of office without a deputy, but the new chief began to look for one. He had a relatively clear idea of what he wanted: someone to whom he could delegate authority, who could deputize for him and be trained as his successor, whose broad experience and professional competence were reasonably well known, who was willing to serve for a minimum of two years, and who could handle congressional relations. Officials of an agency with related interests suggested the name of *Paul Stewart*, who had previously worked in the agency but who was then on foreign assignment for an international organization. The new agency head met *Stewart* and asked him to consider an appointment as deputy. He indicated, furthermore, that he would be leaving at the end of that year and his deputy could look forward to directing the whole operation. In addition, the agency head explained that the organization was being further integrated with the related agency and *Stewart* as the new director would then work in close association with the high officials who had first recommended him.

After considering the matter for some time and making sure he could leave his present employment, *Stewart* indicated he would be willing to accept the deputy post if he were given assurances he would later be made director. He did not want to become deputy and then have another political appointee made his superior. He thought the President and the recruiting officers ought to be able to look that far ahead. He noted, however, that he had one disability: he had registered as a Democrat as a young man, although he then considered himself an independent. He was assured by all concerned that this would make no difference; everyone was enthusiastic about the appointment, and clearances were readily obtained at the White House. His name was also sent to the Republican National Committee, to the Senate, and to the senators from his home state. When nothing happened, the agency head asked about its submission to the Senate, but instead was given a list of new names to consider, compiled by the White House and the Republican National Committee. At this point, it became evident that the nomination had run into trouble. When *Stewart's* name was routed to the two senators from his state, one had given immediate approval, but the other had registered an angry objection. The latter referred the name to the local Republican party organization which replied that it would not object to the appointment, but that it could not approve and support the appointment of a registered Democrat. The senator was angry because his colleague had approved *Stewart's* nomination and because this seemed added evidence that the White House was not giving him adequate support in his bid for reelection that year. He obtained the support of others in the Senate Republican leadership, and then the support of the Republican National Chairman, who was also disgruntled over lack of consideration for national committee personnel recommendations. Attempts to mollify the senators and the national chairman were unsuccessful, and the White House then put pressure on the recruiting officials to withdraw the nomination and consider another candidate. The recruiting officials were humiliated by this, so much so that one of them, a big contributor to the Republican campaign war chest, refused to provide funds for the campaign that year.

At this point, it became necessary to reconsider the whole matter. The agency head looked around briefly for other candidates but finally turned to his own subordinates. *Charles Martin,* his general counsel, had been serving for some months as the acting deputy while waiting for the arrival of the new appointee. He had served effectively in the organization for several years in a number of important positions and was well thought of generally, although not considered seriously for the deputy position until all other prospects faded. As a registered Republican, *Martin* was acceptable on a party basis. He was also acceptable to the high agency officials and the White House. Rather than being opposed in the Senate, *Martin's* work with Congress in the past had made him known favorably to both Republican and Democratic members. When offered the position, he was glad to accept it.

Influence of Special Interest Groups

In contrast to other participants in the recruitment process, including political parties, interest groups have no formal and recognized role. But the relationship between them and the major party organizations is often very close, making liaison on many matters, including appointments, an accepted procedure. Past practice in the field of agriculture is a good example. The Democrats have been stoutly supported in the postwar years by the National Farmers Union while the American Farm Bureau Federation generally found Republican doctrine more appealing. It was only natural, then, that the influence of the National Farmers Union was important both in the development of policy and in the selection of executives in the Department of Agriculture during the Kennedy Administration. Secretary Orville Freeman had strong Democratic-Farmer-Labor Party support in his home state of Minnesota, and that group generally was found in the same policy camp as the Farmers Union. Secretary Freeman chose John Baker, who had previously been director of legislative services for the National Farmers Union, as Director of Agricultural Credit Services. But, in order to broaden the base of recruitment, he also selected important figures in competing farm groups. John Duncan, who became one of the assistant secretaries, had been president of the Georgia Farm Bureau (one of the few Farm Bureau officials in the country to support Kennedy), and Harry Caldwell, the new chairman of the National Agricultural Advisory Commission, was Master of the North Carolina State Grange.

Similar forces operated in other departments and agencies. It would be inconceivable, for instance, that a Democratic administration would select an assistant secretary—or any other Interior Department official —who was opposed to public power. Thus, the selection of Kenneth Holum was natural for the position of Assistant Secretary for Water and Power. He had long been associated with rural electrification in South Dakota and elsewhere in the Midwest, and undoubtedly had the support of the public power interest groups. He also had the advantage of being an ardent Democrat, having twice been the South Dakota Democratic candidate for the Senate.

In a larger sense, interest groups must compete with party politics in their efforts to control appointments. Sometimes preference is given to appointees who have made greater contributions of a party character than those suggested by the interest groups. At other times, if the interest groups are highly competitive in a particular subject-matter area, the selection of someone without known attachments to one or the other group may be advantageous politically. On many occasions, there is no recognized clientele group or groups that can claim dominant interests in particular positions. The efforts of professional accountants, for example, to obtain a political executive position for one of their number went totally unrecognized in one instance during the Eisenhower administration, partly because the group had no clear claim on the post. Joseph D. Keenan, a vice president of the AFL-CIO, was refused a position in the Department of Defense in 1960, even though the appointment had been reported in the *New York Times,* whereas his rejection for a labor post would have been extremely unlikely.[4]

The case studies reveal, too, a pattern of recruitment in which the interest groups play a direct role in only a few agencies and in a relatively small number of instances (four cases out of the 108 appointment studies). When their clienteles are highly structured and clearly identifiable, the interest groups can directly influence their related departments or agencies. Such groups, for example, played a most prominent role in the Veterans Administration, the Department of Labor, the Department of the Interior, and the Department of Agriculture. To a lesser degree, this has also been true of the Department of Commerce.

[4] See *New York Times,* Dec. 24, 1960.

To a certain extent in these agencies, but to a much greater extent in others, interest groups take no active role in recruitment, but provide an important restraining influence on those who do. In the business community there is little evidence of powerful trade associations or general organizations of businessmen, such as the Chamber of Commerce, taking an active part in the selection of political executives, but officials of these organizations are often called upon to evaluate the qualifications of candidates under consideration.

The reasons for this relatively inactive role are fairly clear. Officials seek candidates among their friends and associates, among men who move in the same kinds of circles in which they have moved, whether these be political, professional, or commercial. Thus, a Secretary of State has generally moved in a community of people who have an abiding interest in foreign policy, as represented by members of the Foreign Policy Association. Prominent members of such organizations as the National Association of Manufacturers and the Committee for Economic Development have played important roles in the selection of some candidates, but it was a personal service and seldom related to a clearly perceived professional interest on the part of the organization or the individual who was nominated.

In addition, these organizations seldom wish to risk the identification of a particular appointee as "their" man in an agency. The suspicion that such an identification engenders is too great a price for whatever benefit may be received. Conflict-of-interest regulations and congressional as well as public concern over individuals using government office for private benefit, particularly in the contracting field in the Department of Defense, have a decided impact on interest group roles. The problem has not been one of excessive group influence over appointments, but an unwillingness to allow one of their members to serve in a sensitive post.

The influence of these interest groups, whether individual businesses, organized trade associations, or voluntary organizations of a myriad variety, is found primarily in eliminating certain candidates who might otherwise be seriously considered. An economist who might be a potential nominee for a Treasury post is stricken from the list because his unorthodox views might be offensive to the financial community. A public power advocate whose advanced position on this question has so offended private power interests that the possibility of a workable harmonious relationship is slight, is deleted from the list of candidates for a position in the Department of the Interior. A foreign policy expert whose previous experience has compromised his position regarding foreign policy between the United States and certain nations cannot be appointed.

A case which suggests the subtle veto power and also the competing demands of interest and party politics occurred in the Eisenhower administration. An agency with powerful clientele organizations which were usually unified on policy as well as other matters sought a deputy to the agency chief. One of the most attractive candidates for this post was an experienced civil servant in the agency who was highly regarded both within and outside the agency. His one failing was that he had never been formally identified with the clientele groups when in private life. This disqualified him for promotion to deputy and soon led to his departure from the agency. The agency head considered and rejected a large number of candidates, and finally asked a senator from his state for his legislative assistant who also came from his state and had been very active in party politics. He had the required identification to qualify him, although totally without experience in agency affairs. Despite this drawback, he received the appointment.

Not infrequently, once a candidate is under serious consideration, he is obliged or feels it advisable to approach the interest groups influential in his prospective agency's affairs. One candidate in the Kennedy administration was asked by his agency head to do just this in order to justify his own appointment. The candidate canvassed several organizations, including the one most influential in his agency at that time. This appointee was fortunate in that several of the officials of the special interest group were well known to him because they had all worked together in the Truman administration. A slightly different case occurred when a congressman who was giving strong support to a candidate created much broader support for his nominee by obtaining nearly unanimous agreement in his favor from the interest groups closely connected with the department concerned.

Confirmation by the Senate

The Senate's power to confirm nominations made by the President to policy-making positions gives influential senators an opportunity to play important roles in the original selection of candidates. As David Truman points out, "The subtle element in this control device lies not in the legislative body's refusal to confirm, but in the care taken by an appointing officer not to nominate anyone likely to be rejected."[5]

Today, all department under secretaries and assistant secretaries (except administrative assistant secretaries) are subject to the requirement of senatorial confirmation. In other agencies, there is no firm rule. For example, the administrators of the Veterans Administration, the Housing and Home Finance Agency, and the General Services Administration are appointed by the President with the advice and consent of the Senate, but their deputies are not subject to senatorial confirmation. Neither the director nor the deputy director of the Bureau of the Budget needs senatorial confirmation. The rationale for this arrangement is the President's direct responsibility for the budget and his consequent close personal relationship with the Budget Bureau staff. In contrast, however, in another agency within the White House office—the Office of Civil and Defense Mobilization—the appointments of both the director and deputy director require senatorial confirmation. So also do the director and deputy director of the United States Information Agency.

In selecting his chief administrative aides, the President must consider not only the merits of the individual candidates but also the consequences of appointing someone who is unacceptable to the Senate. Rather than risk a fight on a nomination, he may be forced to accept a second or third choice, or even accept a candidate proposed by an individual or a bloc of senators. In some circumstances, because of overriding personal, political, or policy considerations, he may take the risk of appointing a candidate who is sure to create Senate opposition, using whatever political capital is necessary to get his nominee approved. Normally, however, the impact of senatorial confirmation is felt primarily at the clearance stage of recruitment rather than at the confirmation stage, which is generally a formal verification of an appointment that has already been approved by those who have the power to block it.

As pointed out in the previous chapter, the attitudes of senators vary considerably, although there is a strong tendency for most of them to recognize presidential prerogative in the selection of the official fami-

[5] *The Governmental Process* (Alfred A. Knopf, 1957), p. 425.

ly, which is perceived as including all presidential appointees. Under most circumstances, nominations are referred to the senator of a candidate's home state if he is a member of the President's party. Unless there are powerful reasons for objecting—and this usually means that the appointment would be either a personal or a political affront to the senator or to the state party organization—he will not object. The candidate can be a political nonentity, an independent, or even a member of the opposition party and often cause no stir. In some instances, senators may have alternative candidates to offer, but seldom would they offend the President or his department head by public opposition.

Clearance with the committee and subcommittee chairmen is equally important for appointees who are subsequently going to work with those committees or appear before them. In this type of clearance the issues are less related to home state politics than they are to the substantive issues with which the appointees will deal. Here again, however, the senators are willing to concede the President considerable discretion, occasionally giving an appointee a brief hazing at the confirmation hearing because of some errant views or objectionable past action.

The formal hearings therefore fall into several categories. The large majority are perfunctory introductions of the nominee to the members of the committee, with no searching probe of his ideas, his experience, or his intentions; in many instances no public record is kept. Others provide an opportunity for a candidate to respond to particular questions in which senators have an interest, such as conflict of interest. At some hearings the senators subject a nominee to an intense examination of his ideas and his past actions, but with little hope or intention of outright rejection. In such instances, the committee is concerned more with airing grievances and putting objections on public record, perhaps extracting some commitments from the nominee. Finally, there are the all-out battles in which a determined effort is made by the opposition to defeat a candidate and where there is some chance of success. These provide pyrotechnics which shower political sparks all over the country.

The chief justification of senatorial advice and consent lies in the independent check which the Senate can exercise on both presidential selection policy and individual appointments. Nevertheless, the haphazard manner in which the senators conduct confirmation hearings in the overwhelming majority of cases indicates the ineffectiveness of the confirmation proceedings as a device for screening candidates. Whatever screening there is usually occurs in informal and individual communication among White House and agency officials, the nominees, and power-holding senators. The Senate as a whole rarely advises and nearly always consents. Moreover, in recent years the almost exclusive attention paid to certain problems, especially conflict of interest, illustrates the unwillingness of senators to raise more general objections to the qualifications of presidential candidates. Conflict of interest inquiries appear almost to be substitutes for more searching probes.

There have been relatively few genuine contests over the nominations of under secretaries and assistant secretaries in the executive departments, although, paradoxically, the Senate has been more given to examine the nominees for lower posts than for cabinet offices.[6] The contests that have occurred in recent years—over the appointments of Rexford Tugwell as Under Secretary of Agriculture in 1934, Ebert K. Burlew as First Assistant Secretary of the Interior in 1937, an Under Secretary and five Assistant Secretaries of State under Secretary Stettinius in 1944, Edwin W. Pauley as Under Secretary of the Navy in 1946, and Wesley D'Ewart as Assistant Secretary of the Interior in 1956—have often involved policy issues, but occasionally resulted from personal animosities. Only in a few instances has opposition to the appointment of assistant secretaries become a matter of widespread notice, and only in a very small number of instances, notably in the cases of Edwin Pauley and Wesley D'Ewart, has senatorial opposition resulted in the withdrawal or defeat of a nominee. The Senate has usually applied the same rule to subcabinet posts that it applies to cabinet posts: that the President cannot be held responsible unless he can select his own subordinates.

Strictly speaking, the appointments to political executive positions are not subject to the practice of senatorial courtesy. Senatorial courtesy involves a tradition of deference by the President to senators of his own party in making appointments to federal positions actually located within those senators' states. An appointment as federal district attorney, for example, would be subject to senatorial courtesy. This tradition is buttressed by the usual willingness of the Senate to reject

[6] See Joseph P. Harris, *The Advice and Consent of the Senate* (University of California Press, 1953), pp. 265-66.

nominees if the senator declares them "personally obnoxious" to him. There are instances in which senators have objected to nominees from their states and have forced a reconsideration of these candidates, but normally a withdrawal is made long before the confirmation hearing or formal vote by the Senate on the nomination. In some instances, senators have attempted to apply the rule of senatorial courtesy to national officers, but with only limited success. In deciding whether the rule will be honored with regard to appointments to national office, it appears that the standing of the individual senator in the Senate is an important factor. Among those whose objections have not been honored, for example, were Senators Rush Holt, Huey Long, Theodore Bilbo, Smith Brookhart, and the elder Robert La Follette—none of them in favor with their administrations, nor standing high in the inner circle of the Senate,[7] although La Follette was certainly an eminent senator of great influence.

Hearings

At the beginning of a new administration, virtually all nominees are presented to Senate committees, since the restriction of hearings to a limited number of appointees at a time when a large number are entering the government would appear to be discriminatory. The committees' legislative burden is also less onerous at the beginning of a session. In earlier years the Senate occasionally conducted its confirmation hearings in executive session; but during the past two or three decades hearings have been in open session, at which time the nominee himself and others who wish to speak for or against him are invited to testify. If there is an objection to the nomination, particularly coming from a member of Congress, a hearing will almost always be held.

The discussion here is based on the examination of approximately 110 hearings on confirmations of cabinet and subcabinet officers, agency chiefs, and deputies in the Truman, Eisenhower, and Kennedy administrations. The hearings were held by a wide range of Senate committees. Twenty-nine of them involved case studies.[8]

[7] *Ibid.*, pp. 224-27.
[8] Many of the case studies provided no information concerning senatorial action on the nominations, either because no hearings were held or because no transcript was printed. There is no way to determine the total number of hear-

The newly appointed candidate not infrequently visits with influential members of the Senate committee, including ranking opposition members, prior to the formal hearing. These can be described essentially as courtesy calls,[9] but in some instances they are made in order to gain clearance and may be designed to remove potential reasons for objections by the senators to the appointment.

Because of the difficulties encountered in the past with respect to conflicts of interest, the White House and the executive departments have paid a great deal more attention to the briefing of nominees prior to their appearance before the Senate committees. The traumatic experiences of Charles E. Wilson, Robert T. Stevens, and Harold E. Talbott before the Senate Armed Services Committee in 1953 left an indelible impression upon the minds of appointing officers. Since the Senate Armed Services Committee has required stock divestment as a condition of approval, nominees to the Department of Defense now obtain guidance from the general counsel's office.[10]

In presenting themselves before the Senate committees the nominees are frequently accompanied by the senators from their own states, and it is not exceptional for a home-state senator of the opposite political party to support the nominee. For example, both California Senators, Republican Thomas H. Kuchel and Democrat Clair Engle, supported the nomination of John J. Allen of California as Under Secretary of Commerce for Transportation in the Eisenhower administration. Senator Gordon Allott, a Republican of Colorado, endorsed the selection of Byron White as Deputy Attorney General and both Republican Kentucky Senators, John Sherman Cooper and Thrus-

---

ings held during the period of this study, since many hearings were informal and no record was kept or the records have since been lost. To restrict the discussion to case studies would tend to reveal the identity of the case study appointees because of the use of public documents. This discussion, therefore, is based on considerable research, but not on a random sample.

[9] For example, in 1961, John Connally and Charles Hitch both reported seeing Senator Leverett Saltonstall of Massachusetts, a Republican and the second-ranking minority member of the Senate Armed Services Committee, just prior to their hearings. William Hartigan visited with Senator Joseph S. Clark of Pennsylvania, a member of the Senate Post Office and Civil Service Committee, prior to his appointment as an assistant postmaster general.

[10] See the nominations of Paul H. Nitze and Arthur Sylvester as Assistant Secretaries of Defense, in Hearing before the Senate Armed Services Committee, 87 Cong. 1 sess. (1961), pp. 7, 24.

140 THE ASSISTANT SECRETARIES

ton B. Morton, spoke for Frank J. Welch as an Assistant Secretary of Agriculture in the Kennedy administration. These presentations were little more than a formality, and illustrate the general willingness of senators to accept decisions made by an administration controlled by the opposite political party. Even opposition senators take some pride in the appointment of executives from their own state.

Although relatively few contests have occurred over appointments at the under secretary and assistant secretary level, the candidates have occasionally been scrutinized with great care by the Senate. Nevertheless, the approach taken by the Senate committees, even with regard to those whom they later approve without opposition, varies widely. Some appointees are asked to present only biographical statements and are subjected to no further interrogation, while others are queried with regard to background, previous writings, attitudes, awareness of the responsibilities they are assuming, and administrative relationships. Illustrative of the first type of hearing were the confirmation hearings for Charles S. Thomas, nominated as Under Secretary of the Navy at the beginning of the Eisenhower administration, and Henry H. Fowler, nominated as Under Secretary of the Treasury in the Kennedy administration. Both made brief statements regarding their previous experience and their intention with regard to conflict-of-interest questions. Fowler stated his agreement on policy matters with his chief, Secretary of the Treasury Douglas Dillon. Routine questions were asked concerning possible conflicts of interest and, except for a query whether or not Mr. Thomas was married (he was, and had four children), no further questions were asked.[11] Not always, however, does a nominee escape quite so easily. Undoubtedly the hearing in Mr. Fowler's case was perfunctory because he was known to the Senate, having served two long tours of duty in the federal government, one running from the early depression days through 1945 and a second during the Korean War as Administrator of the National Production Authority and Defense Production Administration. Since he had also been a successful Washington attorney as senior partner in the law firm of Fowler, Leva, Hawes, and Symington, there was little reason

[11] Nomination of Charles S. Thomas to be Under Secretary of the Navy, Hearing before the Senate Armed Services Committee, 83 Cong. 1 sess. (1953), pp. 17-19; nomination of Henry H. Fowler to be Under Secretary of the Treasury, Hearing before the Senate Finance Committee, 87 Cong. 1 sess. (1961), pp. 4-6.

to question his experience or his competence.[12]

One might expect all hearings to include some probing into the background and attitudes of the candidate, but they do not necessarily follow such a pattern. For example, True Morse, appointed Under Secretary of Agriculture in 1953, appeared before the Senate Agriculture Committee and answered a long series of questions dealing primarily with his work in the Doane Agricultural Service. The committee inquired into the company's role in land appraisals where Doane represented in some instances the federal government and in other instances the farmers. The senators were also interested in its management of a large number of farm operations, and its involvement in the publishing field, both in distributing its own digest and in advising other farm publications. Only briefly did they examine Morse's future role in the Department of Agriculture and his attitudes on farm policy. The pattern of questioning developed as a result of one initial inquiry, and the selection of subject matter was random and disconnected.

The Senate Committee on Foreign Relations took quite a different approach in questioning Chester Bowles, who had been nominated for the post of Under Secretary of State in the Kennedy administration. In contrast to Morse, Bowles was a well-known figure to the Senate committee members. He had served both President Roosevelt and President Truman as head of wartime agencies and had been governor of Connecticut. In international affairs he had served as a special assistant to the Secretary-General of the United Nations and as United States Ambassador to India and Nepal. During the one term he served in the House of Representatives he was a member of the House Foreign Affairs Committee. In addition, Bowles had spoken and written extensively on foreign affairs during the period when he was not in the government. The Senate Committee hearing was directed almost entirely to a discussion of Bowles's views on policy issues. In particular, the senators were interested in his opinions on United States relations with Communist China. Those who supported his nomination gave

[12] For a comparable hearing, see the nomination of Earl Dallam Johnson to be Under Secretary of the Army, Hearing before the Senate Armed Services Committee, 83 Cong. 1 sess. (1953), pp. 9-10. Mr. Johnson had been serving as Under Secretary of the Army under a recess appointment and was renominated and confirmed in the Eisenhower administration.

Bowles every opportunity to disabuse any senators who suspected that he was "soft" on the question of recognition of Communist China. Bowles answered other questions concerning Laos, India, other trouble spots in the Far East, and relations between Communist China and the Soviet Union. While it cannot be said that the interrogation was a thorough and comprehensive inquiry into his thinking on these questions, it did provide a picture of his approach to serious policy questions in that area.

Almost no attention was paid to Bowles's conception of his responsibilities in the State Department itself. Diverted by one or two brief questions with regard to his role as deputy to the Secretary, the senators were happy to return to policy questions. Because of the controversy occasioned by some of Bowles's views, the senators spent an hour longer in questioning him than they did his superior, Dean Rusk.[13]

Sensitive Positions

Some nominees must expect a certain amount of unpleasantness in the Senate hearings because of the controversial nature of the programs they will administer, the attitudes of committee members, or because some particular policy issue is currently of great interest. Such a post in the recent past has been that of the Assistant Attorney General in charge of the Civil Rights Division, created as a result of the passage of the 1957 Civil Rights Act. Because the Senate Judiciary Committee, chaired by Democratic Senator James Eastland of Mississippi, has a number of southern members, each of the appointees to this position in the Eisenhower administration and the first appointee in the Kennedy administration experienced delays in confirmation. As Senator Estes Kefauver of Tennessee said during the hearing on the nomination of Burke Marshall in 1961, ". . . there are some who do not feel favorably inclined toward anyone who is going to administer the law."[14] In December 1957, W. Wilson White was nominated for this post by President Eisenhower after service as a United States attorney and as the Assistant Attorney General in charge of the Office of Legal

[13] *Nomination of Chester Bowles,* Hearing before the Senate Foreign Relations Committee, 87 Cong. 1 sess. (1961).

[14] *Nomination of Burke Marshall,* Hearing before the Senate Judiciary Committee, 87 Cong. 1 sess. (1961), p. 7.

Counsel. The Senate Judiciary Committee refused to report White's nomination for seven months because the southern senators on the committee objected to his role in preparing the memorandum which was used as the legal basis for sending troops to Little Rock during the school integration crisis.

Burke Marshall's appointment was confirmed after nearly two months' delay. The Senate Judiciary Committee in this instance did not see fit to hold hearings for a month after Marshall was nominated and required two hearings to consider his qualifications. Marshall had been a member of the American Civil Liberties Union, but had not otherwise been involved with civil rights prior to his appointment. Without a past history to investigate, the senators therefore pressed him for information on his approach to certain civil rights issues, notably the approach his division would take toward voting rights cases. The senators seemed unconcerned about his lack of experience in dealing with civil rights questions, in spite of the fact that his previous legal practice had been primarily in the antitrust field. Nor did they make much effort to determine his views on other areas involving civil rights, such as discrimination in schools, places of public accommodation, and housing.

An example of a Senate committee's attempt to impress a nominee with a particular point of view occurred during the hearings on the nomination of Murray Snyder as Assistant Secretary of Defense for Public Affairs in the Eisenhower administration. The House Government Information Subcommittee of the Government Operations Committee had been criticizing the Defense Department because of allegedly unnecessary restrictions on the flow of information, so that it was natural for Senator Kefauver to inquire into Snyder's attitude on the classification of documents and urge upon him the view that the Defense Department should be more cooperative in giving Congress access to much more information than it had been getting.[15]

Conflict of Interest

The preoccupation of Senate committees with conflict of interest—the Senate Armed Services Committee, in particular—often prevents

[15] Nomination of Murray Snyder to be Assistant Secretary of Defense, in Hearings before the Senate Armed Services Committee, 85 Cong. 1 sess. (1957), pp. 18-24.

any inquiry being made into the background and qualifications of the candidates they interview. The feature of conflict of interest that most concerns senators has been the prohibition against holding an interest in companies or firms doing business with the nominee's agency.[16]

The most famous nomination hearings devoted to conflict of interest were the Wilson, Stevens, and Talbott hearings at the beginning of the Eisenhower administration. But the hearing on the nomination of Robert S. McNamara as Secretary of Defense in 1961 was also almost exclusively devoted to questions about conflict of interest. The senators were particularly interested in a trust agreement which the nominee had proposed as a means of removing himself from any direct knowledge of, or participation in, decisions made with regard to his investments. Since McNamara's proposed plan was a departure from previous practice, undoubtedly it deserved some attention. But the lack of attention to issues of defense policy, McNamara's qualifications for office, or interservice relationships leads to the inescapable conclusion that the Senate hearing was ineffective as a screening device. Brief questions were asked about his intention to stay on the job, his role in recruiting other Defense Department executives, and his attitude on Defense Department reorganization. But these were lost in the overriding preoccupation with conflict of interest.[17]

As a result of the 1960 Senate resolution recommending that an appointee stay in the government as long as the President desires,[18] the Senate Armed Services Committee asked nearly every nominee during the 1961 hearings about his intentions with regard to tenure. Other committees made such inquiries only sporadically.[19] The Kennedy nominees

[16] 76 Stat. 1124.

[17] *Nomination of Robert S. McNamara*, Hearing before the Senate Armed Services Committee, 87 Cong. 1 sess. (1961). Similar single-minded concern for conflict of interest questions is found in the hearings before the committee on the nominations in 1957 (85 Cong. 1 sess.) of Fred A. Bantz as Assistant Secretary of the Navy, Robert Dechert as General Counsel for the Department of Defense, William Howard Francis, Jr., as Assistant Secretary of Defense, and E. Perkins McGuire as Assistant Secretary of Defense; in 1959 (86 Cong. 1 sess.) of James Wakelin, Jr., as Assistant Secretary of the Navy; in 1961 (87 Cong. 1 sess.) of Joseph S. Imirie as Assistant Secretary of the Air Force, John B. Connally, Jr., as Secretary of the Navy, and Finn J. Larsen as Assistant Secretary of the Army.

[18] S. Res. 338, *Congressional Record*, Vol. 106, Pt. 12, 86 Cong. 2 sess. (1960), p. 15705.

[19] See the nomination of Edward Gudeman to be Under Secretary of Commerce, in Hearing before the Senate Interstate and Foreign Commerce Committee, 87 Cong. 1 sess. (1961), p. 8.

uniformly responded, when asked this question, that they were willing to stay as long as the President desired and as long as they felt that they were doing an effective job. Such inquiries and the exaction of such commitments appear to have limited effect, in view of the departures that occurred within the first two years of the Kennedy administration.

Individual Background as a Factor

For purposes of the senatorial hearing, the nominee who has attracted little public notice, has played no part in any controversial decisions, and has committed himself to nothing in print can count himself fortunate. The hearing on the nomination of Paul B. Fay as Under Secretary of the Navy in 1961 is a good example. Fay had an impeccable background which included, in addition to business experience, service with President Kennedy in a motor torpedo boat squadron during World War II, relationship through marriage to Senator Stuart Symington, and participation in Kennedy's campaigns for Congress and the Presidency. The senators could find virtually nothing to ask him. They asked good-natured questions about the fact that he was a Republican who worked for a Democratic candidate, and they took turns bringing to the attention of the nominee the desirability of their own states for naval installations. Chairman Richard B. Russell finally commented:

> Mr. Secretary-to-be, Georgia does not have any naval yard, but we are one of the original States, and we are on the Atlantic Ocean. Please see if you can find anything for us. [Laughter.][20]

Quite in contrast with the experience of Fay was that of Stanley S. Surrey, nominated to be an Assistant Secretary of the Treasury in the Kennedy administration. An expert in taxation and tax law, Surrey had served in the Treasury Department as tax legislative counsel. He had been counsel to a subcommittee of the House Ways and Means Committee, member of several foreign missions on taxation and fiscal affairs, and professor of law specializing in taxation at the University of California and Harvard Law School. He had also written widely in his field. Just prior to his appointment, he had served as chairman of a task force on taxation appointed by President-elect Kennedy. With this as background, a conservative Senate Finance Committee gave Mr.

[20] *Nomination of Paul Burgess Fay, Jr.*, Hearing before the Senate Armed Services Committee, 87 Cong. 1 sess. (1961), p. 4.

Surrey the toughest grilling of any nominee in the Kennedy administration. Senator Wallace F. Bennett, a Republican from Utah, opened his questioning with an amended version of traditional wisdom, "Don't write and fear no committee of the Senate. . . . "[21]

He noted that much of Surrey's ordeal resulted from the statements which he had made, not expecting to be called to account in such a forum. Senator Bennett explained, "But this is a game, and every member of the committee thus far has played it, and I cannot resist the opportunity to continue. So relax and we will go on with these questions of what you have written."[22]

Surrey had particularly offended the Finance Committee because, according to Chairman Harry Flood Byrd of Virginia, he had implied in one of his articles that Congress had abdicated its responsibilities and had given in to seekers of special tax privileges when the Treasury Department had failed to take a strong stand on these tax issues.[23] Surrey tried to explain that he did not mean that selfish interests controlled Congress, but only that Congress tended to approve changes in tax law when the Treasury Department did not take a position, assuming that silence implied that the latter had no objection. He was unable to explain these passages to the satisfaction of Senator Byrd, who continued to see them as a reflection on Congress.

The committee proceeded to inquire into Surrey's views on a number of complex tax questions. He attempted to distinguish between his role as a private citizen and as a public official, but without much success. The following exchange shows the tenor of the discussion:

THE CHAIRMAN. . . . As I understand it, you favor the taxation of tax-exempt interest on State and local bonds, and so forth; is that correct?

MR. SURREY. In testimony before Mr. Mills in the House Ways and Means Committee, as a private citizen, I indicated that I thought that would be a desirable step.

THE CHAIRMAN. Is that your position now as Assistant Secretary of the Treasury?

MR. SURREY. I do think, Mr. Chairman, that a person who changes his role from a private citizen to that of a Government official, has an obligation to consider all problems in a fresh context.

[21] Nomination of Stanley S. Surrey, in Hearings before the Senate Finance Committee, 87 Cong. 1 sess. (1961), p. 54.
[22] Ibid.
[23] Ibid., pp. 10-13.

SENATOR KERR. In what?

MR. SURREY. In a fresh context.

SENATOR WILLIAMS. Does it mean you should be a puppet and not exercise your own opinion?

MR. SURREY. I beg pardon, sir?

SENATOR WILLIAMS. Does that mean he should be a puppet and not exercise his own opinion?

MR. SURREY. No, sir; by no means. I think it does——

SENATOR WILLIAMS. Let me read what he said in connection with tax-exempt interest. In connection with that you stated: "This exclusion is indefensible from the standpoint of income tax policy." Do you still feel that way about it?

MR. SURREY. Could I just make a general statement and then answer this particular question, because I think I would put it this way:

As a professor and as a private citizen, one attempts to get all the information he can with respect to a particular matter. He does not work in a vacuum, and he does attempt to get the information he can. But he is necessarily limited in what he can do.

As a public official, he has access to a great, much greater, mass of information, both solicited and unsolicited.

This information can either confirm his views or it can alter his views. He also bears responsibility, with a number of other officials, to make recommendations.

Now in this particular area of tax-exempt securities, I would like to explore as far as I could the effect of this upon municipalities and their financing, and on the States to see whether initially my views would be confirmed or would be changed as a result of the information.

At the moment, I certainly think that the subject of tax-exempt securities is one of the matters that should be reexamined in any program of tax reform.[24]

When Republican Senator John J. Williams of Delaware suggested that Surrey might have "gone off halfcocked" when he made the statement, Surrey protested that he did not think so, and denied that he had changed his mind, though still arguing that many elements of tax policy should be reconsidered. At the conclusion of the long and rigorous examination, Chairman Byrd commended Surrey for being a frank witness and answering the questions as well as he could.[25]

The public attention given the Surrey hearing, because of the committee's critical examination of his views, caused Secretary of the

[24] *Ibid.*, p. 16.
[25] *Ibid.*, pp. 18, 74.

Treasury Douglas Dillon to write Chairman Byrd to assure him that Surrey had taken his position with an open mind. He explained that Surrey and he agreed that

> . . . it would be important that he put aside his writings as a professor in performing his task as a public official; that it was one thing to write on the outside as an observer or commentator and another to operate within the Government where the responsibility is quite different. [26]

Because Surrey did have an open mind and because the Treasury Department was reviewing many phases of tax law, Surrey was unable to give fixed opinions on many matters.

In spite of this assurance by Secretary Dillon, which came immediately after the open hearing on March 22 and 23, 1961, the Senate did not confirm Surrey's appointment until April 13, 1961, although Chairman Byrd reported that his nomination was approved unanimously by the Finance Committee.[27]

Seldom does anyone except the nominee and his congressional supporters appear before the committee to testify. Although there was controversy over the appointment of Robert C. Weaver as Administrator of the Housing and Home Finance Agency in 1961, only one witness—the representative of the National Apartment Builders Association—appeared to contest the nomination. Possibly other groups were privately antagonistic, but the chief source of opposition appeared to be the senators themselves. Similarly, during the long and bitter hearings over the nomination of Lewis L. Strauss to be Secretary of Commerce in 1959, virtually all of those who testified did so at the request of the committee or were themselves members of Congress.[28] When someone does voluntarily appear in opposition, he sometimes takes the approach illustrated by the one witness adverse to the confirmation of Wilbur J. Cohen as an Assistant Secretary of Health, Education, and Welfare in 1961. She accused Mr. Cohen of subversion and moral turpitude because of his alleged associations with people whom she identified with the "Communist menace," and because, she said, he misrepresented the social security program by claiming that it was insurance.[29]

[26] Congressional Record, Vol. 107, Pt. 5, 87 Cong. 1 sess. (1961), p. 5803.
[27] Ibid.
[28] See Nomination of Lewis L. Strauss, Hearings before the Senate Interstate and Foreign Commerce Committee, 86 Cong. 1 sess. (1959).

Withdrawals and Rejections

Only eight cabinet nominations have been rejected in the entire history of the United States. Of assistant secretaries and under secretaries, very few nominations have been withdrawn and no candidates have been defeated since 1933. It is, in fact, only in exceptional circumstances that senators feel compelled seriously to oppose a nominee, and seldom does this opposition reach such proportions that it results in his defeat.

The opposition to Edwin W. Pauley, nominated to be Under Secretary of the Navy by President Truman in 1946, was based on two considerations. First, his appointment was considered to be a reward for his past political services as an official of the Democratic party and as a supporter of President Truman for the vice presidential nomination in 1944. Second, since the Navy depended on oil for the operation of the fleet and possessed large reserves, it was improper for a man in the business to be appointed to this high position in the Navy Department. President Truman vigorously defended Pauley's integrity and urged support for the nomination, but to no avail. During the nomination fight, Harold Ickes, the last remaining member of the Roosevelt cabinet, resigned, attributing his resignation to the Pauley nomination. Ickes charged that Pauley had approached him regarding a deal in which Pauley would attempt to raise $300,000 from the oil interests for Democratic campaigns, in return for which the federal government would not prosecute its suit to establish federal title to offshore oil lands. Pauley denied this but the senators, with the support of much of the press, felt that it was improper to appoint an oil man to this strategic position.[30] President Truman ultimately withdrew the nomination.

When former Representative Wesley D'Ewart was nominated to be an Assistant Secretary of the Interior in 1956, after having served for several months in a recess appointment, he had two strikes against him. D'Ewart had been a sponsor of a bill in the 83rd Congress which, according to his opponents, would have given stock men a vested interest in the national forests. He was, moreover, the floor manager of a timberland exchange bill which allegedly would have given a few

---

[29] Nomination of Wilbur J. Cohen, in Hearings before the Senate Finance Committee, 87 Cong. 1 sess. (1961), p. 129.

[30] Harris, op. cit., pp. 200-202.

large timber producers advantages in cutting timber in the national forests. He had been roundly criticized for this by the conservationists. Though both bills had failed of passage in Congress, many conservation groups were nevertheless affronted by his appointment and opposed to confirmation.[31]

His second handicap lay in having run in 1954 for the Senate seat then held by the chairman of the Senate Interior Committee, James Murray. Unfortunately for D'Ewart, this committee had to pass on his qualifications for office. The 1954 congressional campaign was notable for the use of campaign material which imputed "left-wing," "pink," or "Communist" sympathies to candidates for federal office. The Murray-D'Ewart campaign was one of those in which such material was extensively used in the Republican attacks on Murray. D'Ewart disavowed any personal responsibility for use of this material during his campaign for the Senate, pleading ignorance. He repudiated its use during future campaigns. All questions directed to him in the hearing concerned his role in this campaign. Representatives of the Citizens Committee on Natural Resources—a committee made up of the leaders of various resource interests, such as the National Farmers Union and the National Congress of American Indians—opposed the nomination primarily on the basis of his conservation record. The representative of the National Lumber Manufacturers Association supported the nomination, as did one former member of Congress. Because of the intensity of the feeling against D'Ewart from conservation groups and among senators who considered themselves defenders of conservation interests, no final action was taken by the Senate and he resigned after the adjournment of Congress. How much the objectionable material in the senatorial campaign played in this opposition is not clear. However, Senator Wayne Morse of Oregon did indicate in discussing the matter on the floor of the Senate that Senator Murray should, and in fact would, object to D'Ewart on the grounds that he was "personally obnoxious."[32]

After receiving testimony during a hearing, the Senate subcommittee or committee meets in executive session to consider the nomi-

[31] *Nomination of Wesley A. D'Ewart to be Assistant Secretary of Interior,* Hearings before the Senate Interior and Insular Affairs Committee, 84 Cong. 2 sess. (1956).
[32] See *Congressional Record,* Vol. 102, Pt. 2, 84 Cong. 2 sess. (1956), pp. 1559-1563.

nation. Occasionally the committee votes in open session, but only in those instances where there is no dissent.[33] If the hearing is conducted by a subcommittee, their recommendation goes to the full committee, which then considers the nomination, votes, and refers the nomination to the Senate. If the committee's action is unfavorable or no action is taken, the nomination is effectively rejected. In most instances, nominations which have failed to gain approval are rejected at this stage.

Consideration on the Floor

Only under exceptional circumstances, when the appointment evokes considerable controversy, is there a formal debate on the nomination on the Senate floor. Usually the nominations are called up on the executive calendar by the majority leader and are approved without objection. In spite of the hazing which Stanley Surrey received in committee in 1961, his appointment was unanimously approved by the Senate. The fact that a nomination is sent to the floor and is permitted to go to a final vote usually indicates that there are sufficient votes to gain confirmation. The rejection of certain nominees is an indication either of miscalculation on the part of the President or determination to have a rejection on record. The rejection of Charles Warren as Attorney General in the Coolidge administration and the rejection of Lewis Strauss as Secretary of Commerce in the Eisenhower administration were the results of miscalculations, while the rejection of Leland Olds as a member of the Federal Power Commission in the Truman administration indicated a desire to have on record that he had been rejected overwhelmingly by a 53 to 13 margin.

The nomination of Wilson White as Assistant Attorney General in charge of the Civil Rights Division occasioned a relatively short debate in 1958. His nomination had been under consideration by the Senate Judiciary Committee for several months before the committee majority recommended his confirmation. The southern senators saw an opportunity to object on the floor of the Senate to his recommendation in the fall of 1957 that troops be used in the Little Rock controversy, while northern Democrats and Republicans supported the nomination.

[33] See the nominations of Edward Gudeman, Rowland Burnstan, and Clarence Martin as Under Secretaries and Assistant Secretary of Commerce, Hearing before the Senate Interstate and Foreign Commerce Committee, 87 Cong. 1 sess. (1961), p. 29.

It is perhaps too much to call the consideration of the White nomination a debate, since there was no confrontation between the two opposing sides, but only the presentation of each side's views. The Republicans emphasized his ability and experience—some even lauding the role White had played in the Little Rock controversy. Senator Everett Dirksen of Illinois emphasized that, as long as there was no attack upon White's character, the President had the right to have in his official family whomever he desired. Senator Richard Russell of Georgia, in opposition, stated that he regretted opposing a nomination because, as a former state governor, he would "lean over backward in an effort to uphold the appointive power in dealing with nominations."[34] Nevertheless, he felt constrained to oppose the nomination because it was a reward for misleading the President. The debate, as is usually the case, was devoted to establishing a record and, in the end, White was confirmed by a vote of 56 to 20.

How much senatorial confirmation of presidential appointments adds to the quality of the candidates is not clear. Professor Joseph Harris concluded that the principal result has been

> . . . to afford the opposition party and insurgents within the ranks of the President's party an opportunity to attack his administration by contesting his nominations.[35]

It has allowed the opposition to make a record against which it can judge the nominee's subsequent performance. Certainly, it has not led to systematic inquiry into capacity or experience. But, if the result is more effective political relationships between those who achieve appointment and the Senate, the practice of senatorial confirmation may still be justified.

[34] *Congressional Record*, Vol. 104, Pt. 14, 85 Cong. 2 sess. (1958), p. 18215.
[35] *Op. cit.*, p. 379.

6

The Appeal of Public Service

RECRUITERS MAY SEARCH OUT suitable candidates for political executive office from the ranks of the federal service itself, in business and professional circles, or on the university campus. But the criteria they set themselves in considering the party platform and policies of their administrations do not necessarily lead to the selection of men who meet these exacting requirements. Many appointments, in the final resort, issue from a series of judgments—with presidential interest, group pressures, and political obligations on the one hand, and the careful balancing of advantages and deterrents to the acceptance of public office on the other.

The men on whom recruiters first cast a speculative eye are generally successful individuals in mid-career who may have shifted about between employers and occupations in their earlier years but who are clearly on the promotion ladder by the time they come to public notice. They are generally the men who have most to lose by a break for government service, and the factors that largely contribute to their acceptance of appointments as assistant secretaries or under secretaries are related (according to their own testimony) more to a sense of public duty, patriotism, and an obligation to put their special skills and experience at the country's disposal than to career considerations.

Nevertheless, despite their stated objectives in accepting political executive positions, the majority of these appointees have one thing in common with most ambitious and successful men regardless of background or occupation: willingness to exchange security and steady promotion in one place, one firm, or one career line for new and more attractive opportunities elsewhere.

153

Mobility in American Life

The capacity of the federal government to attract its share of capable and experienced men depends in part on the general conditions of mobility in American society. Between 1933 and 1961, there was a strong tendency to recruit men with varied careers as political executives, men who felt no undying commitment to private life and who were willing to adventure into public life for a considerable period of their working lives. There was also mobility within the government ranks themselves. Many of the career and noncareer officers who became assistant secretaries had had previous experience in more than one department or agency.[1]

Studies of occupations in the private sector providing the most profitable sources of executive manpower have been reassuring in this respect. Warner and Abegglen discovered in regard to business leaders, for example, that three-fourths of their sample had had experience in more than one firm, the majority at executive level. Although those executives who made less frequent firm changes were likely to be the first to reach the top, at least a few of the group had actually achieved success because of their versatility and willingness to change.[2]

Lawyers, who comprised approximately one quarter of the political executives serving between 1933 and 1961, are probably the most politically motivated occupational group in American society.[3] They are also mobile, and are particularly willing to consider government service as an alternative or subsidiary career. Not only are they prominently represented in appointive positions but they have also constituted the largest single source from which American governors and members of Congress have been drawn; and, according to Belle Zeller, in 1949 they composed the second largest occupational group in the state legislatures.[4]

[1] See note 9, p. 13 above, on the Brookings study by David T. Stanley, Dean E. Mann, and Jameson W. Doig, *Federal Political Executives, 1933-1965: A Biographical Profile.*

[2] W. Lloyd Warner and James C. Abegglen, *Occupational Mobility in American Business and Industry* (University of Minnesota Press, 1955), pp. 126-27, 134.

[3] David R. Derge, "The Lawyer in the Indiana General Assembly," *Midwest Journal of Political Science*, Vol. VI (February 1962), p. 19.

The academic world provided only a limited number of political executives, ranging between 3 and 10 percent according to the administration. Here, as in the business world, the recruiter faced a number of obstacles in persuading professors to leave their ivy-covered buildings.[5] The associate professor (like the businessman in mid-passage) is probably the least mobile among the educators because he identifies success with promotion in his own institution. The successful full professor, on the other hand, is generally able to move from institution to institution without undue hardship. Even after a hiatus in government employment, those with established reputations in academic circles seldom find the door closed to attractive employment opportunities.

Very few executives had either primary or secondary careers in the scientific and engineering fields. But, with the increasing emphasis on research and technology and the possible creation of new assistant secretaryships in this specialized area, recruiters may be looking more and more to these professions in the near future, particularly to science.

Scientists as a professional group are found in a variety of institutional settings and appear to be highly mobile. A 1948 survey revealed that in a sample of over one thousand, 90 percent had worked for more than one employer and 62 percent had had more than one type of employer: the government, private enterprise, or an educational institution. Scientists employed in private industry or government were much more likely to shift from one type of job to another than those in the universities.[6] Other professionals (including engineers) appear to be able to change locale and institutional setting with relative ease, but during this 29-year period, their skills obviously did not appeal greatly to recruiters for political executive office.

---

[4] See George B. Galloway, *The Legislative Process in Congress* (Thomas Y. Crowell Company, 1953), p. 374; Joseph A. Schlesinger, "Lawyers and American Politics: A Clarified View," *Midwest Journal of Political Science*, Vol. 1 (May 1957), p. 26; Donald R. Matthews, *United States Senators and Their World* (The University of North Carolina Press, 1960), p. 36; Belle Zeller (ed.), *American State Legislatures* (Thomas Y. Crowell Company, 1954), p. 71.

[5] Theodore Caplow and Reece J. McGee, *The Academic Marketplace* (Basic Books, 1958), p. 41 ff.

[6] U. S. Bureau of Labor Statistics, *Occupational Mobility of Scientists*, Bulletin 1121 (1953), p. 38 ff.

Social Motivation

A veteran Washington observer commented that President Roosevelt in 1933 and even in 1939, and President Eisenhower in 1953, "could have gotten almost anybody," but that presidential appeals at other periods were relatively unavailing.[7] The corps of top officials from private industry serving in important government positions during World War II indicates the type of response that always occurs when national security is at stake. It included such men as Edward R. Stettinius, Jr., Donald M. Nelson, Sidney J. Weinberg, John J. McCloy, Robert A. Lovett, James V. Forrestal, William S. Knudsen, W. Averell Harriman, Nelson A. Rockefeller, William M. Jeffers, Ralph J. Cordiner, and Charles E. Wilson (of General Electric). Labor and the university campus also supplied many executives, usually at less prominent levels.

The Korean emergency again brought men from industry into the government, although businessmen as well as executives from other segments of American life did not respond so eagerly. John J. Corson reported in regard to two appointments made at this time:

> Ten or more individuals declined the President's invitation to serve as Economic Stabilization Administrator before an acceptance was obtained. Before a Director of the Office of Price Stabilization could be obtained, thirty individuals were offered the position.[8]

It was a threat to economic existence that brought men into the government during the early days of the New Deal. The crusading spirit attracted candidates from the business and professional worlds of New York and elsewhere who had been singularly reluctant to supply an abundance of executive talent during the Hoover era. With Roosevelt's call to service, many people were willing and eager to accept top-level positions in the federal government; and, although this enthusiasm in

[7] Marver H. Bernstein, *The Job of the Federal Executive* (Brookings Institution, 1958), p. 140.

[8] *Executives for the Federal Service* (Columbia University Press, 1952), p. 6. A survey made in 1952 among businessmen who had served in the government indicated that patriotic appeals were effective in bringing businessmen into government only in periods of exceptional emergency. National Civil Service League, "Survey of Business Executives Who Have Held High-Level Government Administratives Posts" (1952), mimeo.

part reflected lack of other employment opportunities, it was also due to hope for a new administration that promised solutions to the day's critical problems. As one observer wrote in 1957: "Neither the Democratic nor the Republican administrations since 1946 have had available anything like the talent that was available in Washington during the depression." The Kennedy administration presented a somewhat similar image in 1961, attracting many who agreed that the United States "must move ahead in the 60's." The economic and social conditions of the "60's" were less critical, but the international situation provided an effective substitute.

When this fervor engendered by war or economic crisis is lacking, relatively few outsiders see any challenge or excitement in government service. Henry Stimson observed sadly after World War II that his successors in the cabinet were having the same difficulties in recruiting as he had in 1931 for the Department of State:

[In 1931] many an outstanding younger man in the business or professional world of New York was hard pressed to protect his family and his career, and Stimson never presumed to judge any individual's decision. But taken together, the series of refusals he received was indicative of the preoccupation of able men in 1931 with their own affairs; the needs of the nation, and the world, were given second rank. The usual reluctance of private citizens of standing and ability to become entangled with government was intensified in 1931 by the economic depression and the evident difficulties faced by an administration which lacked congressional support. And as he pleaded with the men he wanted, Stimson had neither the crusading spirit of Theodore Roosevelt's day nor the overriding appeal of national defense to assist him.[9]

When Truman and his staff were recruiting in 1946 and later, the general desire was to return to private life and there was considerable revulsion to continued government employment after so many years of obligatory service during the war years. Of those who did accept political appointments, the majority stayed for brief periods of time.

Although not so challenging in its impact on the public as national and economic emergencies, every change of administration, particularly at the time of a party overturn, attracts more recruits for executive service than at later periods. Many who have strong policy commit-

[9] Henry L. Stimson and McGeorge Bundy, *On Active Service in Peace and War* (Harper & Brothers, 1947), pp. 194-95.

ments see the door of opportunity opening with the new administration and a chance to influence national programs. This feeling was obviously intense among the Republicans in 1953 who saw the first Republican administration in twenty years as the vehicle for restoring honesty to government, for curtailing or altering certain domestic programs, and for redirecting American foreign policy. Unfortunately, enthusiasm and the desire for public service quickly wane after the selection of the first crew of political executives. Lacking the interest which comes from direct involvement in the administration's affairs, those who have been left on the shore soon find their attention absorbed by private affairs and are less willing to replace the ship's initial complement. In view of the infrequency of party turnover in the twentieth century (1912, 1920, 1932, 1952, and 1960) and the relatively short tenure of many political executives, the nucleus of enthusiastic supporters attached to a new President can supply only a limited portion of the total number of executives required for an entire administration.

Reactions to Appointment Offers: Case Studies

The decision to accept or reject a government appointment is a far more difficult matter for some candidates to resolve than for others. A mid-career executive with a growing family out in the Midwest may feel as great an urge to implement programs and policies he perhaps helped to formulate as a recently retired businessman in the East. But he has to weigh personal and career considerations with much greater care. The reasons he gives for accepting an appointment may also be difficult to categorize. He may emphasize the importance of, say, public duty, as the deciding factor more than it actually was. In any event, it is certain that his background and current circumstances have an important bearing on his course of action. His geographic ties, education, occupation, political interests, and acquaintance with government activities all have their effect on his final choice.

Before going further into the individual reactions of candidates (and their recruiters) to appointment offers, here is a brief rundown of the personal and career characteristics of the men who accepted the 108 appointments under review. Since these appointments were chosen specifically to throw as much light as possible on differing recruitment procedures and selection methods, the appointees' backgrounds only approximate but do not represent those of the total group of federal political executives in office during this period.

Background and Experience[10]

A certain geographic mobility was apparent among these 108 appointees. The move to the Northeast was most pronounced in Eisenhower's administration, probably because of the large number of businessmen he recruited. It is also interesting that there were actually twenty-eight of Truman's thirty-seven appointees already in Washington at the time they accepted their case study appointments; the majority were already in the government. Eisenhower's executives were considerably older than either Truman's or Kennedy's; there was, in fact, a ten-year difference in median age between Truman and Eisenhower appointees. None of Kennedy's appointees in the sample was over sixty at the time of appointment; but Truman's as a group were the youngest. The educational standard of this sample was reasonably high. Fourteen had no college degrees but, on the other hand, well over half had had some form of graduate experience. Law predominated; forty-three had law degrees and two others had been admitted to the bar, one of them without any degree at all. The Big Three (Harvard, Yale, and Princeton) were fairly well represented, providing the undergraduate education for twenty-one of the group. Harvard was prominent at the graduate level because of the thirteen who attended the Law School. (See Tables A.1 through A.5.)

The major occupations of this group of 108 appointees followed a characteristic pattern. Because of their versatility the decision as to primary career interest was in some instances extremely difficult to determine; in others it was well-nigh impossible—eight of the case study appointees had "multiple occupations." Nevertheless, the general pattern appears to approximate that of the total group of men who held office at these levels between 1945 and 1961 (see Table A.6).

Businessmen, public servants, and lawyers were more or less equally represented. Among the Truman appointees, public servants predomi-

[10] Data on the background and experience of the 108 case study appointees are tabulated in Appendix A.

nated and there were relatively few from the other professions and occupations. Businessmen and lawyers accounted for about two-thirds of the Eisenhower sample, but the proportion of businessmen was only slightly higher than that of lawyers, which was not typical of the total group of Eisenhower recruits. Law, business, public service, and the academic world were all fairly equally represented among the Kennedy appointees.

Besides six of the public servants, another twenty-six of the executives had had previous federal appointments at the upper levels before their case study appointments. A quarter of the whole group, however, were without any government experience at all, the largest proportion being in the Eisenhower sample. Again, this was probably due to Eisenhower's greater reliance on his business contacts for recruitment than on the more varied sources (including government) relied upon by his predecessors. Relatively few Republicans had had much opportunity to gain federal experience. In addition to the twenty-four appointees whose chief occupational interest had been the public service, there were another forty-three in the group who had left their private careers for sufficiently long government assignments (generally at lower levels) to be reasonably familiar with some facets of its administration. Thirty-four of these 108 appointees had also been particularly active in political party activities. (See Tables A.7 through A.9.)

Reasons Given for Acceptance

The willingness of men to accept political executive positions depends on such a variety of social and personal factors that it is difficult to discern consistent patterns of motivation either within an administration or within a department or agency. Like everyone else inside and outside the government engaged in any form of public activity, political executives have their own private reasons for accepting or rejecting appointments: reasons that may differ somewhat from the motives assigned them in public—or the reasons that they publicize themselves. Nevertheless, the men who accepted appointments during this seventeen-year period were, on the whole, public-spirited individuals with a keen sense of personal obligation to the national welfare. Extremely susceptible to appeals for help (especially from the President himself), they were the first to set their shoulder to the wheel in periods of national crisis or to support new policies and programs when change and reform were in the air. They reacted quickly, and with little regard for personal inconvenience, to threats of war, economic emergency, international tensions, or the challenges of a new administration.

The case study appointees reflected both this public-spirited attitude and the individual miscellany of private motives characteristic of the average political executive. Table A.10 lists the major reasons for accepting the specific appointments under review mentioned by the 106 executives answering the question. It classifies their responses under somewhat arbitrary headings, showing the frequency with which certain factors were mentioned—not their relative importance in the decision-making process. The weighting of the various pros and cons affecting appointees' decisions is indicated below in relation to individual responses on their reasons for acceptance.

PATRIOTISM AND PUBLIC SERVICE. Nearly one-half of the appointees interviewed who held office during the Truman, Eisenhower, and Kennedy administrations attributed their decision to accept a political executive position either totally or in part to a sense of personal obligation to engage in public service (see Table A.10). In some instances, this commitment took rather a nebulous form, relating to a general sense of duty to undertake some activity that was beneficial to the community and not directly related to self-interest. In other instances, it was closely tied to motives such as policy reform, prestige, or the opportunity to work closely with some of the nation's leading policymakers.

Such an obligation to undertake some form of public service was mentioned as an important factor by recruits from all the major occupational groups. But more business executives referred to a sense of duty as the chief motivating factor than those in the professions. This was probably because they had more to lose both with regard to career and salary than those in other occupations. A large number of lawyers and public servants also gave this reason for acceptance but their answers indicated that they were not unaware of the possible advantages of a federal appointment later on in life. University faculty and administrators stressed the same point although less emphatically, since many believed that they were already fulfilling a patriotic function by dedicating themselves to education. They believed their sacrifice for the public good to be quite considerable already, compared with other private occupations.

The evidence presented here (which is based on interviews with appointees and others involved in their appointments) tends to reinforce the evidence compiled by the Harvard Business School Club of Washington in a 1958 survey. The latter found that 89 percent of the businessmen responding attributed their acceptance of a government position to the desire to be of public service. The 530 career civil servants interviewed during the course of the Harvard survey discounted public service motives, however, as a cover for such personal objectives as gaining prestige and public stature, advancing future business interests, extending business contacts, and learning more about government techniques.[11]

Although a certain skepticism is necessary when accounting for the desire to serve one's country as a reason for accepting a government position, it is obviously still an important factor since recruiters continue to capitalize on such motivation in urging candidates to accept. One Truman cabinet officer, for instance, exploited this form of patriotism in looking for an under secretary. He wanted to appoint a banker with whom he was acquainted who appeared to fit his needs but who protested his lack of experience and his limited financial resources. The banker reported the conversation leading to his acceptance like this:

SECRETARY: "You're not interested only in money."
BANKER: "No, that's true."
SECRETARY: "You had a son in the war, didn't you?"
BANKER: "Yes."
SECRETARY: "When the war broke out, did he say he had too many other things to do, or that the money wasn't enough?"
BANKER: "No, he volunteered."
SECRETARY: "On the same basis, then, you have no right to refuse your country when you're needed. And the government needs you now."

Another successful businessman gave the following reasons for entering the Kennedy administration:

For several years I have thought businessmen should undertake to do some work outside their own business. I mean more than the nor-

[11] *Businessmen in Government: An Appraisal of Experience* (Washington: Harvard Business School Club, 1958), p. 17.

mal activities one engages in in the community. For example, I think a successful businessman should engage in teaching or some phase of education or participate in government. I feel pretty strongly that those who have gotten a great deal from society ought to be willing to give something back. I admire very much those who are willing to take a job in the government when they have gotten much less than I have from society.

And an Eisenhower lawyer traced his sense of public duty to his college training:

> The principal consideration in accepting the position was a feeling of wanting to be of service to the country. When I considered the offer, only then did I realize how deeply the attitude fostered at college had sunk in. Students were always urged at Commencement time to give some time to government service.

His department head had exploited this sensitivity toward public service by reminding the lawyer that he was a reserve officer in the Navy and asking him whether, if the Navy called upon him to serve during an emergency, he would do it. The lawyer responded affirmatively and the secretary then said, "Well, there's a cold war going on, and your country needs you now." Similarly, another Eisenhower cabinet officer told his recruits emphatically, "By God, you've got to take your turn at the wheel."

This motive for accepting political office is stressed all the more by the many executives whose immediate professional and social circles are hostile to the idea of their leaving for government service. Often, businessmen candidates are warned that their careers will be jeopardized if they leave their companies. Clarence Randall cites what he considered to be the typical reaction:

> . . .His business associates are highly disturbed. They tell him that his number two in command is a "fine boy" (he being 48) but not yet ready to take over. His banker suggests that surely there must be someone else. His wife reminds him that his doctor has urged him to slow down, and that she had hoped they might go to Jamaica in the winter.[12]

The experience of a company president who wished to take an appointment in the Eisenhower administration and who was violently opposed by his board of directors illustrates what some appointees were up against:

[12] *The Communist Challenge to American Business* (Little, Brown and Company, 1959), pp. 189-190.

[The board] pointed out the financial sacrifice I would be making, leaving in a period when the company and the profits were growing; they invoked my loyalty to the company and to the people who had joined in the expectation that I would continue my connection. And they pointed out that I was already exerting an important influence in the field I would work in while in the government.

Nevertheless, the company president took the position "because of my concern over the course the United States government was taking and would take; and because of my conviction that able people should go to Washington."

An investment banker in the Truman administration accepted a most difficult assignment in spite of ill health and long previous service during and after World War II because

. . . it was perfectly obvious that great problems were building up into a virtual national emergency. We were increasingly losing ground to the Russians and it was imperative that the trend be reversed. . . . Life in Washington is not as pleasant as life in my home town but it is very stimulating. I have very little patience for those who grumble about life in Washington. It is a privilege to serve the government.

POLICIES AND PROGRAMS. The above explanation by an investment banker illustrates how complex the reasoning is for accepting political appointments. It shows, too, how closely meshed with a sense of public duty and patriotism in the minds of appointees is the desire to promote their own policies and programs, to be in on the ground floor when new projects are being planned by an incoming administration.

In some instances, appointees may have taken an established stand on specific issues and their wish to influence the trend of future government activities would be limited to their specialized interests. They may wish, for example, to formulate new policies toward colonial areas, advocate reduced subsidies for agricultural commodities, or change the tax laws. In other instances, appointees may want to help fashion much broader government programs with more general implications for the country as a whole. They may want to decentralize the functions of the national government, leaving more discretion in the hands of the states; they may want to change the national defense posture or the nation's image abroad.

Understandably, such policy issues, whether broad or specific, assume much greater significance after a party overturn. Both Eisenhow-

er and Kennedy appointees were highly motivated by policy considerations, generally holding views which differed from those of their department or agency predecessors and looking upon their political service as a means to restore the ship of state to an even keel. Each group
saw the election of their President as the harbinger of major policy
shifts.

Truman, on the other hand, taking office in midstream, made few
such dramatic policy reversals, the notable exception being in the area
of foreign affairs. Truman, of course, also tended to promote people
from lower political or career positions into the ranks of assistant and
under secretaries. This group gave less emphasis to policy convictions
which were probably incidental to their main reasons for accepting
political appointments and subordinate to such career considerations
as promotion, prestige, and higher pay.

Over a quarter of the executives interviewed, however, were attracted to public office because of their preconceived ideas of the challenge of government work or of the specific programs and projects for
which they would be responsible.

Many shared the attitude of the Labor Department executive in the
Truman administration who looked at the proffered job as an opportunity to break new ground for the labor movement.

> The thing I liked most was the challenge of the job offered. It
> gave me an opportunity to show that a trade union man could do a
> job impartially. I was the first person from my federation given a
> major political appointment in my state government and also the
> first to serve as an assistant secretary.

Not infrequently, certain individuals become the unofficial spokesmen for a particular policy approach so that, by the time their party
comes to power, they have committed themselves so strongly to their
particular portion of the party platform that refusal of appointment
would be difficult. An instance of this—although not one of the case
studies—would appear to be the appointment of Wilbur Cohen. A former civil servant, Cohen was the Democratic candidate's adviser on
health issues in the 1960 campaign and the head of President-elect
Kennedy's task force on health problems during the pre-inaugural period. He was later appointed an Assistant Secretary of Health, Education, and Welfare.

Emphasis on policy as a motive for acceptance of appointment is
the more important in those departments where current issues are

most controversial and critical. This is true of the Department of State, where one Eisenhower official explained his acceptance of a position in the following terms:

It was one of the hardest decisions I ever had to make and I went through quite a period when I didn't know what to do. I was led to accept by the tremendous mess in our China policy which needed to be straightened out. There were elements in America which continued to believe that if we gave all our attention to European affairs, things in Asia would work out. I didn't agree with this and felt that our world position was at stake in Asia.

Another State official in the same administration agreed to enter the government for a limited period of time because of the importance he attached to certain policy recommendations which he had helped to formulate.

I felt that this was a job that was necessary; the recommendations were good and needed to be implemented right away. I knew the subject well and felt fully qualified. I was one of the very few people who could do the job and did not feel that I could refuse.

Highly charged policy issues are likely to be found in the Department of Agriculture, and its recruitment pattern during the three administrations under review reflected this conflict. Dedication to reform and new programs was, of course, very pronounced when the Republicans took over in 1952. One Eisenhower appointee commented when interviewed that there was "a public service job to be done. I was concerned with the direction of agriculture programs and government spending and was interested in helping to change that direction." Another described himself as a political team player, and emphasized both the party and policy considerations in his acceptance.

I was anxious to see the first Republican administration in twenty years be popular and make good. I thought I could be of help and benefit the party by taking the job. I also felt there was a real need for new agricultural legislation and that if the Republicans could put in a workable program it would be good for both the country and the Republican Party.

Like agriculture, the management of natural resources also involves difficult policy issues, such as the development of the hydroelectric energy resources of the country. One assistant secretary in the Truman administration actively sought his position in order to put his ideas on regional development into effect. He believed in the Tennessee Valley

APPEAL OF PUBLIC SERVICE

Authority and wanted to work for the creation of similar valley authorities in other regions. Later, two Eisenhower appointees—both with law backgrounds—were concerned about the general departmental policies followed by Truman and his predecessors, particularly those associated with TVA. One "had long been concerned about the trend toward socialism which characterized departmental policies in recent years." The other "wanted to participate in the renovation of the government, to get rid of some of the things and some of the people I did not like in the government."

Not surprisingly, few political executives indicated concern for policy questions in accepting positions in the Bureau of the Budget, General Services Administration, Department of Justice, Office of Civil and Defense Mobilization, or the Post Office Department. While they are of major importance in these agencies, policy issues are seldom clothed in the same dramatic guise as issues in foreign or power policy.

Somewhat more surprising is the fact that none of the Treasury executives interviewed indicated that policy considerations influenced their judgment in accepting positions. This illustrates, perhaps, the narrow latitude within which officials of such an influential department must operate because of conflicting pressures on revenue policy and the heavy cost of federal functions.

INFLUENCE OF THE RECRUITER. The direct approach is often decisive in persuading some candidates to accept appointments. Thirty of the 106 appointees who responded attributed their acceptance either totally or in part to the drawing power of the recruiter, whether he was President, Secretary, or White House aide. In many instances, this influence was based on strong personal ties developed over a period of years. But, based on a personal relationship or not, the President's invitation was of course the most effective form of persuasion. As one observer stated:

> The appeal of a President is still almost irresistible, even from a Republican administration to a life-long Democrat. If the President of the United States sees a job for an individual to do and will go to the extent of personally inviting him to talk with him about it, it is mighty hard to turn the President down.[13]

Only occasionally does the President directly concern himself with

[13] Bernstein, *op. cit.*, p. 143.

the selection of subcabinet members before the choice has been narrowed down to the single candidate whom a particular cabinet member wants. However, the Kennedy administration provides some interesting examples of such direct intervention. One active participant in the 1960 campaign was preparing to return to his business after the election when he received a call from the President-elect asking him to arrange his affairs so that he could take a post in Washington. The businessman explained:

> My reaction was immediately favorable. I had come to know the President very well during the past four years and I had tremendous respect for him. During this time I was working for him at my own expense. I was very pleased to think that he had enough confidence in me to offer me a position in his administration. I was happy that he knew me well enough to want me to help. I also knew that when he said something, he meant it.

Another executive, who had earlier refused to be considered for another Kennedy appointment, also succumbed to presidential pressure.

> The most important consideration in my accepting was the direct request by President Kennedy. He asked me to take the post because he felt that I could make a contribution and not out of any sense of political obligation. I was impressed with the President's concern for this area of activity and his clear indication that he felt I could be helpful to him.

One recruiter in the Eisenhower administration made a practice of having the President's secretary call a prospective candidate and ask him to come to Washington to see the President, assuming that in a personal confrontation the candidate would be less likely to resist. Indeed, when Eisenhower himself asked a close personal friend to serve as assistant secretary the latter "regarded it as an order from the President," and accepted because he "felt an obligation to the President personally."

In most instances, however, it is the secretary's influence that determines whether the prospective recruit will accept or not. One young lawyer who was serving in a subordinate post in the Eisenhower administration was anxious to return to his practice when the secretary offered him an assistant secretary post. With this,

> . . . all sorts of emotional dams broke. I could not refuse because of my personal loyalty and attachment to the Secretary. I would never have accepted the job if [the Secretary] himself had not personally

asked me to, and in addition, asked me in such a way that to refuse would have grievously wounded him. I had come to honor him second only to my own father. I accepted also because of the pleasure of working with the ablest man I've met in government. He has done a tremendous job and it is fun to work for a big man, a leader.

A prominent Truman executive displayed the same kind of emotion in accepting a critical post:

> The principal reason I accepted was that the secretary asked me to. If anyone else had solicited me I would have thought about it a great deal longer. He had already made one of the great contributions to the country and after serious illness he was still willing to serve. I don't understand how anyone could refuse such a man.

Nor is this personal relationship found only among people who move in and out of government. One Foreign Service officer was called back from an ambassadorial post and reluctantly accepted an Assistant Secretary of State position "because over the years I have tried not to let the Foreign Service down, and if I refused then I would go down in Loy Henderson's esteem."[14] A civil servant in the Truman administration thought little of a suggestion by his department head that he was being considered for an assistant secretary position until the secretary made a sales pitch and said, "I want *you*." After thinking it over, he concluded that the secretary was the kind of man he wanted to work for, and that generally "it was more important to choose a good boss than a good job."

The absence of presidential interest or even of secretarial interest in recruitment often has an adverse effect on candidates. Men who might otherwise be attracted to government service are in fact offended when the recruiter is himself relatively unknown. A New York executive in 1959 lamented recruitment procedures in the latter half of the Eisenhower administration:

> . . . We only hear from second- and third-rank officials if they want someone from our company. It's easy to say no. If an Administration really needs a top-flight man, the President can always get him. You just can't say no to the White House.[15]

---

[14] Loy Henderson was a distinguished Foreign Service officer, now retired, who rose to the post of Deputy Under Secretary for Administration in the Eisenhower administration.

[15] "Nobody Wants a Washington Job," *Business Week* (February 28, 1959), p. 30.

CAREER CONSIDERATIONS. In the careful weighing of pros and cons that decided whether individuals would accept or reject political executive appointments, career considerations were frequently on the debit side of the balance sheet. The majority of the executives interviewed regarded their government appointments as somewhat of a threat to their established careers in private life; but over a quarter of them saw some form of advantage from a short-term assignment. This may have been because they welcomed a change and a political appointment offered a valid excuse for breaking away from a settled and somewhat monotonous existence; they may have wanted to lay the groundwork for another career line outside the government later on; and, if they were civil servants or lawyers, they may have seen political office as promotion or at least in their career interest. Only three appointees saw any monetary gain from a change to public service.

It was, of course, the men already in the government, particularly in a subordinate policy-making or confidential post, who really considered a presidential appointment as a definite step up in their careers and not as a resting place between jobs. A significant number of "assistants to" made this jump successfully. One Treasury official in the Truman administration, for example, explained why he had accepted:

> I felt flattered. I thanked [the Secretary] and told him I would accept. I accepted principally because with this appointment I had moved into the big leagues. Having been in the Department for several years I thought my experience qualified me, whereas I had turned down a job in another agency because I didn't think I was qualified. I think the Treasury Department is the greatest institution in the government.

And he remained in the government "big leagues," returning later after a brief absence to a highly prized government post. Another Truman appointee who had had many years' experience in both government and private enterprise felt that his experience as assistant secretary "would be a great asset to him in his career, as a source of contacts and enhanced personal prestige." He had seen his career in private industry "blow up" and he was frustrated in his subordinate position in another federal department, so that the subcabinet position appeared extremely attractive to him. Hoping for a future in the government (which he substantially realized) he looked on his assistant secretary post as "a real glamour job."

Lawyers, on the other hand, who served as political appointees in the Department of Justice saw not only a chance of promotion in the assistant attorney general positions but also a means to obtain later appointments on the federal bench. One of these Justice lawyers who had political connections looked upon his advancement in the first instance as a "career appointment, part of a general practice of bringing up people from within the ranks to the higher posts." Assuming that it was his "successful performance" on a very sensitive assignment that brought him to the attention of the Attorney General (although he admitted others were working on his behalf), he was "gratified and highly flattered to be appointed assistant attorney general, viewing it as great recognition and one step beyond" the recognition he had received in other posts he had previously held. After his government assignment he was awarded a federal district court appointment; and, in his interview, made the following general observations on the possibilities of obtaining a judgeship:

> There is no real expectation of being appointed a judge because of successful experience in the Justice Department but there is a hope. Many have gone from the Department to the federal bench. Such appointments are an outgrowth of experience in the department and persons in these positions hope to invite attention by sufficient competence.

He also compared the appointment of assistant attorneys general to district court judgeships with the appointment of attorneys general to the Supreme Court.

Of course, this generally accepted view that visibility in the Justice Department encourages consideration for a later bench appointment must not be too obviously espoused by the prospective candidate. One Assistant Attorney General reportedly told the Attorney General that he would accept his Justice appointment because he could then go on the federal bench as a friend of his had done. Unfortunately, the Attorney General was displeased at this candid expression of what obviously lurks in the minds of many Justice appointees and the later performance of this particular lawyer did not lead to further advancement. A similar example was the assistant secretary who had been a prominent labor leader in his own state and who had looked well ahead.

> I intended eventually to go back home and run for state office. I already have an adequate background in [his previous occupation] and I have developed a close association with and the confidence of a large section of the state's people. I feel that I have the confidence

of perhaps 40 percent of the voters. I think it is necessary that I establish certain other identities. One of these is that of an administrator and I hope to gain this through service in the executive branch. I am also anxious to gain the identity of a businessman; so I intend to go back and enter business. Once I have done that I will go into state-wide politics.

Unless he is a lawyer or public servant, a political executive seldom has a specific goal in mind when he accepts a political appointment for career considerations. As a Truman deputy described his own motives:

> There is hardly a better way for a man to make contacts and broaden his career opportunities than by service in an executive position. I felt that my experience would serve me particularly well in giving me further background in urban development planning, and in the administration and supervision of engineering projects—fields in which I am interested and in which I have specialized.

But like many others, he gave a multitude of reasons for wanting the job, including improved pension rights, prestige, and the challenge that the job itself presented.

The situations vary—some involve men of independent means; some those who are ready to retire and who are seeking other interests; others, men who are immersed in their private affairs but recognize a public assignment as an opportunity for an exciting experience. One 60-year-old executive explained:

> I was perhaps unique in my business situation because I felt my son was ready to take over the family business. I was freer to consider government service than I might have been otherwise. I was not in a marginal position financially in the sense that I couldn't have afforded to leave if my son hadn't been available to manage the business. I was over 60 and more or less in the twilight of my career in my business; I wasn't forsaking a position on a corporate business ladder.

Another executive noted how favorably he had been situated in that he "owned controlling interest in a banking firm and could leave whenever and for as long as I pleased. I have a reliable business partner whom I can trust to manage the firm efficiently in my absence." And an active figure in state politics explained:

> I hadn't been doing too much since I left [public office]. I was living in semi-retirement on my ranch and was getting a bit restless and anxious to get back into public life of some kind. I didn't have any real financial worries and my son did the actual management of the ranch so I felt that I was leaving the ranch in good hands.

Understandably, too, in every administration there is a small group of men who try to "use" public office to their own career advantage. One former political executive described them at a Brookings round table in this fashion:

> . . . there was also a great number of men who sought political appointments pretty vigorously on a rather crass, commercial basis. They regarded government service as a chance to develop a reputation, to make contacts they could capitalize on later on. I don't want to overstate this element, but it is a part of the process.[16]

The appointees in the case studies did not, as a group, appear to exhibit much interest in this aspect of political office nor was the "crass" approach particularly prevalent. In any event, executives with long experience in the federal government, a strong orientation toward the public service, and pronounced policy commitments recognized that political appointments might enhance their reputations and tended to be influenced by this factor in their decisions to serve. It was less true of those from private occupations. One Eisenhower executive who had held office during World War II and had served later in several important federal and international posts during the Truman administration, accepted a political executive assignment within his area of specialization "because I felt that in the long run the government experience would be worthwhile in broadening my career opportunities, especially in the kind of consultant work I was interested in." In addition to this consideration, he was a Republican who genuinely wanted the Eisenhower administration to succeed; he enjoyed government work and felt he could make an important contribution in his area of interest and competence.

PRESTIGE. Ranged beside the relatively small number of appointees whose purpose is to "use" political executive office for their own advantage are the many candidates who are in agreement with them in one respect—that there is considerable "glamour" and prestige attached to the senior policy-making posts in the government. This prestige value of a political executive position depends on the perspective of the candidate. There are men who have marked recognition in private life and tend to disdain government as an institution. A political executive appointment would enhance neither their own self-esteem nor their public image. For the many, too, who have already seen long service

[16] Bernstein, *op. cit.*, p. 148.

in prominent government positions an additional appointment has little to offer in the way of added prestige. Nevertheless, nearly a quarter admitted that the prestige and public notice of these positions played an important part in their favorable decisions.

Recent studies at the Brookings Institution indicate that the attitudes toward political executive positions must be clearly differentiated from those toward civil service positions. Business executives, engineers, natural and social scientists in businesses and the universities—some of the groups from which political executives are recruited—rated senior political appointees extremely high on capability, honesty, ability, interest in serving the public, drive to get ahead, and respect. In some instances, they rated them higher than executives in private industry. The better educated the rater the higher the ratings given.[17] These findings suggest that, by and large, political executive positions are attractive and reputable even to men who are in highly professional and generally respected positions.

The perspective of men outside the government, however, may be quite different from those inside. One secretary noted that certain people were "unattainable," because they would not consent to serve at a particular level or in a particular kind of position. Business and professional men have attained certain standing in their own circles which is measured in many ways: public visibility, income, memberships in clubs and organizations, clientele, and so forth. Their responsibilities are often broad and involve the welfare of large numbers of people and important institutions. When asked to take a position in the government, they measure the importance in terms of the responsibilities they carry in their present position. If the position in the government is not only less remunerative, but also less visible publicly, narrower in its responsibilities, with a relatively less renowned agency (and dealing primarily with people either inside or outside the government who may be characterized in the same way), there is a strong likelihood that they will refuse. They can argue that such positions may be occupied effectively by persons of less experience and status while they continue to carry out what they consider to be more important responsibilities in private life.

Of course, to men who rose to assistant secretary rank from subordinate government positions—as many did in Truman's administration—

the prestige value of these appointments assumes significance and involves career considerations as well. One Treasury executive expressed his delight at becoming an under secretary in the following terms:

> I think the under secretary post is the most desirable position in the government. I have aspired to this position since the 1930's and have actively sought it for three years. This job is especially interesting because the under secretary is in on everything. He goes to cabinet meetings when the secretary is out of town or is ill, and he serves as an alternate on the National Security Council.

The lawyers interviewed appeared to value appointments in these terms almost as much as public servants. Undoubtedly it was valuable to them in their later professional work. In contrast, businessmen seldom indicated that prestige was a factor in their decision to accept or reject. The absence of evidence is hardly conclusive but it is reasonable to assume that businessmen, with a suspicion of "politics" even in the administrative branch, considered such service less exalted than their own occupations.

The position and the agency concerned were particularly important to the political recruit. No matter what the actual reasons given may have been for turning down some of the harder-to-fill appointments, the majority of them were at subcabinet level in the less attractive or less highly regarded agencies. A cabinet member in the Kennedy administration was turned down by a college president and at least one foundation head when he asked them to serve as his under secretary. He explained in his interview:

> The most serious obstacle to their accepting was the financial question. But money is not the most important motivating factor involved with the top jobs since the financial issue would be subordinated when one received the highest honor—the cabinet post. There isn't as much meaning attached to a subordinate post in a department, and then money did provide a stumbling block.

In another case a candidate, first sounded out for a position at the bureau chief level, declined because "the position was not very influential." He felt his present position was "a better spot for public service." Later, he was induced to accept a position as assistant secretary. A businessman in the Eisenhower administration stated that "one cannot say no when asked to serve the government in time of stress, and I wouldn't say no to such a request at a level of appropriate responsibility."

APPEAL OF WASHINGTON. Life in the capital city, the glamour and social whirl, are particularly attractive to the wives of many political executives. A cabinet member in the Truman administration said, "Nine times out of ten, Mama wants to come." One experienced recruiter in the Eisenhower administration stated that "wives are not too unhappy about coming to Washington. As a matter of fact, they are often the helpful ones in getting a man to accept a job." The wife and children in one family were actively pushing an appointee toward Washington even before he was seriously considering an appointment himself. Another wife was described as "enjoying the life of a big shot," and therefore she enjoyed Washington. One, amazingly, preferred Washington weather to that of her home state. Others were "delighted" or responded immediately, "Let's go."

For the most part, however, the wives left the question of moving to their husbands, accepting their judgment about their future. A frequently reported reaction is, "It's up to you to decide," or, "I'll be glad to go if that's what you want to do." Wives share vicariously in the prestige and influence (and the turmoil and troubles) of their husbands, but they have a much more direct interest in the environment they find in Washington than in their husbands' conditions of employment. To many wives, the disadvantages of uprooting themselves and their children from their home communities were counterbalanced by their exciting new life in Washington.

Drawbacks to Political Appointment

Some recruiters maintain the fiction that no one ever refuses a presidential appointment by never making a direct offer until a candidate has committed himself. This is the reason why it appears that some cabinet members had difficulty in obtaining qualified staff, while others who served in the same administration, and even in the same agency, had no trouble at all. The former were probably looking for the "best" man, the latter tended to accept whoever was suggested to them. Some cabinet heads knew where to look for competent executives while others did not; some were restricted because their field of recruitment was demarcated by certain interest group and technical boundaries while others were not because there was no "natural" recruitment source.

One prominent Eisenhower cabinet officer who professed no problems at all in recruitment illustrated these different approaches by this confusing comment:

> Almost everyone who accepted wished we hadn't asked him. No one we asked really wanted the position because they were top men and they had much to do as it was. Getting them to accept, however, was not difficult because they recognized their obligation to serve. This was the most important reason for their coming.
>
> If anyone gets a refusal, they've asked the wrong man. There is no use asking a man who has a big family and who has a big job and obviously can't come.

Similarly, a Kennedy executive who was responsible for bringing in a large number of people at the assistant secretary level commented: "The reason recruiters are turned down by prospective candidates is that the recruiters go to the wrong people." In his opinion, the likelihood of rejections among the business executives was great because of their inability to adapt to public service.

One Truman cabinet officer, on the other hand, described assistant secretary posts as "second-string jobs." He regarded the appointments he made as *"faute de mieux"*—for lack of anything better. He obtained nearly all of his political executives either by promoting career officers or by accepting the recommendations of the Democratic National Committee. Another Truman cabinet officer who said he never had any problems recalled that he rewarded one man with a presidential appointment because of his loyal party service and because it would help him get an increased annuity upon retirement. Under such circumstances, it is understandable why the secretary believed the problem to be overemphasized.

No one factor, of course, explains why a man finally refuses a political executive appointment. One Eisenhower cabinet officer related the variety of responses he had had when seeking an assistant secretary:

> I was trying to find a businessman who could look after certain business functions in our department. I was looking for a young man who had had some experience in large organizations, who was on his way up and could still stand the gaff.
>
> I took several months in looking for the right candidate, I went to the presidents of several companies. The presidents told me to pick the man I wanted and they would approve the selection. In one instance I did pick a man but he would not accept, even though the president of the company urged him to take it. Apparently the man

hoped to obtain a higher position in the company in the very near future. I think the candidate's supervisor probably advised him to stick around.

Later I found a vice president of a utilities company who seemed like just the man for the job. He was interested and was all set to come until his wife decided that she didn't want to move to Washington and have to change the kids' schools.

A third man had retired at the age of fifty-five, after reaching the top of his profession. I knew him personally and also knew the president of his company. I was certain he wasn't doing anything and would be available. I got him to come to Washington, but he would not tackle it. He was very much interested in activities in his own small town and didn't want to leave them.

This cabinet officer's problem was not unique. Special problems and circumstances conditioned the response of each man. In probing for candidates he had to find the man whose inclination to serve dissolved his understandable reasons for refusing.

Certain reasons for this reluctance are recurrent, and common to many prospective appointees; but others are specific, such as the one given by the Negro who declined an appointment as an Assistant Secretary of State because he would not reside in Washington owing to its segregation practices, or that of the candidate who was about to adopt a child and would have jeopardized the adoption by transferring legal jurisdictions.

PERSONAL CONSIDERATIONS. Every potential executive has to think not only of the effect of occupying a political appointment on his career but also its effect on his private life and on his wife and children. The break from familiar surroundings—from home, school, and community —may be very hard indeed for his family. So also may be the stresses and strains of Washington life and the heavy drain on family financial resources.

These personal difficulties, rather than career considerations, appeared to create the biggest obstacle to acceptance in the minds of most appointees who debated seriously whether or not they should come to Washington. Three-quarters of those who responded mentioned either financial difficulties, the problems of uprooting their families from their home communities, or both (see Table A.11). Of course, these drawbacks to acceptance were closely interwoven with job-related questions. Salary is dependent on promotion; professional or business success is dependent on community visibility; and many individuals are reluctant to leave not only their friends but also their secure working environment.

Financial Drawbacks. First and foremost among the obstacles facing many political executives and their families was the severe cut in salaries most of them had to absorb in the face of heavily increased expenses.[18] As one Secretary of Defense put it:

> Only those who have money to come down to Washington are able to accept. As a result, most assistant secretaries are people who have money. This is the only way we get people. We should either increase the salary or give a tax-free allowance.

The sacrifices which many executives in higher income brackets without independent means have to make may seem unreal to those whose income is considerably lower. But few men who depend on salary or earned income find that they have excessive income. They invest any money left over from living expenses in life insurance, expensive educations for their children, and savings. A political executive in the Kennedy administration explained his reluctance to accept:

> I don't have a family fortune nor does my wife have an independent income. Besides, I have spent half of my career in the government. We have had a lot of illness in my family and the expense of this, combined with trying to keep up a good insurance program, has taken quite a bit of my income. I haven't accumulated a fortune so I can live off interest and dividends; my only source of income is earned income. I have been making around $100,000 per year in recent years. I don't think it's decent to go beyond that. I don't suppose that accepting this job was a sacrifice for me personally but it is for my family.

Another candidate said he told the President:

> I'm not a man of independent resources so I depend on my salary. The salary in the position offered me is high for government salaries, but it will be less than 50 percent of my present earnings. This is important because I have to educate my kids and build an estate for my family since my family isn't the beneficiary of a trust.

A businessman who had taken part in the 1952 campaign on a full-time basis and was recruited early in the Eisenhower administration explained how important it had been to him to have a private income:

[18] See Chap. 10 for discussion of federal executive salaries.

I had some difficulty in deciding whether to accept or not. Officially, I was still with my company but I knew if I took this post I would be through there. I am not a man of great means. At [my company] I was earning $25,000 per year and the deputy post paid only $20,000. I had two boys in school and it would have been a tough decision if it had not been for a small independent income from an inheritance.

These reductions in income are often severe. A Truman appointee gave up a $65,000 per year partnership in a business counseling field for his $15,000 per year salary as an assistant secretary. An Eisenhower appointee, who felt an obligation to serve when asked directly by the President, remarked that the financial loss involved would have had a compelling influence under other circumstances:

I felt I had to give up all connection with the company, selling my stock and renouncing my pension rights in addition to resigning my official connections. My salary as assistant secretary—$15,000 at the time—would be less than half of what I was earning. My children were either of college age or nearing it.

A somewhat different problem arose for a businessman who resisted an appointment in the Eisenhower administration because of the financial sacrifice involved. In his fifties and near the top of his organization, he was getting ready to retire. He finally succumbed to the President's pressure but eventually had to go back to his company and continue working past the age of retirement because of the need "to get some of it back."

Several appointees who were making in private life little more and sometimes even less than the salary paid political executives recognized the additional financial burdens they would have to carry in Washington. One university administrator who served in the Eisenhower administration knew he "wouldn't be making anything in the bargain" in spite of his $3,000 increase in salary "because money doesn't go quite so far in Washington." A union official who had served as a state administrator noted that there was no monetary advantage since assistant secretaries were paid only $10,000 during the Truman administration (until 1949). A Kennedy appointee faced serious difficulties because, although the political executive job he was offered paid more than his position in the news media, he would now have to pay many more expenses out of his own pocket which he had previously put on an expense account. In addition, his expectations of substantial pay increases he might receive in his news job were not likely to be realized in the government. For some, the mere cost of moving to Washington is a considerable barrier, although on its own it seldom justifies rejection of an appointment. At least three of the Kennedy appointees in the limited sample of twenty-four had to borrow money (one as much as $3,000) to make the move.

Department and agency heads seldom identified money problems as an important factor in the decisions of those who declined appointments, and their testimony ran counter to the testimony of the appointees interviewed in the case studies. One Secretary of Commerce was emphatic about it:

> I don't think higher salaries are an answer to the problem of getting people to accept. For example, I tried to get [the president of a prominent company who was very active in party affairs], but he wouldn't have been able to come if I'd been able to offer him $50,000 a year instead of $18,000 or $19,000. You can talk to him for two hours and he'll tell you exactly what I tell you: he was too tied up in his business to take a turn at the wheel.

Nevertheless, the fact remains that appointees were seriously perturbed about the financial losses they had incurred during their government service and it was a recurring theme during the majority of the interviews. It may be, of course, that their economic trials and tribulations stood out sharply in relief after their terms of office were over and that they had not been an overriding consideration at the time the appointments were accepted. Be that as it may, one unfortunate result may be that department heads and White House officers who are active in recruiting still tend to restrict their search for suitable candidates to those who have private incomes and can afford substantial losses.

Disruption of Family Life. The financial expenses of moving to Washington and salary cutbacks are not the only personal factors of importance to a political executive. Many candidates find upsetting the family, maintaining two places of residence, changing schools, cutting off ties with old friends and associates, too burdensome. Many who try it once are reluctant to try it again.

Some, particularly from smaller towns and cities, have real affection for their communities. One Kennedy appointee expressed reluctance to leave his city because it was "as nice a community of medium size as there is in the country." An assistant secretary in the Eisenhower administration, who came from a small college town, said, "I consider it to be God's country and both my wife and I want our children to grow up there." They resisted moving to a large metropolitan area. One political executive from a small southern town took an important job in industry after his government service and even persuaded the heads of the company to transfer their headquarters to his locality. And some candidates were reluctant to accept for even more specific reasons, such as the one given by a Kennedy appointee who had just had a new house built and had landscaped the grounds himself: "We felt we had, for the first time, a permanent home." His children were all in school and one child in high school was very much opposed to moving because it meant leaving all her friends.

Of considerable importance in the decision-making is the wife's reaction to the appointment. Among the case studies where her attitude to the appointment weighted heavily her husband's decision to accept or reject a position, she was more often than not in favor of moving to Washington. But a minority were reluctant or actively opposed: one because she "didn't mingle," and her distaste for Washington caused her to spend much of her time in her previous home; others because they were concerned about their children's schooling or the formidable and more imminent problem of the move itself. At least two wives of candidates who accepted refused even to come to Washington, in spite of separation from their husbands. Either the wife or husband spent weekends shuttling back and forth between Washington and their home town. For some wives, it was difficult to trade the settled, comfortable existence they had found in their home towns for the faster pace of the capital city. Others were less opposed to the location than they were to their husbands' jobs. The wife of one political executive who lived in the Washington area opposed his acceptance of a position in the Kennedy administration because she knew the burdens which high-level service would impose upon him.

Foreign Service officers were among the most reluctant to leave their assignments to serve in Washington as assistant secretaries. Upon hearing of his candidacy, one Foreign Service officer, who was then serving as an ambassador, remarked that "it would be very sad" to leave his station, even though it would be a step up professionally. Compared with his foreign post his standard of living would decline 20 percent and he would have "fewer visible accomplishments than one has abroad where one plants seeds and helps institutions grow and develop." Another Foreign Service officer-ambassador was not at all pleased at the prospect of returning to Washington since he was forced to take his children out of school in the middle of the year and de- part—which involves much diplomatic ritual—in less than two weeks. Only one of the cases studied seemed genuinely pleased at the pros- pect of coming back to the United States for State Department service.

JOB-RELATED DIFFICULTIES. Uppermost in the minds of most men who are candidates for political executive positions are the career implica- tions of such service. Testimony of both recruiters and recruited leads to the conclusion that uncertainty associated with government employ- ment and anxiety over harmful effects on one's present status in a company, university, or law practice constitute a serious hindrance in the recruitment process. Sixty-one percent of the appointees inter- viewed mentioned some factor connected with their jobs that made them seriously debate the advisability of accepting the government offer (see Table A.11). Their replies were worded in many different ways: they would lose advancement; they preferred their present jobs; their employers were too dependent on them; conflict of interest and lack of promotion would require too much financial sacrifice. They were all essentially career considerations and fear of the effect of government service on future prospects.

When this issue was raised before a Senate subcommittee, Marion B. Folsom, who could draw on his own varied experience in the gov- ernment, testified that the principal reason for reluctance to serve was

> . . .the fear on the part of the younger executive that, regardless of promises by the company, he would find upon his return that he might have lost an opportunity for advancement.[19]

And Professor Bayless Manning of the Yale Law School asserted at the same hearings:

> It is the question of what happens to his job while he is gone. Where does he stand on the company ladder or the law firm ladder or the university ladder when he comes back? Was it an escalator he was standing on that kept going up while he was away? Or will he

[19] *Organizing for National Security,* Inquiry of the Senate Subcommittee on National Policy Machinery of the Committee on Government Operations, 86 Cong. 2 sess. (1961), Vol. 1, p. 480.

find that people passed him while he stood still on the same rung of the ladder? [20]

Among the case study appointees, an assistant secretary related his experience in trying to find his own replacement. He was successful only after having received twenty refusals:

> The man I most wanted for the position was up for promotion in his company. He had worked his way up from office boy to vice president and within six months was to be made president of the company. Had he accepted the position in Washington he would have thrown over his life's ambition.

A Secretary of Defense tried to fill an assistant secretary post with a man who held an important position in a company headed by a president who had served the government several times and who encouraged his men to enter public service. The Secretary obtained the company president's support for recruiting the man in question, but the candidate refused because of his fear that he would lose out in the competition for a higher post in the company. Ironically, he lost out anyway. This Secretary reported that similar situations had arisen in a number of cases he knew of.

Like the company president above, some employers or partners may encourage acceptance of a government post, indicating their desire to have the candidate return to the fold, but this is not entirely reassuring. Anything may happen in a two- or three-year absence. In other instances the candidate is told either that he cannot leave or that if he leaves he is through with the company. One Eisenhower recruiter said that in trying to find an assistant secretary he recommended the executive secretary of a business association in one of the nation's largest cities. The candidate was excited over the prospect but it was necessary to obtain the approval of his board of directors for a two-year leave of absence. When the recruiter broached the subject with the president of the association, the latter said, "I'll allow him to go over my dead body. I'm not going to allow the association to be wrecked while I'm president." Because he felt he owed everything to the association, the candidate declined.

Top executives in business or professional firms are bound to feel a natural obligation to their organizations, companies, and partnerships

---

[20] *Ibid.*, pp. 457-58. Professor Manning was at the time serving as the staff director of the Special Committee on Conflict of Interest Laws of the Association of the Bar of the City of New York.

—whether they are owners or employees. If they are good potential political executive material, they have come to occupy responsible policy-making positions and their departure might lead to serious reper-
cussions for their organizations. One president of a small company, for
example, turned down an important appointment in an agency that operated in his own specialty, the transportation field. After carefully analyzing the situation in his own company (which he had founded), he
came to realize that his presence was not just needed but was critical to
the success of its operations. In another instance, the vice president of
one of the country's largest companies who had served many years in the
government rejected an offer because he had recently been appointed
head of a large research division.

Of course, in recent years, many executives have attempted to cir-
cumvent some of the most serious disadvantages of government service by insisting on short-term assignments. Quite a few, particularly
during Eisenhower's presidency, accepted appointments on the clear
understanding that they would stay a limited period of time, often for
no more than one year.[21] This ran counter to the wishes of the recruiters that appointees should serve a sufficiently long period to become
familiar with their jobs (often pegged at two years); and Kennedy
even sought commitments, not always successfully, for the entire presidential term.

Many appointees found that they were obliged to remain longer
than their original commitments. Some companies and universities were
willing to grant leaves of absence for one year, but their willingness
diminished rapidly with the addition of more years. Besides, there was
no guarantee that their employees would not ask for additional leave
in order to complete a particular task, to accommodate the secretary,
or to meet an emergency situation. The uncertainty of such a situation
made commitments to re-employ extremely shaky.

Businessmen, labor leaders, university professors, foundation
officials, and lawyers alike, therefore, had to recognize that acceptance
of what appeared to be only a temporary appointment in the federal
government might constitute a rupture in a settled way of life. They
had to recognize that a large percentage of them would have to
change their private employers, their place of residence, and occasion-

---

[21] Among the case studies, three of Truman's appointees and seven of Eisenhower's stipulated that they would only stay one year. The numbers who stipulated two years were two and eight appointees respectively.

ally their primary occupation. They had therefore to make a decision that affected their entire future, not just a three- or four-year interval in a flourishing career elsewhere.

If executives welcomed this break as an opportunity to start afresh in the government, they were likely to be disappointed. Few remained in office for more than one administration. Oscar Chapman and Wilfred McNeil were exceptions. Chapman started his government service as an assistant secretary at the beginning of the Roosevelt administration and rose to the secretaryship at the beginning of the second Truman administration; and McNeil served as a political executive in the Department of Defense through most of the Truman and Eisenhower administrations. The maximum length of service for most executives was likely to be eight years—or only four, if the administration changed hands after one term.

For those already in government, the chances of further promotion were quite slim. About one-third of the cabinet officers and under secretaries who served during these three administrations had previously been employed in subordinate political executive capacities within their departments. But there were only a limited number of such posts available and competition was intense. The step from assistant secretary to under secretary might not appear so great by any measure—prestige, salary, and often even responsibility—but advancement to the cabinet post constituted a great stride upward in the hierarchical structure. During this seventeen-year period, two-thirds of the appointments to this top rank were given to individuals entirely outside the departments concerned.

Political executive service has apparently not been too propitious a launching platform for careers in elective politics, either. Only 1 percent of the executives under review made the grade, and in 1962 Clinton Anderson, Thruston Morton, Stuart Symington, and Bradford Morse were the only former appointees in Congress.

Conflict of Interest. A report of the Association of the Bar of the City of New York, while noting the difficulty in assessing the impact of conflict of interest considerations on decisions to accept appointments, nevertheless felt that the available evidence "supports the conclusion . . . that the conflict of interest restrictions have substantially contributed to the government's difficulties in recruiting executives."[22] Harold

---

[22] *Conflict of Interest and Federal Service* (Harvard University Press, 1960), p. 154.

Boeschenstein cited "the vagueness of the laws and regulations dealing with conflicts of interest as the most serious obstacle in recruitment."[23] The impact has been felt most acutely in the Department of Defense and the military departments since the Senate Armed Services Committee has been most unyielding in its interpretations of the statutory requirements. But every committee has been concerned with these questions. An Eisenhower Secretary of Defense asserted that its restrictive influence was felt most keenly in the number of people automatically ruled out as suitable candidates; and another Defense executive reported that half of the men on a list containing fifty-seven names were kept from accepting positions because of conflict of interest problems.[24] An Under Secretary of Commerce suggested that the most serious implication of these laws is "the mentality underlying them, the short-sighted presumption of guilt which discourages able people from accepting positions."

Interviews with recruiters and appointees revealed a deep concern for conflict of interest problems but gave little indication that they constituted serious barriers to recruitment except in the Department of Defense. Although definitely impeding recruitment efforts, conflict of interest was mentioned as a deterrent by only 13 percent of the appointees. The group hardest hit were lawyers and those who owned and operated family businesses. Rising young executives were affected by the statutes forbidding outside compensation as they generally had heavy financial obligations which did not permit a slash in salary. Senior executives were affected more seriously by stock divestiture and denial of pension rights.[25]

Careful attention to conflict of interest regulations in 1961 helped Kennedy appointees to avoid many of the pitfalls characteristic of the experience of the early Eisenhower nominees. Virtually every committee which considered nominations in 1961 asked for statements by candidates regarding their financial holdings and the dispositions they were making of those that might constitute the basis for conflict of interest.[26] Very often these matters had been discussed with the committee chairman and staff before hearings.

[23] Organizing for National Security, Vol. 1, p. 415.
[24] Bernstein, op. cit., pp. 158-59.
[25] See letter from James L. McCamy in Paul T. David and Ross Pollock, Executives for Government (Brookings Institution, 1957), note on pp. 26-27.
[26] For example, see the nomination of John Leddy to be Assistant Secretary of the Treasury, in Hearings before the Senate Finance Committee, 87 Cong. 1 sess. (1961), p. 2.

Unfavorable Publicity. Public criticism, even to the extent of censure, is generally regarded as an occupational hazard by political executives, the price to be paid for public prominence. Seldom is dislike of such exposure so great as to constitute a serious obstacle to acceptance of a top-level position. Nevertheless, the vituperation of partisan politics may be a deciding factor if a man has other more substantial objections to public service. As one business publication put it:

> A certain amount of criticism of government officials is always healthy. But the same rules should apply to political criticism that apply to big game hunting: You don't hunt so hard and shoot so murderously that you wipe out the breed. In this country, the evidence shows that a very valuable breed of potential public servants is in real danger of becoming extinct. It's time that we took some elementary conservation measures.[27]

Cabinet members and other recruiters shared this view. One Secretary of Defense said:

> In many cases of people whom I interviewed, they observed the process of politics in Washington and would say, "Why should I disorganize my life to take that sort of stuff?" Columnists and politicians are always taking pot shots at you. A lot of people don't want to expose themselves to this kind of thing.

In 1954, when several political executives in the Eisenhower administration were being subjected to congressional and newspaper attacks, a recruiter tried to find a new under secretary for a major department:

> I approached twelve people who were qualified and who could have made a real contribution to the government but they refused. I feel those men under attack were devoted, hard working, public servants who were interested only in the good of the government. Perhaps they did make mistakes in judgment but they were crucified by the newspapers and by political hacks in Congress. My own lawyers advised me not to come to Washington because there was too much risk of an attack on the grounds that I was a representative of big business. These attacks constitute a real danger both to the firm for which one worked and the firm's clients.

Occasionally, recruiters referred to the remark attributed to President Truman: "If you can't stand the heat, get out of the kitchen." But another former executive pointed out that the potential appointees may not be used to such heat.

[27] *Business Week* (August 10, 1957), p. 156.

Many of the people contacted for top positions have had no active political experience. Business and university people are not used to heat and are not calloused. They tend to be sensitive and their families are sensitive too. They don't know how to protect themselves against the kinds of attacks that are made on them. The fellow who is most valuable in Defense in the top administrative and policy-making jobs is generally not seeking publicity and is therefore gun shy over the kind of publicity he receives in Washington.

Some singled out the press for their reporting and editorial attacks. One Truman cabinet officer said:

Many refuse to come to Washington because they don't want to get into the political mess where their names will inevitably be tarnished. All you have to do is to read the Drew Pearson column to see what can happen to one's name.

Another Truman cabinet officer explained that many refused because of "the awful drubbing you get from the press and Congress. You get your brains beaten out around here."

It is rather remarkable, however, how few of those who accepted political executive positions mentioned the problems of dealing with Congress or of being attacked in the newspapers as major factors in their decisions to accept or reject appointments.

Summary

Regardless of the prevailing atmosphere of the times—and whether there is general eagerness to participate in government affairs in periods of stress and challenge or not—a variety of personal reasons are weighed in the balance with each candidate's decision to accept or reject political appointments. Those frequently mentioned by appointees during the last three administrations were patriotism and public service (at all times, not only in times of crisis), personal relationships with the recruiters, attraction of public life, prestige, and the possibility of personally influencing policies and programs. Career considerations generally deterred acceptance, but there were a number of individuals in every administration, particularly among those already in the government, who considered a political appointment one more step on the ladder to the top.

Bayless Manning distinguished between two classes of potential appointees: those who "have arrived at a status of life where they would be interested in serving the Government on a short-time basis in what might be described as the capstone of their careers," and a second group of middle executives in the age bracket 35-50 who are living 7 percent above their income this year in the hope that they can live 10 percent over their income next year. This latter group are the type needed for subcabinet positions, he asserts, but financial and career problems prevent them from moving. Manning further noted that the problems facing men from different occupational categories vary widely. The conflict of interest statutes have the greatest deterrent effect upon lawyers. For top men at universities the problem relates to their professional advancement, "how many more books could have been written, how many more articles published. . . . "[28]

[28] *Organizing for National Security,* Vol. 1, pp. 457, 459.

7

The Pros and Cons of a
Political Appointment

ALMOST WITHOUT EXCEPTION, political executives who held office during the three administrations under review were glad that they had accepted their political appointments. They may have had a long list of legitimate complaints about their various assignments. They may have commented on—or complained about—long hours, heavy responsibilities, pressure of work, and complicated relations with Congress, the career civil service, and interest groups. They may have talked of financial cutbacks because of lower salaries and increased expenses, lack of family life, a demanding social round, and a host of other features—or serious drawbacks—characteristic of a Washington assignment. Yet, despite all this, only two of those appointed during this period from 1945 to 1961 out of a sample of 108 whose appointments were studied in considerable detail wished that they had never served. What, then, did they find so appealing about political executive office and their life in Washington?

Sources of Satisfaction

Three words are found most frequently in the vocabularies of political executives who enjoyed their government service. These words are "stimulating," "exciting," and "challenging." Virtually no one found high-level government service dull or routine; and the number of executives who were ready and willing to return to the political arena for a second time—in spite of all its drawbacks—indicates the degree of fascination that working at the nerve center of the nation held for many appointees.

They liked working closely with the key political figures of the day, taking a hand at fashioning government policy themselves. They liked a senior executive's latitude of action, the corollary to his heavy responsibilities; and many also liked living in Washington with their families and the prestige and glamour attached to their senior government jobs.

It is, of course, true that some men have the happy capacity to rationalize and even to romanticize extremely trying experiences, so that an assistant secretary may look back over a span of ten years and feel rather warm about assignments that gave him nightmares at the time. But even with this caveat, the testimony is so overwhelmingly favorable toward political executive service that one need have no doubt about the satisfying nature of these experiences.

Challenge and Responsibility

Even those appointees on their first term of service with the government, who were on the whole flabbergasted at the incredible variety of their duties and responsibilities, reacted to this feeling of challenge and to the exciting knowledge that they might be "fashioning history" (see Table A.12). Like the executives who sat in at the Brookings round table, over two-thirds of the appointees interviewed were "without sentimentality or superficial emotion . . . deeply convinced that service in an executive post in government can be immensely rewarding and satisfying."[1]

Not untypical of the reactions of the novice political executive are these comments by businessmen interviewed during the study:

My work as an assistant secretary and government service in general have been very exciting and a great challenge. Once a person coming in from the outside gets by the initial hurdles and makes a reasonable adjustment to government work, he almost always finds the experience stimulating and worthwhile. I know many business people who have served in the government who are positively nostalgic about it and who would jump at the opportunity to get back into the government on virtually any terms.

✿ ✿ ✿

[1] Marver H. Bernstein, *The Job of the Federal Executive* (Brookings Institution, 1958), p. 219.

I happen to enjoy the stimulation of challenges. I seem to thrive on them. The rewards of government service can be one of the richest experiences life has to offer. It has a tremendous broadening effect and gave me a sense of accomplishment in having participated in something really important. I have many, many fond memories.

❀ ❀ ❀

My job was more rewarding than I ever expected it to be. Mainly in intangibles, such as doing something for others without adequate compensation. It's a hell of an experience if you don't expect to accomplish too much.

❀ ❀ ❀

There are many intangible benefits. My experience as under secretary was a great enrichment of my life. It broadened my understanding immensely. In fact, my whole life has been broader as a result of this experience. I would unhesitatingly advise a man to accept a government position if he asked me for my opinion.

And a State Department official during the Truman administration commented:

My experience in the government was challenging beyond any expectation I had of it. It changed my entire outlook on things. The world we live in became smaller and I developed different notions about issues that are important in the world.

Specifically:

The Marshall Plan was a tremendous and thrilling enterprise and feeding Berlin and holding on to Greece and Turkey were sources of great satisfaction to me. I was also involved in setting up NATO and that was just about as much fun as you could have.

He added that he was pleased with his good relations on Capitol Hill and with the fact that President Truman had given him full support in his work.

This fascination with the challenge and stimulation of public life was particularly true of second-term appointees. Not a few Kennedy executives, for instance, were Truman appointees who had sat out the Eisenhower administration. One who had been in the government for nearly twenty years before 1953 thought that he really should stay out of government because he knew that a top-level job "consumes" a person. But he was willing to accept a position in one department in 1961 because of the unique and intriguing nature of its problems, toward the solution of which he felt he could make a contribution. Two State Department political executives, who had served during World War II and the Truman administration, retained their active interest in foreign affairs throughout the Eisenhower years and were fully prepared to reenter the government at the political executive level. One would have been willing to stay on during the Eisenhower administration had the Republicans wished to retain him. The other believed his previous experience both in and out of the government had "put him in training" for an appointive position. Although he was prepared to be selective, he "saw Washington under the Kennedy administration as a potentially exciting frontier at the center of the world."

Many shared the mixed feelings of the Kennedy under secretary who had seen long service in the government, but who had spent the eight years prior to his appointment at subcabinet level in a comfortable, secure position in a local public agency. He observed, "If you can stand it emotionally and financially and in every other way, then you have a chance to get a Ph.D. in governmental relations at the expense of the government." He stated in his interview:

> All of my arguments against taking the job were based on one thing: my desire to be comfortable. Not that I necessarily wanted to be completely secure, but that I wanted to have things relatively easy. I liked my job and felt secure in it, but I asked whether I had gotten to the point where I was ready to retire. At the age of [46] was I ready to say "This is it?"

Men of varied occupation or profession were equally ready to return to public office on the basis of their prior government experience. A lawyer in the Defense Department in the Kennedy administration, with long experience during World War II and in the Truman administration, expressed his point of view as follows:

> I was familiar with the compensations and satisfactions of government experience from my service in wartime. The problems of national security and other large public problems are considerably more interesting and exciting in a personal way than private problems, such as profit-making for a businessman, or, for a lawyer, the question of "whose pig got run over."

And an academician, also with long government service to his credit, observed:

> I suppose most people who had some connection with the WPB could not go back to the Widget factory because they felt they had dealt with things which seemed to them that much more significant.

An extreme view was taken by a prominent lawyer who served in subordinate positions during World War II and in political executive positions in both the Truman and Eisenhower administrations. "All of us would like to stay with government if we could afford it." While his view is undoubtedly atypical, it nevertheless portrays an attitude that is more prevalent than is generally realized.

An Eisenhower Defense appointee, a former businessman who had served in the Navy during World War II and in the State Department in the Truman administration, recalled that "it didn't take much persuading" for him to accept an assistant secretary post in one of the military departments. He considered it "the nicest job in Washington." Another businessman who had served on numerous advisory committees during World War II, the Korean War, and the early Eisenhower administration developed a great interest in foreign trade. He accepted an appointment in the Commerce Department because the challenge of it "hit me where I live."

A judge, too, who was recruited during the Eisenhower administration, welcomed a return to more active political life because of the restraints imposed on him as a jurist.

I felt a challenge in this extremely responsible job. I had led an active life before going on the bench and chafed a bit at the restrictions of the bench and was eager to get back into active political life.

Successful Performance

No executive can react enthusiastically to the challenge and responsibility of his less routine assignments unless he has confidence in his own ability to perform well in office. And few executives feel on top of their jobs unless their own backgrounds and experience are in some degree relevant to their agency's specific areas of operation. The more substantive knowledge an individual has the more likely he is to derive satisfaction and a sense of achievement from his government service.

The converse is also true. The novice political executive with little prior acquaintanceship with government operations is likely to feel very uncertain of himself; and his ignorance of the substantive work of his department or agency in the face of his more experienced career colleagues whom he is supposed to guide in policy decisions can lead to strained relations. He can, of course, learn on the job but a great deal of valuable time and energy will be wasted in this way and it is much better if he is already familiar with his organization's activities before appointment. One high military officer, for example, recalled a conversation he had had with his political superior in the Department of Defense:

> From the questions he had asked, I knew that he had a good knowledge of radar and this made it easier to explain things to him. After all, he had had experience in the Department and overseas. He knew what it was like to serve both on the firing line, where he was decorated, and also in an administrative situation. Although he had been away from the service for some time, all of this background was helpful.

If political executives are ignorant, too, of the type of control that will be exercised over their actions by Congress and the degree of their accountability to legislative committees and political and interest groups, they may be in for sharp setbacks once in office. Those appointees who appreciate the importance of establishing good relations with the legislative branch, who have previously worked with Congress and are well known in political circles, are more likely to have their programs and policies approved.

To be sure, successful performance does not always depend on previous experience and established contacts. A measure of luck enters into the picture as well. Some congressional committees are less critical of executive action than others. Some areas of activity are less prone to crises and publicity than others; information on their specialized area of operation is more easily acquired. Some departments and agencies, too, require only broad administrative abilities of their political appointees.

Nevertheless, like the Defense Department official above, those who are thoroughly familiar with their organization's operations and who have had previous experience that relates in some way to its major activities are those who tend to enjoy executive office the most.

Interviews with officials in all departments and agencies and at all levels in the Eisenhower and Kennedy administrations confirmed the importance of this type of substantive background and experience in resolving the problems associated with the 1960-61 transition. A Foreign Service officer who was succeeded by a former Truman political appointee stated:

Transition difficulties were not nearly so severe as they might have been since we had been good friends for years. He was a consultant to the National Security Council and was familiar with many State policies. Generally speaking, it was an unusually happy transition.

A deputy assistant secretary emphasized that he had had a scholarly interest in the area for which he was now responsible which permitted him to grasp the problems of the area much more quickly. Similar expressions were heard in the Department of Defense and military services. Two assistant secretaries emphasized that what must be learned are procedures and details. One had been a consultant to the Department of Defense during the previous year and had been engaged in work similar to his new duties. He said, "If you have some background in the field before you come into the Department, you can pick up the details quite easily." The other had had many years of experience on a contract basis with the Department of Defense and therefore knew the substantive problems well; finding himself in a rapidly changing budget process, however, he wanted to know how the budget cycle worked and the procedures followed in the preparation of the budget.

While a large majority of the political executives interviewed mentioned in general terms how much more exhilarating and interesting their case study appointments were than they had anticipated (compare Tables A.10 and A.12), a third of them referred to specific projects which they had managed to bring successfully to a conclusion. More Eisenhower appointees mentioned this source of satisfaction than those in the Truman sample. Truman's appointees did not take office after a party overturn. Many came from the subordinate political or career ranks and the domestic programs they followed—the New Deal and Fair Deal—had lost the original dynamism generated in Roosevelt's day. With his party deeply divided, President Truman, as Samuel Lubell notes, sought above all else to buy time for the future. "Far from seeking decision, he sought to put off any possible showdown, to perpetuate rather than break the prevailing stalemate."[2]

Republican executives entering the government in 1953, on the other hand, considered themselves part of "the great crusade" which would reverse what they viewed as dangerous trends in domestic policy and more effectively deal with the problems confronting the na-

[2] *The Future of American Politics* (Doubleday & Company, 2nd ed., 1956), pp. 9-10.

tion in the foreign policy field. One Assistant Secretary of State, for example, stated that his primary source of satisfaction lay in the fact that he had helped to establish a "good realistic policy" in his regional area. He had also the satisfaction of knowing that "we were right" and that his policy was accepted by both political parties. Still in office in 1956, an election year, he was gratified that Congress passed resolutions supporting the policy which he had helped develop. Later, a Kennedy State Department official called his job "utterly absorbing." He characterized as the "guts" of the job the relating of the policies he developed to the two important forces operating in the underdeveloped regions of the world—nationalism and modernism. He could draw on his background and on his competent staff in the formulation of policies that he felt would make a difference in the world in the next few years.

As one might expect, this source of satisfaction appeared to be more prominent among executives in those departments where the policy issues were more marked, such as the Department of State, the Department of Agriculture, and the Department of the Interior. In the latter, where the policy issues were very sharply drawn, several political executives welcomed the opportunity to change the direction of government resource policy. One Eisenhower executive was pleased with one achievement in particular:

> We substantially redirected the Department's attitude in the power field away from federal domination and in favor of local control. We took up the fight in favor of local private power and against public power when we drafted the administration's power policy.

In a less controversial area, another Interior executive expressed satisfaction in such accomplishments as setting up the administration of the continental shelf lands and selling large amounts of public land which realized sizable benefits to the federal treasury.

In contrast, hardly any executives found substantive satisfaction in their work in the Post Office Department. Lacking public notice and room for maneuver, executives in such a department were seldom able to derive any pleasure from this aspect of their jobs.

Although few executives denied the importance of previous experience, some were better able than others to make good their deficiencies in knowledge on the job. Many appointees who entered the government with some trepidation about their ability to perform well in an entirely new setting were agreeably impressed with their own ability to work effectively under high pressure. Said one lawyer who had had little administrative experience: "I was very pleased to discover that I could be an effective executive and even enjoy it." Sometimes this learning situation in which many executives found themselves led to specific career appointments in private life. One former assistant secretary, for instance, attributed his later successful career in the transportation field to the knowledge he had gained and the contacts he had made while in the government.

A career executive considered his experience as a deputy administrator had given him a different perspective on his career duties, and that he had acquired a new insight and understanding into the broad range of government activities. An attorney, who specialized in tax law during his tenure as an assistant attorney general, said that he was pleased at the opportunity to examine a great many cases that private tax attorneys would never have had an opportunity to see.

In conflict with stereotypes of federal administrators as automatons in an unwieldy machine, several executives commented on the satisfaction they had in administering the affairs of their divisions without outside interference. One lawyer who served as an Assistant Secretary of Interior said the following about his Secretary:

> He gave his subordinates their responsibilities and expected them to carry these responsibilities out. The Secretary wanted to know the results and wanted to be consulted if necessary, but he didn't want to meddle in the affairs of his subordinates.

Perhaps because of the scandals in the Department of Justice during the latter part of the Truman administration, several assistant attorneys general commented on the freedom they had in administering their affairs without being subjected to political pressure. One said that his greatest satisfaction came from "the knowledge that I was clearly charged with the responsibility for my division. The work was my own and my responsibilities were clear cut. It was my baby and whether it turned out well or badly was entirely my own responsibility." He could not recall a single instance in which any one of the three department heads whom he had served had ever exerted any pressure on a case under his jurisdiction, and for this he was grateful. Another Truman assistant attorney general said that, although his position had certain political overtones, there was no political finagling in his division during his tenure: "Despite all the talk of corruption in public office, my record in office was clean. No actions were brought by the Eisenhower administration as a result of anything done in my bureau."

Such freedom to work depended in large measure on the degree of mutual confidence and respect developed between the political appointees and their department heads and career staff. By and large, those who held office during the three administrations under review were reasonably happy in their interpersonal relationships. One assistant attorney general, for example, mentioned the pleasure he derived from staff meetings with the Attorney General and his other assistants, men for whom he had the utmost respect. He also enjoyed the social life that was attached to his high position, and he had made some of the finest friends of his entire life while he was in Washington. A number of assistant secretaries emphasized their pleasure in serving under competent and inspiring leaders. To one young assistant secretary the Secretary was a second father. And another, a Foreign Service officer, found great inspiration in the high caliber of the people with whom he worked, particularly Secretary John Foster Dulles "who was devoted to his staff and his colleagues." For one under secretary it was a particular thrill to meet President Truman and to work closely with him on policy matters.

There were a number of others, of course, who tended to lay a large portion of the blame for their ineffectiveness and dissatisfactions in office on poor rapport with their department and agency heads. Usually this complaint was associated with other dissatisfactions.

A different set of problems was posed for the political executive in his relations with his career staff. In most instances a political executive entered an organization manned by civil servants whose tenure long exceeded his own and whose substantive knowledge was obviously much greater than his. Their relationship generally began somewhat warily on both sides, with executive and staff assessing each others' capabilities and methods of operation. More often than not, however, this developed into an association of mutual trust and respect.

Two Truman appointees in the Department of Commerce provided good examples of this reversal in attitude that resulted in more effective use being made of the career staff. One appointee described himself as a loyal party man, but said his earlier notions of "clearing the bastards out" gave way to great respect for the civil servants. He came to believe that the career men virtually ran the government and that the political executives had to rely on them to get anything done at all. The other appointee, who had agreed with much of the criticism he had heard of the bureaucracy prior to his service, was impressed with its sincerity and dedication. "I was fortunate in having three bureau chiefs under me who were outstanding public servants."

This change of attitude on assumption of office was particularly noticeable among Eisenhower appointees. One assistant attorney general became convinced that the government had some "extraordinarily dedicated career people" and that one of the most important qualities a political executive should possess is the ability to sense the mood and morale of the excellent people who work under him. Another assistant attorney general said he had not anticipated the high quality of the lawyers in the Justice Department, and particularly in his division, "where I found the caliber of lawyer to be far higher than in the bar in general and with a high degree of dedication." And an Assistant Secretary of State from the business world, who worked in one of the most highly charged regional areas, reported:

> I could never have hoped for better type people. I have great admiration for the Foreign Service. They are hard working, dedicated, and they never complain. I found the performance of the Foreign Service inspirational.

One of his greatest sources of satisfaction while in the department was the support he received from his subordinate career staff. Two Assistant Secretaries of Labor, both from labor backgrounds, came to Washington with dim views of bureaucrats, one feeling that they would be inflexible and the other that they were lazy. Both found their fears to be groundless, one observing that government workers are greatly "underrated."

The general approval of the civil service by political executives was extended to military personnel also. One Truman Defense executive who gained a high opinion of them called them "remarkable to work with." An Eisenhower executive left the Defense Department with a "profound respect for the military."

> I was surprised to find that they were adaptable and willing to discuss matters and even change their minds. Like many other people, I thought military promotions came only when the guys up-

stairs died off. But I found that the military services have done a good job in moving their ablest men to the top.

Approbation for civil servants was not unanimous, however. Among the Eisenhower appointees were those who were extremely critical of their career subordinates. Some did not change their minds about them during their term in office, and left the government with views similar to the Assistant Secretary of Commerce who observed that "career executives are people who know how to get around the rules and skirt policy rather than execute it."

A source of amazement to many incoming executives was the enormous amount of time they had to spend in establishing rapport with their congressional committees, catering to their demands for written reports and formal statements, and attending hearings. Businessmen in particular were surprised at the extent of this aspect of their work. As one explained who had had some experience in practical politics during the first Eisenhower campaign:

> I had no real image of Congress or of what dealing with Congress would be like before I came to Washington. After I had been in the government awhile, I realized how important Congress is and how much dealing with Congress was a part of the job. You're bumping into Congress all the time. This is particularly true when the Congress and the executive branch are controlled by different parties.

Establishing good relations with Congress was on the whole an extremely trying and difficult job for the average executive. Those who did look back on their congressional experience with satisfaction more often than not couched their responses in terms of having accommodated and pacified a potential enemy. An Assistant Secretary of Commerce recalled that he did encounter pressure from Congress, particularly at appropriation time, to get public works for particular localities; but generally his relations were "pleasant." An assistant attorney general said that he was "always pleased to have congressional and public inquiries." Serving during a period when the Justice Department was under congressional investigation, he was pleased to have the opportunity to demonstrate the integrity of his office.

One State Department appointee expressed pride in his good relations with Congress. He observed that one had no trouble if one's department established a basis for trust with its parent committees. The

State Department, he noted, was run on a nonpolitical basis, even though there was a Republican Congress and a Democratic administration, and he described Senators Arthur H. Vandenberg and Walter F. George as "great men."

The majority of the assistant secretaries and under secretaries were perhaps more likely to agree with Robert Lovett who testified before the Senate Subcommittee on National Policy Machinery:

> . . . I think appearances before the congressional committees are a part, and a very important part, of the responsibility when you take your oath of office. It is a very time-consuming necessity. There is no question about that.
>
> . . . if I had to choose between having a congressional committee breathe on the back of my neck as a form of performance audit or riding some particular conviction or belief to the point of defeat I would choose a congressional hearing. . . . Appearing before committees is time consuming, it is exhausting, sometimes terribly irritating, but on the whole, as long as we have our form of governmental system, I think it is a necessary part of it.[3]

Few would have agreed with the Defense official who said:

> Congressional relations were more fun than any other aspect of the job. I had dealt with Congress before when Congress investigated a firm I was connected with during World War II. You get a feel for congressional hearings, and if you are wrong you tell them so and explain what you are doing to tackle the problem. In this way you can get rid of congressional investigators in two minutes.

Attraction of the Washington Environment

Many political appointees and their wives became Washington addicts. They loved being at the hub of national affairs. An Eisenhower executive with two decades of residence in New York said that both his wife and he "had come to like Washington better than New York as a result of living here since 1940."

Not all political executives participate in the Washington social whirl, nor does it appear necessary to do so, but some found it attractive (although only two appointees interviewed specifically mentioned it). An executive of one of America's largest corporations recalled his

[3] *Organizing for National Security*, Inquiry of the Senate Subcommittee on National Policy Machinery of the Committee on Government Operations, 86 Cong. 2 sess. (1961), Vol. 1, pp. 26-27.

service in Washington during the Truman administration in a most favorable light.

Government work is stimulating and exciting. There are opportunities for travel under unique conditions and there is the satisfaction at the solution of problems. Washington is a pleasant place to live and outside associations are stimulating. My wife loved Washington. There were good schools and a cosmopolitan atmosphere for the children. There is no snobbery—and not *too* much good living.

An executive from business who served in both Truman and Eisenhower administrations corroborated this view.

Washington life was stimulating for the children. Although one child was quite young, the rest gained an interest in public affairs they would not have picked up otherwise. My family, and particularly my wife, had an interest in intellectual things. In Washington one obtains a sense of the historical currents of the time.

Life in the capital city with its exciting and exhilarating atmosphere is particularly appealing to those who have already experienced it. Few perhaps would have put it as strongly as this ex-congressman turned political executive, but he nevertheless conveys the type of attraction Washington has for some people:

Washington has a fascination—an appeal. When the bug bites, it's almost fatal. This is the heart of my life. There is lots of excitement in Washington and I don't see how I could live without being here at least part of each year. Besides, my wife couldn't be blasted away from here.

Dissatisfactions and Their Role in Some Departures

Although only two of the Truman, Eisenhower, and Kennedy appointees interviewed wished that they had never accepted their political appointments at assistant secretary and under secretary levels, almost all of them had specific grievances and felt considerably dissatisfied with certain aspects of their work.

Most of those interviewed expressed concern over their extremely heavy workload, the scope and variety of their duties, and their heavy responsibilities. Many chafed at the unwieldy government machinery and the process of approval that made it well-nigh impossible to put through any major changes in policy. Others had poor working relationships with cabinet head and career staff or they could not get along with Congress and resented the degree of interference in executive affairs. These conditions of work irked many appointees. Few cited them as cause for departure, although it is obvious that men who are discontented with their environment are more responsive to opportunities elsewhere. Sources of dissatisfaction most frequently mentioned by case study appointees are shown in Table A.13, and their reasons for departure in Table A.14.

Pressure of Work

Long hours and the heavy burden of responsibilities to be assumed by even the novice executive are for most appointees the two most unexpected features of their induction into the government. A source of astonishment to some, to other executives this heavy workload constituted a major grievance and, for the few, a reason for leaving. The pressure of work is felt not only in the State and Defense Departments where crises abound but also in the domestic departments where solutions to problems can, and often do, take decades to work out.

In large part, the long hours are the result of the open nature of the American political system which makes access to policy-makers and administrators relatively easy. Congressmen, interest group leaders, party leaders, officials in other agencies, presidential aides, individual citizens, and departmental personnel—to say nothing of itinerant scholars—all claim the executives' attention. They find their office day lengthening to twelve or fourteen hours, and although few appointees come to Washington expecting to be drones or social butterflies, many are totally unprepared for the amount of work that is loaded on them.

An Interior Department executive commented:

> I was most surprised at the enormity of the job. I was amazed that I had so many different responsibilities each of which was overpowering. I worked from 9:00 a.m. to 8:00 p.m. nearly every day and a large part of Saturdays and Sundays as well. The responsibilities of that job were almost beyond human management.

An executive in the State Department who had had long experience in a military department during World War II accepted his job knowing it "would be hell—and it was. The only difference was that it was even more demanding than I thought it would be. I was working 90 hours a week, but there was great satisfaction in getting the work done." A newly appointed Assistant Secretary of Labor reported that "there has been an unbelievable demand on my time. It's ridiculous but nevertheless a fact that I didn't meet two members of my staff for an entire month after I arrived because of the demands on my time." One highly regarded Assistant Secretary of Commerce emphasized

> . . . the tremendous amount of factual information one had to acquire to perform his job effectively. I spent much of my time simply studying after I came to Washington. When you take a job like that you study harder than you've ever studied in your life. . . . You always are conscious of budgetary considerations and this requires a careful, detailed knowledge of many minor administrative matters.

A deputy administrator who knew nothing of his duties prior to assuming office said he spent "80 to 90 hours a week, 7 days a week, learning all of the ramifications of my job and becoming familiar with every part of my agency."

Nor do the burdens become much lighter as one gains experience and familiarity with the problems the executive faces. One Defense Department official with long tenure reviewed his service and concluded succinctly, "It's damned hard work!" And an experienced executive in the Department of Commerce explained that he was surprised

> . . . by the rush and bustle atmosphere of government work and the necessity to improvise under pressure. I found it true both during wartime and peacetime. An assistant secretary is subjected to a great deal of pressure because things have to be done in a such a great hurry. Our philosophy of government is to meet problems as they arise, on an *ad hoc* basis, and the result often is a wild scramble. Frequently I was given assignments that were impossible to fulfill in the time allotted. The burden of the job usually begins to affect political executives while they are in office.

For quite a number, one tour of duty was enough. An assistant attorney general, comparing his experience to the Honolulu yacht race, said that it was "something you want to do all your life—but never want to do again."

> The job involved a lot more work than I expected. I had no idea of the amount of time I would have to spend on the Hill and on interdepartmental relations. I was involved in these things because I was on very cordial relations with [the Attorney General]. I was a little more mature than some of the other assistant attorneys general so he had me sit in for him on three cabinet committees and he gave

me other responsibilities. My ability to deal with senators meant that I was sent to the Hill to represent the Department as a whole, not just my division. That meant lengthy preparations going on into the wee hours of the night. On top of that, it was my practice to keep my finger on everything in my division in order to have a grasp of what was going on, although I would have been a better administrator had I delegated more. At the same time I was active in extracurricular activities, including presidency of my fraternity and bar association.

It was too much of a load. I don't mind working from 8:00 a.m. to 7:30 or 8:00 p.m., which includes a working luncheon with the Attorney General, but after a steady diet of it for two or three years it became pretty damned tiresome.

Some appointees found the job pressures sufficiently hard on their health that they sought other job opportunities after a relatively short time. Ill health was not mentioned specifically as a reason for departure by any of the case study appointees, but it quite obviously affected their decision to look elsewhere. One Truman under secretary accepted his assignment only for a short period because he had served in the department all through the war and was completely worn out. Another emphasized the strain of his particular job, dealing with political complaints from senators and congressmen: "It was too much of a madhouse for me."

Those departments dealing with questions of national security undoubtedly impose greater tension on their executives than those dealing with more routine matters. One appointee in the State Department observed that the pressure in the department was so severe and sustained that he believed it was probably one of the most important reasons for high turnover rates. At least three of the case studies in that department were affected by health problems which contributed to their decisions to leave office. One assistant secretary explained that he became an ambassador after three years in office only because he "needed a rest," but an acquaintance explained that the man was reassigned to "let him live a little longer."

Not only do political executives work under heavy pressure, but their attention is fragmented among a large number of often unrelated activities. Some come to office expecting a relatively narrow range of responsibilities and find that they are involved in a wide variety of activities that include relationships with many departments, many bureaus, and even other nations.

Several of the Department of Agriculture appointees, for example, registered their surprise at involvement in international affairs. One Under Secretary of Agriculture with long experience in the government recited several things that were notably different from what he had expected:

> First was the sheer volume of work I was confronted with. Secondly, was the extent to which the Department dealt with foreign affairs. And thirdly was the extent to which the Department was the center of interest to economic groups throughout the country. These groups were interested not only in policy matters but in personnel as well. Everyone had a candidate for every job. I believe there is more general interest in the Department of Agriculture than in any other department in Washington, perhaps even more than in the State Department. There are trade groups and commodity groups without end. I'm constantly invited to meetings, conventions, and conferences. And we are literally inundated by foreign agriculture attaches and delegations from other countries.

Similarly, an Assistant Secretary of Commerce emphasized the amount of time he spent on interdepartmental administrative problems, particularly with the Departments of State and Agriculture on international negotiations. An Under Secretary of Interior said he "was constantly involved in meetings with representatives of State, Commerce, and other departments in working out problems which affected them all," although he felt these meetings often accomplished very little because many of the committee members failed to do their homework.

Frustrations in Achieving Goals

A source of frustration often mentioned by the political executives who were interviewed was the difficulties they encountered in attempting to meet their own policy objectives. They were unprepared for the emphasis on procedure and the prescribed routines common to all branches of the public service. They longed to be free from the excessive officialdom (which they called "system" in business) to accomplish the jobs before them. Eighteen percent of the case study individuals during the Truman and Eisenhower administrations voiced dissatisfaction with red tape, and 23 percent chafed at the legal and political restrictions. Cabinet members and career civil servants corroborated this type of frustration as a major reason for appointees' early departure from office.

Political executives in the Eisenhower administration especially deplored the obstacles they encountered in trying to get things done. Businessmen were particularly irritated, often to the point of leaving the government sooner than they had intended. They found it hard to adjust to the multiple clearance system for every policy proposal or administrative decision, and to the legal and political restrictions upon their freedom of action. One former industrial leader, an Eisenhower department head, said:

> Perhaps the hardest thing for a businessman accustomed to making decisions to adjust to in government life is the situation in which so many people have a *legitimate* right to be heard in making a decision. There are so many implications touching various departments. Representatives of all of these sectors—both in government and out —demand, with right, to be heard. Some men just don't have the patience for this kind of thing. It's tough, but this is part of the democratic process.

Another department head was less kind to the businessman *per se,* but pointed out the same problem:

> People from industry are usually not interested in such posts. As they get older they become set in their ways and unable to face change. They develop a certain pettiness. They get used to pressing buttons and having things done. And they can't take the humbling experience of appearing before a congressional committee.

Often, the novice executive from the business world arrives in Washington prepared to clean house and reorganize. As one high-level civil servant put it:

> They first come down here expecting really to run things and put affairs in order, but they run into great frustration in their initial contact with the job. The usual assistant secretary thinks the job isn't worth a damn for about the first 90 days [because they feel they can use their business background to make things more efficient], but they soon realize that the government is far more efficient than they imagined.

Other businessmen shared the concern of the department head who said, "There is no yardstick with which to measure effectiveness—either of yourself or of others."[4] This man admitted retaining certain individuals whom he might not have tolerated in private business, primarily because there was no way to chart their real effectiveness. A lawyer

[4] *Cf.* Bernstein, *op. cit.,* p. 35.

also complained of the same problem and compared his own impact on public policy with the effect of sticking his finger in a glass of water. His finger in the glass made a slight difference to the water level, but not significant enough to be measured.

Certain incoming executives had had exaggerated notions when they took office of both what was necessary in the way of major organizational and policy change and what could be accomplished. They were later considerably disgruntled at the modest impact they were able to make and if they decided to quit their jobs unseasonably soon, their departures were at least partly attributable to a sense of having outlived their usefulness. Their views were expressed in a variety of ways and from a variety of perspectives. Of two Assistant Secretaries of Agriculture, one stated simply, "an assistant secretary is all shot to pieces after two years and might as well get out"; the other emphasized the importance of fresh ideas, believing that turnover in a position every two to four years was desirable. He felt that men were not sufficiently flexible to adjust to rapidly changing conditions, and he observed that when one operates "in a goldfish bowl, a man can't help the department much after he has made a commitment to which he sticks when conditions have changed."

Several assistant secretaries expressed satisfaction in their own achievements, but left nonetheless because they felt that they had done all that they could and that the other problems facing them were insoluble. One man, after noting the constructive work he had been able to do in certain areas during his tenure, pointed to the other difficulties he had been unable to budge: "There's a limit to the things one man can get accomplished." The combination of frustration and accomplishment led to an overpowering urge to go back home.

Another executive had this unusual but perhaps not unique explanation of his disenchantment with the government that finally led to his resignation:

I felt I was losing my integrity in the sense that I was losing my independence of judgment. After someone has been on the job for several years he tends to lose the initial spark he brought to the job and the independence of viewpoint which allowed him to make decisions solely on the basis of what he thought was right. He tends to develop an organization point of view which precludes him from making the decisions he should make.

The Personal Factor

Part of the frustration in not achieving goals could also be laid at the door of policy disputes and the difficulties of effective personal communication between the appointees and their department heads, career staff, and congressional committees.

Many political executives enter public service with only the vaguest notions of the responsibilities they will have and the nature of their relationships with their superiors. This is particularly true at the beginning of an administration when a department head is recruiting his initial team. Except in those instances when the head has had previous experience in the organization he supervises, he can seldom provide much guidance for his new executives. Job descriptions and statements of responsibility are frequently so ambiguous as to be meaningless. Moreover, a new executive head may change entirely his predecessor's organizational framework; he may be ignorant of his secretarial duties and allocate staff responsibilities on a trial and error basis that is confusing to his subordinates. For this reason, not a few political executives have been surprised, sometimes pleasantly and sometimes unpleasantly, by the duties they have had to assume at one time or another during their term of office.

Some had thought that their chief function would be to supervise their subordinate units and were amazed to find that they were expected to operate at the highest policy-making levels, involving not only the top staff of their own department or agency but also White House officials and representatives of foreign governments. One Eisenhower Assistant Secretary of Commerce, for example, found that his position differed "in every way" from what he had expected. Instead of dealing in administrative matters strictly within his own jurisdiction, he was deeply involved in international negotiations which brought him into contact with officials in the State Department, the Department of Agriculture, and the White House. Perhaps this was not entirely a source of dissatisfaction, but he found himself involved in entirely unexpected and complicated negotiations at a level and with people outside his previous professional orbit.

Others expected exactly this kind of policy-making and negotiation and were disappointed by the relatively narrow range of duties assigned them. One Assistant Secretary of Agriculture expected to operate at the highest policy levels in the department, leaving administrative details to his career subordinates. Instead, he was excluded and seldom had contact with the Secretary on policy matters.

There were no staff meetings to set up policy. This was partly due to the Secretary's own inclinations, but also to his frequent absence from Washington. Then, shortly after I was appointed, three new assistant secretaries were appointed and responsibility for the various subdivisions was distributed among us. I was frustrated because I felt the need for more contact with the Secretary in order to understand more of his philosophy. I had to operate almost in a vacuum, deciding on important policy matters without much guidance from above.

One assistant secretary who actually resigned because he had no part in the policy-making gave the following explanation:

I had very little contact with the Secretary. I had to find out what his policy was from his speeches instead of from personal contact. I had to look to the under secretary for leadership but he was not able to give it. I was concerned about having to operate by myself, without participation in the over-all activities in the Department. I have a high regard for [the Secretary] but I couldn't see that I was helping him win his battles because I really wasn't part of the team. I didn't feel that I could do anything to enhance [the Secretary's] program by staying on.

Many department heads have to devote so much time and attention to negotiation with other agencies and groups outside the department or agency that they tend to neglect the needs of their assistants, who sometimes feel isolated by this lack of communication. In extreme cases, this exclusion is deliberate. Several political executives found themselves essentially "fifth wheels," having few functions of any importance. Lacking faith in their ability, or having had to accept them because of political exigencies, the secretaries gave them dignity but no responsibility. It is perhaps not without interest that the two women in the case studies were both described in these terms. Since their chiefs had accepted them only because of insistence from outside the department, they were loath to give them major responsibilities. Some males fared no better. A deputy administrator, when interviewed by the administrator before accepting the position, was told that he would have whatever duties the chief prescribed. These were eventually described as "public relations," a euphemism for idleness. Noting the chief's firm hand over the organization, the deputy commented, "I sure thought I'd have something more to do." Another deputy actually resigned because he had "absolutely no duties except as an alter ego of the director."

He was a difficult man to work with, doing things and deciding things without telling anyone. He even put me in the embarrassing position of having to argue with an admiral at a National Security Council meeting on a matter he had first advised me of one hour before the meeting began. I was simply a fifth wheel with responsibility but without authority.

An executive who was asked to stay on in the Eisenhower administration after service under President Truman left very soon after his appointment, in part because, as the new secretary explained it, there were "differences in our way of doing things." The departing executive felt that it was high time the new team proceeded on its own.

Strained relations led to the departures of three assistant secretaries in the same department, each of whom cited conflict with the same secretary as one of the primary reasons. One complained that the secretary vacillated constantly on all subjects and was especially willing to defer to the views of senators. Another mentioned that he felt that the secretary was "feeling uncomfortable" with him after they had become involved in a policy dispute. A third assistant secretary found himself in conflict with a subordinate whom the secretary supported in the dispute.

Actual policy disputes, however, figured in decisions to move out of government service in only four cases out of the thirty-seven who left of their own volition. This suggests either that the selection process has been fairly effective in bringing men with similar policy orientations into an agency at a particular time, or that political executives develop a unified perspective and mutual tolerance while working together so that, although perhaps dissatisfied, they prefer to settle their differences without resorting to threats of resignation.

The most publicized example of a departure caused by a policy dispute occurred in 1949 when Secretary of the Navy John L. Sullivan and his Under Secretary, W. John Kenney, resigned in protest over the "scuttling" of an aircraft carrier by Secretary of Defense Louis A. Johnson, allegedly in violation of a previous agreement. There were departures because of policy disputes in another department in the Truman administration when several executives with strong policy convictions left over a period of several years because of their difficulties with the secretary. Two Eisenhower Defense officials also left because of differences of opinion over defense objectives. One explained that a number of things "mounted up," and he found himself "in basic disagreement with the administration and in no position to make his voice heard." The other's resignation was in part due to a policy dispute that had earlier caused his secretary to resign. According to one observer, his continuance in office would have appeared as a failure to support his chief in a situation where it was felt the President had let his subordinates down.

Differences of opinion with career staff are not so likely to lead to early departures as disputes with department heads but they are nevertheless the cause of considerable exasperation. Dissatisfaction with career people in the Eisenhower administration reflected in part the deep distrust felt by some appointees for the public service generally. It also indicated the failure of some departmental personnel to adjust their policy orientation to the Eisenhower administration after twenty years of Democratic rule. The appointees' initial dislike and distrust for civil servants were often dissipated during the course of the administration, particularly during Eisenhower's term of office, but even so a number continued to hold a most pessimistic view of their career subordinates' ability. In the Department of the Interior, one under secretary found the attitude of his bureaucracy to be his only source of dissatisfaction in government service: lacking the objectivity and detachment of the civil service in Great Britain, he said, "many career people saw no disloyalty in running to the opposition in Congress whenever something doesn't suit them with the Department." This was discouraging and frustrating to a leadership that felt it "had done nothing to warrant that kind of behavior." An assistant secretary in the same department said he was impressed with the ability and dedication of the high-level bureaucrats, but felt that civil servants generally were "not worth the powder to blow them to hell." He accused them of being timeservers and laggards and would have liked to fire many of them or at least transfer them elsewhere. And an assistant postmaster general complained that "there was indifference and defiance even among the civil service people. They would complain to

Congress. They would give you one set of figures one day. A few days later they'd give you another figure and you had already given the first to Congress and were embarrassed because it was wrong." (It should be noted, however, that this particular executive thought everyone else was against him too.)

Lack of Experience and Substantive Knowledge

Many department heads and other observers of the work of the political executive tend to depreciate the importance of substantive knowledge as a qualification for a government position. Emphasis is placed upon innate ability and broad experience in analyzing the characteristics of successful political executives. Nevertheless, it is clear that many executives congratulated themselves on the advantages of their previous specialized experience, while others felt keenly their lack of substantive information and the necessity of working extremely hard to acquire rapidly the basic facts which were needed to make decisions. Those who had such information "hit the ground running" while others were tooling up. The information had to be acquired and, in some instances, those who were forced to learn quickly and under fire often became eminently successful executives. But this form of pressure was a source of dismay—if not actual dissatisfaction—to even the successful executive.

The novice political executive felt particularly disillusioned. Regardless of background and profession, in a very real sense he found he could really only learn his job by experience. No reading or secondhand commentary could give him the "feel" for government service or a sensitivity to the problems he had to face in his new capacity. His formal indoctrination—if he had any at all—tended to be hurried and, almost from the beginning, he was faced with the necessity to make decisions on matters which others (including his career staff) had taken months and years to study. He was forced, in fact, to cram a long educational process into a few weeks if he hoped to be successful.[5]

The executive branch today is so diversified in scope and its ramifications so vast that it is doubtful whether any appointee was ever adequately prepared for his assignment unless he had held a sub-

[5] For additional analysis of a panel of experienced executives and observers, see Charles A. Wilson, *Developing Responsible Leaders* (Oceana Publications, 1963).

ordinate political or career position in the same department or agency beforehand. Although about four-fifths of the executives serving during this period had had some form of previous public service, relatively few had had experience that was related in any way to their new appointments as senior political executives.

Take, for example, the type of knowledge that is required of some Defense Department appointees. The ultimate goal of the Defense Department, to defend the United States in the event of an attack, has little comparability with the overall goals of any organization outside the federal government. Nevertheless, there are certain functions such as personnel and logistics which are not totally unrelated to functions found in the private economy. The context is quite different, of course, in that recruitment may be by conscription rather than by voluntary employment, financing is through the appropriations process in Congress, and logistics involves the acquisition of commodities on a broader scale and of a wider variety than that found in any private institution. Experience in one of the military departments, particularly direct experience with these functions, often is the best background for assuming these duties. Because of his lack of this experience, one Kennedy defense appointee said:

> The offer hit me cold. I hadn't been thinking about this kind of job at all, particularly in this department. I had never served in a military department; in fact, I never even had a Western Union uniform on. The Secretary convinced me to take the job because he needed someone who could do liaison work with Congress and who had experience in legal and organizational problems. In some ways it is better than I had anticipated, but it is a handicap not to know more about military organization and military problems.

Another lawyer recruited to the Defense establishment in the Truman administration observed that neither he nor his department head knew what his job would involve since the post was really a new one. He was simply on "general assignment." Having no conception of the prerequisites of high political office, he even horrified the old hands at the Pentagon by driving his own car to work the first day.

On the domestic front, a former newspaperman and national party committee official was appointed assistant postmaster general with responsibility for its transportation functions. He had expressed reluctance to take the position because of his complete lack of knowledge of transportation. He told the President during an interview, "Mr.

President, you want me to take a job heading the biggest transportation operation in the world and I've never even driven a truck." Unfortunately, his predecessor had left long before and there was no one available to teach him his responsibilities. Moreover, he was faced immediately with an important rate case. To make up for his lack of knowledge he worked on the case from seven in the morning until midnight for four months. As he looked back on his experience, he felt that this lack of basic information was his primary source of dissatisfaction with the job he had held.

Another assistant postmaster general, whose previous career had been almost entirely in the field of practical politics, found himself responsible for personnel functions of the department. Like many liberal Democrats, he previously had been mainly concerned with more sweeping problems—foreign affairs, federal aid to education, defense—leaving such routine matters as the Post Office to others. With his fellow novice executives, he had to put in 13- to 14-hour days to catch up.

Congressional Supervision

The tutelary role of congressional committees and their critical appraisal of executive actions are a source of major concern to many appointees. Quite a number who left the government of their own volition cited their relations with Congress as a contributive factor to their discontent with government service; but only five individuals (or 6 percent) said that it was a major reason for leaving (see Table A.14). The feelings of these men on the matter were often very intense.

This is really not to be wondered at. A new executive is faced with a board of directors 535 strong, each with an insatiable appetite for inquiry. As individual congressmen and as members of committees, these representatives and senators maintain an unceasing vigil over administrative performance not only to insure conformity to legal prescription, but also to guarantee recognition of their constituents' interests and consideration for their own policy views. The political executive is kept aware of congressional thinking through a battery of communication techniques: innumerable appearances before legislative oversight and investigating committees, referral of constituent problems and requests, calls either in person or by telephone on official business, speeches on the floor of Congress, and even casual conversations at the many formal and informal affairs where high-level dignitaries gather. Even an Assistant Secretary of Commerce who had had long experience in public life observed that among the most surprising and frustrating parts of his subcabinet job were "the unreasonable demands made upon my time and energy by Congress. I had a very hard time adjusting to Congress' role and perhaps I never did adjust." In his opinion, many of these contacts were little more than harassment.

The focus of these contacts between Congress and the executive branch differs from department to department and with each subject area. Attention may be devoted to matters of high policy or to administrative detail and partisan sniping. For high-level officials in the Department of State, for example, the stream of communication with Congress relates primarily to the substance of foreign policy, although even here some political executives, such as Dean Acheson, have complained about the excessive detail with which Congress attempts to inform itself.[6] In other departments and agencies, contacts relate primarily to the interests of the congressmen's constituents. For example, both an administrator and his deputy in the General Services Administration reported a great deal of congressional interest in GSA decisions. One administrator noted, "It is difficult to serve fifty masters. Congressmen, as well as others, are always trying to tell the administrator and his staff what to do; including such things as who should get contracts, what color of brick should be used in buildings, and so forth." His deputy commented in a similar vein:

> Congressmen represent people who want to do business with the government and who are much concerned about what GSA is doing in construction and placement of orders. GSA can do much for a state or for a community by the timing and placement of its orders. And in deciding for one community and against another, GSA can even affect the result of a congressional election.

Interference in administrative matters provoked this comment from a Defense Secretary:

> Efforts on the part of Congress to administer the Department should be stopped. For instance, service rivalries were made more severe by the existence of three subcommittees in the House Armed Services Committee. Each of these subcommittees handled matters pertaining to the three service departments and the members got at-

[6] See Dean Acheson, A Citizen Looks at Congress (Harper & Brothers, 1956).

tached to a particular service and tried to make trades with each other. They are actually prejudiced advocates in places of political power. The closer Congress gets to establishing general laws and the farther away from supervising administration, the better things will be. I know this is difficult, particularly where the problem concerns money and appropriations. It is difficult to appropriate if you don't know exactly what the money is going to be used for, but realizing there is a thin line of distinction, some reasonable compromise should be found.

Congressional interest occasionally laps over into personal abuse and some executives are extremely sensitive to such criticism. A Deputy Director of the Bureau of the Budget, a favorite target for congressmen, recalled his experiences with a senator of his own political party:

Senator Malone was always attacking me because of the foreign aid program. I answered him in one of the Finance Committee hearings by telling him that the United States government was giving more aid to the citizens of Nevada than it was collecting in taxes and I compared this with our foreign aid program. The result of this statement was a long diatribe by Malone. I disliked intensely those long congressional hearings where I had to be everybody's servant. And in addition to the hearings, congressmen were always calling up on the telephone demanding information which frequently took a long time to prepare.

Businessmen may be least prepared for the constancy, intimacy, and contumacy of congressional contacts, but they are not alone in their deprecation of congressional meddling, attacks, and burdensome inquiries for information. In addition to businessmen, those who complained about their relationships with Congress included former state officials, trade union officials, lawyers, farmers, and even a former congressional staff member. Nor does it appear that long tenure in public service results in a more tolerant acceptance of the role of Congress. For some, even with long and distinguished political careers, negotiations with Congress were a constant source of annoyance.

Part of the difficulty is the sheer amount of staff time that is consumed in congressional hearings. Busy secretarial and subordinate personnel, who had their hands full administering the affairs of their department, often found the burden of congressional hearings intolerable.[7] The executive may face not only questions about broad

---

[7] And they are unlikely to become more tolerant. Note the problems facing Defense officials because the Armed Services Committees are trying to recapture influence from the appropriations committees at the expense of the Defense De-

policy within his department or agency, but he may be interrogated with regard to detailed operational decisions. The executive must "bone up" by learning and digesting all of the information he may need in the hearing and may even go through a mock hearing in order to prepare himself for the grilling he may take. A Secretary of Defense was unhappy both about the strain of his appearances and also about the publicity which they received.

> . . . I was put under terrific strain by the need to be constantly testi-fying on the Hill and in other ways getting my name in the papers. I am not the type of person who likes to have his name in the papers. On days when I had to appear on the Hill at a hearing, I used to get up at 4 a.m. to study the problems.

Complaints on congressional relations spread across the entire exec-utive establishment. An Assistant Secretary of Agriculture deplored the constant heckling: "Even when the congressmen were good personal friends, the sniping went on at the hearings. Much of this is just killing time." An Assistant Attorney General expressed his annoyance at the "harassment" by the press and by members of Congress: "There was never a week without some kind of needling from Kefauver or Celler." A deputy agency chief similarly complained about the innumerable petty requests and complaints sent to him or registered in other ways by congressmen and senators. Moreover, they were always putting pressure on him to appoint people to posts for which they were not qualified. Because of unfavorable publicity which his agency had re-ceived as a result of congressional investigation, it was less able to re-sist such pressures. An Under Secretary of Labor expressed dismay about the way in which good legislation sent to the Hill was sat on by committee chairmen, whom he described as "the old fogies." An Assis-tant Secretary of Commerce, who had had long experience in the gov-ernment, was the most vitriolic:

> Congressmen are often politically minded and badly informed, and sometimes just plain stupid. Oftentimes I would use charts to explain things to Congress, but some of them couldn't even cope with simple graphs and charts. On the other hand, some of them were pretty sharp, but many of these were simply out for your scalp.

---

partment, whose officials will have to testify even more often. See Bernard K. Gordon, "The Military Budget: Congressional Phase," *The Journal of Politics*, Vol. 23 (November 1961), p. 689.

Financial Problems

Executives who accept a severe drop in salary with their government appointment and who have no other financial resources may ultimately have to face the fact that they cannot suffer such losses indefinitely without jeopardizing their family's financial security. Even the few who receive a raise in pay as a result of federal service seldom find it to be an increase in real income.[8]

Financial loss was a recurring source of concern mentioned by the case study appointees. Thirteen executives mentioned it as a major source of dissatisfaction and seven gave it as a reason for leaving. An executive in the Truman administration reported that he lost $12,000 in the year and a half he was in the government. He was offered a position in private industry that paid over $60,000 per year in contrast to the $10,000 he was paid by the government. He felt that he should not turn down such an opportunity since he intended to remain in the government only two years in any event. A lawyer in the Eisenhower administration reported that he lost $4,000 the first year (at a time when the salary for an assistant secretary was $15,000), and that he was using up his accumulated capital rapidly. He felt that he had to return to his law practice to recoup his losses.

Reduction in income is often coupled with increase in expenses in the public service. Certain positions, particularly in the State Department, require a great deal of travel and entertainment, and Congress has seldom seen fit to provide sufficient funds to cover the cost; appointees generally have to shoulder the burden themselves. Again, extensive travel may be one of the chief attractions of political executive service for some men, but it is also a major drain on personal income. Even political executives in the domestic departments frequently are called upon to make speeches at various conventions and on-the-site investigations of current problems; they have to consult with field offices and attend international meetings. Travel and per diem funds are frequently inadequate and the executive often has to make up the difference out of his own pocket.

A union official noted the expense of high-level service as an important factor in his departure since his position required him to engage

[8] See Chap. 10 for discussion of federal executive salaries.

in a great deal of expensive traveling. A businessman-lawyer likewise complained of the expenses associated with political executive service. He had entered the government for a two-year stint with considerable enthusiasm and left when the two years were up because he had spent his savings in keeping up with his job.

Lack of Upward Mobility

Many, if not most, men look at any specific job in terms of its potentiality for advancement. As indicated earlier, the practice of promoting men to higher positions is common but above the assistant secretary level in many departments and agencies the opportunities are fewer and fewer. Departures from high-level posts are occasionally the result of failure to be offered advancement to secretarial or undersecretarial posts. In some instances, the expectation of advancement is built into the original offer, although this appears to be exceptional. At other times, there is serious misunderstanding over whether any commitments for advancement were made or not.

One assistant secretary, for example, felt particularly frustrated over his failure to achieve the undersecretarial post because of his inability to win clearance from an interest group that worked closely with his department. Having acted as under secretary and even as acting secretary over a considerable period of time, he found it galling that his previous record of service was ignored in the face of opposition that was based primarily on the symbolism of his appointment since he came from a rival interest group. He felt that continuance under another under secretary would be in effect a demotion and he would not accept it. Feeling "stymied in my position," he observed, "I felt that since I could not move up, it was better to get out."

In another case, a deputy assumed from the discussion with his agency chief at the time of his appointment that he would follow the path of his chief by being advanced to the top position when the latter left. Unfortunately, the agency head had no such understanding. Partially as a result of this, the deputy left after a year and a half for another government position.

Some political executives feel that they deserve a chance at the top job in the department after long years of service and resent the intrusion of someone appointed from outside. One under secretary admitted his hope for the secretarial post and claimed support from the outgoing Secretary as well as many members of the Congress. In this instance, however, the President awarded the appointment to a member of his own staff for loyalty and past services. Although the under secretary was asked to stay on, he refused with a strong indication to the President of his displeasure. Another case involved an assistant secretary in the Truman administration who believed that the Secretary had promised him advancement to the under secretary post, but discovered that the job had been promised to other assistant secretaries as well. He became ill from overwork and worrying about whether he would be promoted or not, so he decided to leave the department.

Reasons for Leaving Unrelated to Dissatisfaction

There is no single overriding reason causing men to leave political office. In any event, most men consider public service at this level as a temporary interruption in their careers. Knowing that they are more than likely to lose their positions at the end of an administration, they make a virtue of necessity and are open to other job offers before their term in office is over. Disillusionment and all the other sources of dissatisfaction listed above served as incentives to some appointees to take advantage of timely opportunities (inside and outside the government) much sooner than they or their recruiters had anticipated.

A large number of federal executives, particularly among Eisenhower's recruits from the business world, never intended to remain long; and a change in administration forced many more out of office. Discounting these appointees and others who accepted further government assignments, there were relatively few among the case study appointees who left of their own volition. Eight of the latter attributed their departures in large measure to job opportunities elsewhere.

Executives in financial difficulties were, of course, more amenable to overtures from industry, the universities, professional groups, politicians, and the like than their better-off colleagues. But many would not have been considered if they had not demonstrated a high level of competence and achieved considerable public visibility while in the government service. Two secretarial appointments are instances in point: the departure of John Connally in December 1961, after only eleven months' service as Secretary of the Navy, and the departure of Elvis Stahr on May 1, 1962, after fifteen months' service as Secretary of the Army in the Kennedy administration. Connally resigned to prepare his campaign for the governorship of Texas, while Stahr resigned to become the president of Indiana University.[9] Stahr stated to the press that he left because of "the opportunity to lead one of America's great universities," an opportunity which was "one in a lifetime," although there was considerable speculation at the time that his relations with the Secretary of Defense were not entirely satisfactory.[10]

Among the eight case study appointees who left to take up jobs in the private sector was a Truman assistant secretary who had been approached just as he had accepted the government post by a company doing business in an area of his particular competence. Because of his public commitment, he turned down the offer at that time. But when, two years later, the company offered him the presidency, he felt he had to accept. This Truman executive firmly believed that every political executive should remain for his four-year term in the government "but, on the other hand, one has to consider private interests also at some point." Another appointee, an Eisenhower businessman, had succumbed to pressure when he accepted his government appointment in the first place; he had lost $60,000 because he had had to sell all his stock. He said: "I wanted to return to the business world and did so when I was offered a good position." And a former labor union official serving in the Labor Department left because an attractive offer from

[9] In the Senate confirmation hearings Mr. Connally said to Chairman Richard Russell:
. . . I can only say that I, of course, would be willing to serve as long as I do so at the pleasure of the President and so long as I feel that I can make a substantial contribution to the Navy and to the Defense Establishment.
. . . I have no plans to leave after any specified period of time. I have no plans to go back to any particular employment. I have no obligations, no commitments whatsoever with respect to that.
Mr. Stahr stated to Senator Cannon:
It is my intention to remain on the job as long as the President and the Secretary of Defense wish me to, and as long as I feel in the depths of my own conscience that I am doing an effective job.
Nomination of John B. Connally, Jr., Hearing before the Senate Armed Services Committee, 87 Cong. 1 sess. (1961), p. 7; *Nomination of Elvis J. Stahr,* Hearing before the Senate Armed Services Committee, 87 Cong. 1 sess. (1961), p. 5.
[10] *Washington Post and Times Herald,* May 3, 1962; *New York Times,* July 8, 1962.

a private association provided him with an income substantially greater than either his income as a labor union official or as a government
executive. A lawyer in the Eisenhower administration had an accumu-
lation of grievances, including serious financial losses, which led to his
dissatisfaction with government service. He therefore accepted a part-
nership in the law firm from which he had originally been recruited,
asserting that it was simply a question of "how long I was willing to
go on putting out instead of taking in . . . " Others who were familiar
with this lawyer emphasized the financial considerations, particularly
the fact that the law firm in question had a big case pending.

The question of returning to one's former affiliation was often complicated for political appointees by conflict of interest regulations. Frequently, those concerned with this aspect of their public commitment
had had to sever ties with their previous business or professional concerns upon appointment, but there was often a tacit understanding
that they could and would return at the conclusion of their tours of
duty. Men in such circumstances were sometimes extremely worried
that additional delay would jeopardize their careers, and the Eisenhower lawyer who returned to his law firm pointed out the career implications for a member of his profession.

> I lost a great many contacts in my practice while I was in Wash-
> ington and these outweighed any gains, especially when you take into
> consideration the financial losses I took in the first place. I felt I had
> to return to private practice to prevent losing further ground in my
> career.

After a certain period of time all hope of returning to their previous
employment may be lost to political appointees. A former state official,
for example, had to face the question after two years in office of
whether to stay in his federal post or return to the state office from
which he had been given a leave of absence. He finally decided to return to his state position. In another instance, a union official left the
federal government after less than a year of service partly because of
an opportunity to take over the presidency of his union. He recognized
that if he did not return at that moment another person would take
over.

For the owner of a small business the need to maintain a close
watch on the firm's affairs may be extremely pressing. In one case, a
political executive cut short his tour of duty to return home to save his

business. Unfortunately, he was unsuccessful and eventually had to sell out. Two Eisenhower executives left for similar reasons, one stating that he was afraid his firm "would fail if I were not there." Not all executives owning small business firms felt the same pressure, of course; one under secretary remained six years because of the confidence he had in his business partners and finally left only for personal reasons.

Various other reasons besides those cited above are assigned for decisions to leave the federal service. Some men are fearful about the effect of engagement in partisan politics on their careers. Roger Jones, in testifying before the Senate Subcommittee on National Policy Machinery, stated that a policy executive sometimes believed that "if he stays beyond a certain point he . . . will become contaminated with politics in the partisan sense, in a way which will interfere with his subsequent business or professional career."[11] A lawyer, speculating on the effect of government service on his career, expressed concern not for its partisan connotations but for the suspicion raised in the minds of many people who are accustomed to distrust government and anyone who works for it.

If one is not going to cut his ties completely with private affairs, and adjust to a permanent government career, there is a point beyond which one cannot remain in government service. If I hadn't returned to private life when I did, I don't believe that I would ever be able to. The American people are terribly suspicious of persons who work for the government so they prevent them from engaging in certain lines of activity when they leave the government. And a lot of us feel that we must stay as far away from government as possible for a considerable period after getting out of the government. I believe that if I had remained any longer both my law firm and I would have been seriously hurt.

Congressional harassment, which is frequently mentioned as a deterrent to accepting political executive positions and as a major cause of dissatisfaction, was mentioned by five men in the sample as an important factor in their departure; but it was of primary concern to only one of these executives. Even in this case there were other considerations which were more important in his decision to leave. Politics, in the sense of pressures of a partisan nature on making decisions, was mentioned only by two who left. Others left because of desire to

[11] *Organizing for National Security*, Vol. 1, p. 437.

run for political office. Only in three instances was there clear evidence that individuals were asked to resign, and in two of these instances, both within the Truman administration, an element of scandal was involved. In the third case, occurring in the Eisenhower administration, the individual was generally considered to be a hopeless incompetent.

Only in a small minority of cases were decisions to leave related to a real distaste for federal employment. The fact that such a large percentage accept other posts in the government is a strong indication of satisfaction. Many had extremely rewarding experiences and left with regret. Financial stress, concern for one's career, personal problems, changes in administration, personality problems, and disappointments at not being promoted far outweighed dissatisfactions with conditions found in the public service. Political executives had cause to complain and they were often exasperated at the unwieldy nature of the administrative procedures they had to follow, but seldom were such inconveniences a factor in their departure from office.

The Problem of Short Tenure

Regardless of the reasons for departure, the fact that so many assistant secretaries and under secretaries found it necessary to leave before the end of the four-year term caused considerable concern to recruiters in every administration.

Marion B. Folsom pinpointed the difficulty when he said at the 1960 hearings before the Senate Subcommittee on National Policy Machinery:

> It is difficult to get able people down here. By the time [political executives] get well trained, they leave. I know it would be very difficult to run a business on that basis.[12]

Folsom spoke as a former Secretary of Health, Education, and Welfare and as a senior executive of Eastman Kodak Company. His concern over the short tenure of senior political executives in office is shared by many inside and outside the government who query whether a country can be run efficiently with officials who have an "in-and-out-in-12-months" perspective on national policy issues. Recruiters' de-

[12] *Organizing for National Security,* Vol. 1, p. 488.

termination to exact even a two-year commitment from appointees has obviously been relatively ineffective in view of the continuing shortage of qualified manpower to fill senior political posts.

Reviewing tenure of Truman and Eisenhower executives, for example, the average length of service of the men who held the eighty-four case study appointments was just over two years; only thirteen had a position tenure of four years or more and there were eight who left before twelve months were up. Truman's appointees stayed a slightly shorter time in office than Eisenhower's; the median tenures per position were 2.2 years and 2.5 years, respectively. This was in spite of the fact that fifteen from Eisenhower's sample compared with five from Truman's had stipulated a two-year term, or less, as a major condition of acceptance.

The general turnover picture for executives from general counsel to cabinet rank is even more depressing. The average official held his appointment for 1.6 years under Truman and 2.1 years under Eisenhower. More than one-fifth of Truman's executives left the government before the end of the first year, presumably because many of them had been inherited from Roosevelt and, when Truman had firm hold over the reins after six months or so, they either left of their own accord or were replaced. About one in six of Eisenhower's recruits left within the first twelve months. There were also relatively few with long tenure: about one Truman appointee in five and one Eisenhower appointee in four stayed four years or more. During the longer period from 1933 to 1961 (which included Roosevelt's administration when many executives had longer tenure), over one in three of the appointees at the first and second levels left the government before two years were up, whereas only three in ten stayed four years or more.[13]

Although this general anxiety about the rather brief tenure of political executives has not been misplaced, especially when considered in relation to the much greater length of service of their career colleagues, the assumption that the government is headed by men who never remain long enough in any one appointment to become effective executives requires modification. Many assistant secretaries have had considerable government experience before their political appoint-

[13] These generalizations are based on the premise that about fifty executives were considered to have been reappointed by the incoming President (Truman or Eisenhower) when they remained in a specific position six months or more after the change of administration. For source see note 9, p. 13. Averages include cabinet secretaries, agency heads, and general counsels.

ments and many have also moved from one federal executive position to another. Some have been career people, others have made the public service a concern secondary only to their major occupations and have been in and out of public office in some capacity all their working lives.

An interesting example of this extended experience is furnished by the accompanying table which shows the tenure of the nine men who served as Deputy Secretary of Defense between 1949 and 1960.[14]

NAME	DATES	TENURE IN POSITION		PRIOR GOVERNMENT SERVICE	
		YEARS	MONTHS	YEARS	MONTHS
Stephen T. Early	8/49– 9/50	1	1	12	6
Robert A. Lovett	10/50– 9/51	–	11	6	6
William C. Foster	9/51– 1/53	1	4	4	10
Roger Kyes	2/53– 5/54	1	3	–	–
Robert B. Anderson	5/54– 8/55	1	3	1	3
Reuben B. Robertson	8/55– 4/57	1	8	1	7
Donald A. Quarles	5/57– 5/59	2	–	3	8
Thomas S. Gates	6/59–12/59	–	6	5	8
Average		1	3	4	6

Although average position tenure was 15 months, most of these men were experienced political executives who had had extensive government service, primarily in the military departments. Prior to the time of appointment as Deputy Secretary of Defense they had served an average of 4 years and 6 months in high policy positions. Unquestionably, the constant turnover was cause for concern, but the appointments of Robert Lovett, William C. Foster, or Thomas Gates, for instance, must be distinguished from the appointment of Roger Kyes. The former three were all acquainted with the major problems they faced before appointment and were therefore able to assume their responsibilities with a minimum of difficulty. Turnover in this and other similar posts, in fact, reflects the tendency to promote able men to more responsible positions when they become vacant.

Between 1933 and 1961, nearly 150 individuals held more than one federal executive appointment; about forty held three or more; one man actually held five. Their knowledge of senior management and

[14] Source: Office of the Secretary of Defense, mimeo. (*circa* 1959). Prior government service includes civilian service only. Donald A. Quarles died in office.

policy problems was therefore considerable. Well over half of these appointments involved promotions or reappointments within the same department or agency. The tenure of the average appointee of the first or second echelon during this period was consequently close to two and a half years in each agency, as opposed to just over two years in each position. And they had had much nearer three years' employment as a federal executive somewhere in the government. In addition to this, nearly three-quarters of the appointments made during this period were filled by men who had had some form of administrative experience at the local, state, or federal level of government prior to their federal political executive appointment. The proportion varied from four-fifths of the Truman appointees to two-thirds of the Eisenhower appointees.

Among the case studies (which, of course, were not representative of the group), twelve had had previous relevant experience at the federal executive level before accepting their case study appointment; four of them had been assistant secretaries who had been promoted to the undersecretaryships. Eight among the sample of eighty-four Truman and Eisenhower appointees went on from the case study position to the next echelon—to become either under secretaries or secretaries in their respective departments.

Despite this somewhat cheering evidence of previous experience on the part of many of these assistant secretaries and under secretaries, the problem raised by frequent turnover in these positions still remains. No one, even with a thorough background in department activities, can be truly effective if he remains as short a time in office as too many of these executives did in the Roosevelt, Truman, and Eisenhower administrations.

However, there are other factors besides turnover to be taken into account. Serious though such short tenure in office is, it is perhaps less serious when viewed in the perspective of necessary changes in control of the government and the normal process of shifting men about in the federal service as they are needed. Continuity in office is only one value which must be balanced against the total needs of an administration, a party, department and agency heads, and the personal desires of the executives. If continuity is assumed to be *the* critical factor in ensuring adequate administrative performance—a doubtful assumption—some radically altered system for filling these offices—such as reliance on the career service—may be required.

Another possibility—that of compelling candidates to commit themselves to a specific term in office as suggested by Senator Henry Jackson in Senate Resolution 338—would appear to be difficult to execute and might inhibit many potential executives from accepting appointments. Commitments change with new opportunities.

8

Effect of Government Service
on Subsequent Careers

CANDIDATES WHO HESITATE about accepting political office, who withdraw after a few months, or who refuse even to be considered for an appointment as assistant secretary or under secretary do so in large measure because they are fearful of the effects of government service on their private careers. What will happen to the former businessman, for instance, to the former professor, or to the former lawyer when he returns to his previous occupation and finds that he has been replaced or superseded by his old associates?

"A few companies, a few law firms, a few universities, a few unions, have made it possible for their members to take office and come back without penalty. But this is exceptional," states the Task Force Report of the Second Hoover Commission on Personnel and Civil Service:

> Normally when a man leaves his business, his profession, or his labor organization to hold public office, he loses out. He may have no place to go back to when his term of office is up; or, if he is taken back, he finds that he has fallen behind the procession and that his former associates are away ahead of him. Most men have had to choose either business or politics. They could not do both.[1]

Macmahon and Millett, reviewing the subsequent careers of under secretaries and assistant secretaries who served prior to 1938, concluded that, except for those who served in the Departments of State, Treasury, and Justice, "the overwhelming majority of the occupants of

---

[1] Commission on Organization of the Executive Branch of the Government, *Task Force Report on Personnel and Civil Service*, p. 42.

these posts have not been prominent afterwards either politically or professionally. The few exceptions, indeed, make the obscurity of the mass more striking."[2] Their evidence is limited but they conclude that, on the whole, political executives rose from the anonymous masses to take up their public assignments and returned to these shadows at the end of their service. Macmahon and Millett may be measuring "obscurity" by lack of public note. Activities of a prominent private citizen are seldom as newsworthy as those of a senior government official. Indeed, although less well known in their private capacities, the subsequent careers of appointees who served during the period 1933 to 1961 strongly indicate that men at the political executive level retain the stature—usually high—which they held prior to public office and that they have gone on to do very well for themselves in whatever career line they later choose to follow. Sometimes they are better known as a result of their government service and often such service has contributed much to their later success in private life.

One measure of prominence taken by Macmahon and Millett—that under secretaries and assistant secretaries seldom were chosen to be department heads—has not been validated in recent administrations. It is in sharp contrast, in fact, to the practice of both Truman and Eisenhower—and even of Kennedy—who frequently promoted subordinates in the major departments and independent agencies.[3] But there are many more posts at subcabinet than cabinet level; therefore, although subordinate officers were often given preference for vacancies, relatively few could be selected.

After their term in office, a large proportion of the executives appointed during the Roosevelt, Truman, and Eisenhower administra-

[2] Arthur W. Macmahon and John D. Millett, *Federal Administrators* (Columbia University Press, 1939), p. 301.

[3] In the Truman administration, Dean Acheson, Robert Lovett, James Forrestal, Louis Johnson, Kenneth Royall, Gordon Gray, John Sullivan, Frank Pace, Dan Kimball, Howard McGrath, Tom Clark, Jesse Donaldson, Charles Brannan, Oscar Chapman, Watson Miller, and Frederick Lawton advanced from subordinate posts to head one of the departments or agencies. In the Eisenhower administration, the list included Christian Herter, Robert Anderson, Thomas Gates, William Franke, Charles Thomas, James Douglas, Dudley Sharp, William Rogers, Fred Seaton, Frederick Mueller, James Mitchell, Marion Folsom, Arthur Flemming, Rowland Hughes, Percival Brundage, Maurice Stans, and James Smith. In the Kennedy administration, the first political executives to move up to key positions were Dean Rusk, Douglas Dillon, Fred Korth, Eugene Zuckert, Willard Wirtz, and Bernard Boutin.

234 THE ASSISTANT SECRETARIES

tions switched employers, established new careers, shifted professions, or continued in the government in other posts. Their prospects were generally all the brighter for the change in direction. Taking the long-term view (and discounting former Eisenhower appointees who had not firmly established themselves in either private or government careers by the end of 1961), it is striking that during these twenty-nine years less than one in five returned to his former place of employment. Over 10 percent actually changed their professions or occupations and an astonishing proportion—about one-half—joined new enterprises or set themselves up in their own concerns.

The obvious lesson to be drawn is that acceptance of political executive service implies not only a temporary interruption in a career with a business, a law firm, or a university but also usually leads to a complete breakaway from old associations. This may be because the executive's old job has already been filled and there is no place for him at his former firm or institution. It is more likely, however, that government service has changed his own perspective. With greater visibility, a record of public accomplishment, and broader contacts than ever before, the former under secretary or assistant secretary is much more in demand in the job market and can look further afield for new opportunities. He has probably relocated his family, too, and made new friends. In fact, the same hesitations and uncertainties in his personal life that made him a little dubious about accepting a public appointment in the first place now operate in the opposite direction—his ties with his old home community are more tenuous and he wants to settle down in or near Washington amid now-familiar surroundings.

The expression, "They never go back to Pocatello," is therefore applicable to many political appointees as well as to congressmen. Executives tended to remain in the eastern part of the United States, especially in the vicinity of Washington, D. C., after their public service was over. In the Roosevelt and Eisenhower administrations, about half as many again remained in Washington as the number recruited there. Truman's appointees tended to relocate in the vicinity of New York, join the population surge on the West Coast, or take foreign assignments. Many of these men had seen such long government service that it was natural for them to look further afield when the 1952 party overturn occurred.

During this period, political executives were not only drawn primarily from large urban complexes but were siphoned off permanently from the smaller population centers and the less populous states. The natural attraction of the busy metropolis for the up-and-coming small-town executive meant that few felt inclined to return to their home towns if they happened to be in the West North Central or East North Central regions.

This change in living habits and environment—and also the desire to remain at the hub of things—led not a few executives to desert the private sector for public office on a more-or-less permanent basis. About one-fourth of the executives between 1933 and 1961 decided to remain in the government after their first term of political duty. (A certain proportion, of course, had been recruited from the government in the first place.) The majority of these men were reappointed to the political executive ranks and continued to serve as assistant secretaries, under secretaries, or secretaries. Former Foreign Service officers loomed large in this group, for the most part remaining in high policy positions almost on a career basis once they had achieved secretarial rank. A small number in all departments and agencies valued government service enough to take positions at subordinate political executive levels rather than leaving to make their own way outside the federal orbit. Others became federal judges, secured ambassadorships, or accepted appointments to regulatory commissions and other commissions and emergency agencies.

Case Study Appointees: Subsequent Careers

The subsequent careers of case study appointees resembled in some degree the later experiences of the total group of political executives who held office during this period. Truman's officers showed a definite preference for government employment. Nearly half of them remained in the federal service after their case study appointments, whereas only about one-fifth returned to their former business or professional affiliation. The sample chosen from Eisenhower's recruits, on the other hand, showed no marked inclination in any one direction. About one-third remained in the government, another third returned to their former pursuits, and the remaining third tried out new ventures, generally in their previous career lines.

For some executives, the case study appointment was their second or third government assignment. Four under secretaries, for example, had been promoted from assistant secretaryships, and seven others accepted their case study appointments while occupying some other fairly high, relevant position as general counsel, division chief, or assistant to the department secretary. In fact, although half of the sample of eighty-four appointees selected from the Truman and Eisenhower political teams were recruited from outside the government, another twenty-three—over a quarter—who came originally from the private sector were already engaged in some form of government assignment at the time they accepted their case study appointments.

Other executives recruited directly from business or the professions decided to remain for another tour of duty, or at least on a short-term commitment, before returning to their private occupations. Eight were promoted, some to the secretaryships, others to the undersecretaryships. In all, thirty-one of these eighty-four appointees went on to other federal posts; although fifteen of them left fairly soon afterwards to return to the private sector. The subsequent career picture varies, therefore, according to the time interval after the termination of the case study assignment (see Tables A.15 and A.16).

To a certain extent, the flexibility with which some executives moved in and out of government employment depended upon occupation or profession. Individual testimony from the appointees indicated, for example, that lawyers appear to have at least as much to gain as to lose from federal assignments whereas the careers of businessmen invariably suffered from too long a stretch in the government, especially when such businessmen operated their own enterprises. If businessmen did not hurry back to their own concerns, in fact, they generally went into entirely new ventures. Of the twenty-one appointees who changed their occupations, ten were businessmen, three were lawyers, one was a public servant, and the rest had a miscellany of career interests. All but four of these twenty-one men went into some form of commercial undertaking—in transportation, advertising, banking, or manufacturing. The remaining four joined nonprofit organizations.

The complicated career patterns of this group of eighty-four public officials are traced below according to occupation and profession prior to the case study appointments. Their variety of interests and their mobility in moving from one career field to another—taking government service in their stride—are characteristic of the majority of executives who held office during this period.

Lawyers

Seven of the seventeen appointees who had spent a major portion of their careers in the private practice of law had actually come to their case study appointments from other federal government positions. Two more came from municipal positions and only eight came directly from private practices. At the conclusion of their case study appointments, five of the seventeen returned to their former practices, though one remained for only a year and then accepted a municipal appointment; two others took higher government positions but eventually returned to their former practices. Five of the remaining twelve lawyers went into new law practices, three of them relocating in Washington rather than returning to their former places of residence. Two other lawyers received federal judicial appointments in their home regions, one after another spell in the executive branch; the remaining three entered business, one after two more high level federal positions. Another of these three lawyers-turned-businessmen returned later to a high level government post for some five years.

Government Employees

Nine of the twenty case study appointees who had made their careers in federal government service had law degrees, but only four were in positions where they made use of their training. One lawyer-turned-public servant left his case study position to accept a federal judicial appointment, and three went immediately into private law practice. Two others entered private law practice after serving in other government positions. One of the latter was promoted to another federal executive post before he practiced law. One case study appointee had resigned from the government to become president of a business organization about a year before accepting the political executive post. When he left the case study appointment nearly two years later, he returned to his former business position. Eight other appointees continued to work for the government: four were Foreign Service officers who returned to diplomatic posts; two accepted lower federal positions;

one was promoted to a higher post, retiring when that tour of duty came to an end; and one eventually went to a state government post. Three men took positions with international organizations, but one left after only a year to take a job with an industrial organization for which he had qualifications. Two appointees retired immediately after the termination of their case study appointments.

Businessmen

Twenty-six of the case study appointees were businessmen, although six of them were in other federal posts when they accepted the case study position and four others had held high level federal jobs previously. They included men from banking, investment, manufacturing, transportation, and public relations. Four of them had law degrees, but only two were making some use of their training. Nine of these businessmen had no previous federal government experience, and another five only minor experience.

Nine of the appointees returned to their former business connections and homes when they completed the case study appointments. Six accepted other federal government posts; three of them eventually returned to their former businesses, though one made his headquarters in Washington; two retired; and one remained in public life. Nine men made new business connections, some even changing industries, moving from investment counseling to manufacturing, from transportation to advertising, and from banking to transportation. Of these nine, only three returned to their former homes, one having made acceptance of the new position contingent on being allowed to remain at home; three remained in Washington; two went to New York; and one located in the South. One of the men possessing law degrees who had broken his ties with his corporation (which asked him to come back) remained in Washington to establish a law practice; he had bought a house, and was living fairly close to his wife's East Coast relatives; he said that 90 percent of his new practice business was with the federal government and was channeled to him from all parts of the country. The twenty-sixth man, an investment banker who had previously held a number of government jobs (including another at the federal political executive level), also remained in Washington with a nonprofit organization working closely with the government.

Others

The twenty-one remaining case study appointees comprise small groups of individuals from several diverse areas—the academic world, farms, trade unions, journalism—and some men who did not confine their careers to a single dominant field but moved from one pursuit to another, or more than one—chiefly combinations of law, business, and government. Eight of the appointees returned to the job from which they were recruited for political executive positions—including three farmers and three from academic institutions, although one of the latter took a banking position within a year's time. Eight went to other positions in the federal government, but two of them soon moved on to new businesses and one to a new law practice. Four joined new organizations, chiefly nonprofit; and one man went directly from his federal executive post to a new business connection.

Effect of Government Service on Career Prospects

An appointee's own assessment of the effect of government service on his future career is subjective at best and does not really lend itself to statistical comparison. But there are recurring factors in the evaluations of forty-nine executives from the Truman and Eisenhower administrations who were questioned on their subsequent careers that can be related in some measure to the experience of the whole group of second-level executives who held office between 1945 and 1961.

Most political executives, for example, concluded that their service had favorably affected their careers. Sometimes they expressed this only in terms of some vague notion of "prestige" or "experience." In other instances they measured the effect in terms of jobs, income, contacts, and type of work, where the relationship between government service and later employment were unmistakably clear. They shared the view of the lawyer now practicing in Washington who said that from the standpoint of his career, the post he had held in the government was "the best job there is."

Of these forty-nine appointees, thirty-three believed that political executive service had been of benefit to them and twelve that it had had little or no effect. Two had mixed reactions and only two considered that their careers had been damaged and wished that they had not served. The only marked difference in judgment between Eisenhower and Truman political executives was the tendency for Eisenhower businessmen to regard government service merely as an interlude in a profitable career elsewhere. Otherwise, there was little variation among occupational groups in either administration. Except for bankers and farmers, a majority in each career line looked back on their public service with satisfaction. Lawyers and government employees were slightly more impressed than the others.

Opinions of appointees differed somewhat according to agency. In all of them except the Post Office and the State Department, for example, a majority of the executives felt that their government appointments had been useful to them; in fact, eight of the nine Defense executives were glad, from the career point of view, that they had served. The case studies did not support the commonly held assumption that executives of prestige departments—State, Defense, and Treasury—gained the most from their government service. Other domestic agencies such as Post Office, Labor, or the Veterans Administration might not hold the same attraction for prominent men but since their executives are generally younger and have not made their mark on the world, they are quite likely to consider political office a real boost to their careers. On the other hand, a number of men were like President John Hannah of Michigan State University who was willing to serve as assistant secretary in the Department of Defense, but who would probably not have been tempted by a post in any other agency. Having already achieved a certain level of success in their own private occupations, the career value of government service weighs very little with these individuals.

No general rule seems to explain why certain State Department and Post Office employees were somewhat negative about their service. Two executives in the Post Office, for instance, were older men, relatively unconcerned about long-term prospects. One remained in a fairly senior government post while the other set up a new business in a field with which he had been familiar before entering the government. A third Post Office executive was asked to resign because of his alleged misbehavior. Among those in the State Department were two bankers, neither of whom could see any particular relationship between their permanent careers and the service they had performed in the government. A third was a career Foreign Service officer who returned to an ambassadorial post—the same level from which he had been originally recruited. The fourth man retired after long service which threatened to break his health.

Younger men were most likely to relate political executive service to enhanced career opportunities in all departments. On the whole, it was the men who left the government between the ages of 36 and 55 who had a strong tendency to look favorably upon their political executive service. Among the case studies, three out of four men in this age bracket who left in the Truman and Eisenhower administrations believed that their appointments had been beneficial to their career prospects. Few thought that it had had no effect and even fewer that it had actually hindered them.

Individual Reactions to Government Service

So much for the tabulation of appointees' responses. More revealing are the views held by individual executives on the relationship between government service and their future careers.

Some pointed, for example, to a direct—and positive—relationship between the two. One Truman assistant secretary traced his present position, which he considered a real advancement, directly to his government post. "It's obvious," he said, "that no one would have recommended me otherwise." He went on:

I could easily have left the government in January 1953 without having achieved any advancement over the job I had before entering the government. The knowledge I gained of government procedures and about other departments has helped a lot too. I got to know how things are done in Washington.

And another in the same administration—a career civil servant who had obtained a law degree while in the government—"picked up his union card" upon leaving the government and went into law practice in Washington where cases relating to his former department were now his "bread and butter."

Several Defense officials were equally impressed with their government experience. One who served in two administrations became the head of an important trade association and later joined one of the large defense contractors at a high level. He explained that he was especially fortunate because:

I served in both administrations and I had charge of a wide variety of functions—including the financial management, logistics and procurement, and manpower and personnel. This gave me a total approach and perhaps helped my chances with prospective employers. In addition, I had certain international experience which was a major plus in my book.

Another who returned to his previous employer, a large Defense contractor, said that at first he was doubtful that his government experience had been of any value to him at all in his private career since he found that his ideas were ignored by his superiors and he was considerably restricted in the kinds of defense activities in which he could engage. Later, however, he had been given full responsibility for his firm's Defense contracts, and he attributed this in part to his knowledge of Defense operations. A third executive considered that his appointment as head of a private scientific organization engaged in defense work was largely due to his Defense experience. The executive himself noted that his political appointment had made him acquainted with the scientific community and the "government ins-and-outs."

Quite a few of the appointees pointed to the advantages of their government contacts in giving direction to their future careers. One Eisenhower executive reported, for example, that his prospects had been enhanced, "not by the prestige of the job but because I met the man who offered me the job I now occupy." Another in the same department said that his government work had been important, "since it taught me everything I know about transportation and gave me contacts in transportation circles." The man who makes his career in government benefits most, of course, from such associations. The assistant attorney general who becomes a federal judge is perhaps the best example, but others include those who have gone to positions on the White House staff, and to memberships on regulatory and other commissions. In particular, access to the White House which the position of an assistant secretary or above often provides may lead to long-term government service in other capacities.

Learning on the job was another advantage mentioned. As one former assistant attorney general stated:

> Much of my present practice is in the same field I handled while in the government as a result of my work in the Justice Department. Although the conflict of interest rule prevents me from participating in a case that involves a claim against the government for two years, and it would be unethical for me to switch sides on a case begun

while I was in office, these rules have not prevented me from handling a substantial number of related cases. There is no problem in handling new cases and much of this type of practice involves preventive counseling anyway. My knowledge of government helps me give my clients sounder advice.

Another former assistant attorney general who went into law practice found useful both his substantive work and the contacts he made.

Probably more mail is sent out from my old division than from any other in Justice. I was known to all 94 U.S. Attorneys who served when I was in office. When they went out of office and needed an attorney in Washington they naturally turned to me.

And an assistant secretary who became, first, head of a trade association and, second, a private consultant explained, "I can open any door now." The opportunities afforded a lawyer as an agency deputy helped him "tremendously."

The advantages are not always in the career line, however. A former businessman who had lost business because of his identification with a party and a political philosophy, maintained that, on balance, he was glad he went to Washington because of his own personal development. Another appointee, a banker, entered the government for a relatively brief period of time to accomplish a specific task and later asserted that this period "was the most satisfactory I have ever had," in spite of the considerable sum of money he had lost.

It was also a banker who had served in several high-level federal positions who observed that his government experience had not made him a better banker—a point made by others in the banking field—but it had nevertheless been enlightening, even "thrilling." He was instrumental in setting up an important international organization, and he felt that that experience was "about as much fun as you can have." In the same vein, an official in the Defense Department who realized no appreciable career gain through his service, remarked that "it was even more fun than I expected it to be." A State Department assistant secretary who bitterly resisted accepting his post and retired after service, noted that he couldn't "turn off" his interest in foreign affairs, particularly in the area that had formerly been his responsibility. Local events in his own community no longer seemed so important.

There were adverse reactions to government service too, of course; but on the whole individual responses were favorable. Perhaps the general tenor of the replies is best summed up in the words of the

Eisenhower executive in the Department of Agriculture who said:

Looking back, I wouldn't have missed the experience. It greatly broadened my outlook on life. It gave me broader contacts with people both in and out of agriculture. I made many friends in Congress, including some southern Democrats, who asked me to stay on in my post. I gained a greater appreciation for men in public life and found they are more able and patriotic than newspaper accounts indicate.

9

Evaluation of Political Executives

RECRUITERS ASSEMBLING the new executive team of an incoming administration have to bear in mind that their role is essentially a political one. They are subjected to so many conflicting pressures in the appointment of any one individual at the second-echelon level that past experience and personal qualifications have sometimes been the least important criteria. The type of person who would be the "best man in the job" is never well defined as the "job" itself varies so much from administration to administration and from department to department that it is hard to assess the abilities required for a specific position at any given time. A post mortem inquiry therefore on the effectiveness of a particular assistant secretary may appear to be of little value. Nevertheless, at least a few of the recruiters base their search for new blood on a combination of qualities and background that have provided the most successful recruits in the past. Some have definite objectives in view when they select, say, an under secretary for the Department of the Interior or a deputy administrator for the General Services Administration. They may consider political balance important, expertise, a business background, or general administrative ability. They may have to compromise in their final selection and accept the "best man available" who fills the bill—more or less—in the judgment of as many participants in the recruitment process as possible.

Who is this "best man available"? And what relationship does his background have to his successful performance? The President may be the actual recruiter or he may work through the Donald Dawson, the Sherman Adams, or the Robert Kennedy of his particular administra-

245

tion. But no matter who influences the candidate's appointment in the first place, it is his political and career colleagues who can best assess how the appointee measures up to his responsibilities once in office as a politically sensitive decision-maker and risk-taker, as an able administrator and program planner.

What, for instance, does a cabinet officer think of his under secretary and assistant secretaries whom he may have had thrust upon him from outside recruiting sources or whom he may have chosen himself for any number of reasons other than related experience? What does the senior career executive who carries the load of day-to-day routine from one administration to another think of the men chosen to guide him in policy issues? Is there any particular type of environment, experience, or ability that produces better assistant secretaries or deputy administrators than others?

Performance Ratings of Political Executives, 1933-61

In order to assess the value of generalizations concerning the relevance of background and personal characteristics to capability in office, highly placed political officials (usually department heads) and senior career officials were asked to evaluate the performance of the political executives who had served in their departments or agencies and whose work was familiar to them. Ratings were given by forty-three men, twenty-nine political appointees and fourteen civil servants. They reviewed the effectiveness of 317 subcabinet officers with whom they had been associated during the Truman and Eisenhower administrations. Included also were a small number from the Roosevelt and Kennedy administrations. In most instances, at least two evaluations were obtained on each individual.

It was recognized that raters' assessments were based on personal experience and bound to be subjective. Therefore, they were asked to explain the varying assumptions upon which they based their judgments of performance. Ratings were assessed on a ten-point scale, with one end representing the most successful performance and the other the least successful. The evaluations given by agency heads and career officials had a high degree of correspondence: there was significant disagreement in the evaluation of only 10 percent of the 317 executives.[1]

Ratings by Previous Occupation

The ratings given raise serious doubts whether there is any important causal relationship between occupational background and performance. Successful executives were recruited in nearly the same proportions from all the major private occupational groups, about half of those from business, law, and other professions being given good or excellent ratings.

Except for those in elective politics, government officials as a group were considered to be better executives than men who came exclusively from the private sector. Remarkably few public servants were, in fact, believed to be below average: only 10 percent compared with 27 percent of both the former businessmen and lawyers and 40 percent of those from other professions such as education, engineering, and science. Their successful performance emphasizes the importance of on-the-job experience in filling these policy-making positions. This is perhaps the major reason why men from private occupations who had also had a considerable background in government work were rated higher than those with no public service experience at all. As Edward Banfield suggests, "A businessman who enters government service leaves behind him a specialized skill in making judgments; if he remains in government service long enough, and if he subjects himself to suitable training, he will, presumably, acquire a set of specialized skills appropriate to his new environment."[2]

[1] Tabulations are given in Appendix B. The ratings on the ten-point scale were translated into the five classifications found in the tables. Since the raters used different numerical points on the scale to indicate success or lack of it, it was necessary to make a translation of these figures into a common scale. In order to test the reliability of translating these figures to a five-point scale each author independently made such translations and it was found that they agreed in 90 percent of the cases. Only the 284 appointees on whom the authors agreed as to ratings are included in the appendix tables. They form the basis on which generalizations are made in the text. The number of executives rated are divided per administration as follows: Roosevelt, 15; Truman, 107; Eisenhower, 158; and Kennedy, 25. The figures do not add up to 317 because of those executives who held office in more than one administration.

[2] Edward C. Banfield, "The Training of the Executive," in Carl J. Friedrich and Seymour E. Harris (eds.), Public Policy, Vol. 10 (1960), p. 36.

The raters also considered the more versatile men as better executive material than their single-minded colleagues. Thus, a businessman who had had a long history of service as a public official was most likely to achieve a high rating, and someone who had combined his business experience with the practice of law or who had had a variety of business interests was more likely to be successful than those who had remained with a single enterprise.

Ratings Related to Government Experience

Success as a political executive has a positive correlation with previous public service and with specific types of service. About 70 percent of the political executives and career employees were rated good to excellent, and about 55 percent of other noncareer personnel fell in the same categories. In contrast, much higher percentages of those who had had no service or whose contact with government was in Congress, party service, or part-time associations were given inferior ratings. Only 27 career officials were rated as compared with 169 in the noncareer ranks, but the findings appear to indicate that the generally held view that the career service produces men lacking in imagination and ability to adapt themselves to changes in party or philosophy is untrue; and that they are fully as successful as those who rise to political executive positions after having served in subordinate noncareer posts. Perhaps the career service constitutes a very valuable yet neglected source of potential political executive talent.

Raters were somewhat ambivalent as to the effect of public service at the state and local levels on successful performance as assistant secretaries. Sixty-seven executives had had experience of this nature. Only 4 percent of those with nonelective backgrounds were considered below average. Elective experience apparently has little effect on performance, although governors and men in similar positions had a larger proportion with excellent ratings.

Emphasis on prior knowledge of government procedures was all the more apparent when appointees were rated according to the length of previous administrative experience at all government levels. There was general agreement, for example, that those with less than two years' service did not measure up to their colleagues with longer terms in government.

Ratings According to Type of Business Background

A large proportion of those rated had had business backgrounds; and there were such marked variations in the performance ratings of men with different business experiences that further tabulation is called for. Men from primary careers in banking and finance, for instance, were given the highest ratings, over two-thirds being rated either good or excellent, and only slightly more than 10 percent either below average or poor. Executives from private industry, on the other hand, on which greatest reliance has been placed in the past—the manufacturing executives—were given much poorer ratings. Only 45 percent were better than fair and one out of every four was rated poor. Men from other types of business—trade, mining, and transportation—were assessed at approximately the same level as those from industry.

A significantly higher percentage of former businessmen who had held either subordinate positions in large companies or senior positions in smaller corporations became successful political executives. In fact, over 60 percent of the businessmen who came from such jobs were rated good or excellent as opposed to 40 percent of the top executives in largest firms. While hardly conclusive, these figures suggest that the latter found the transition to government service at subordinate levels a difficult one to make. Some top business executives became outstanding successes, but the majority were either only adequate or did not measure up to any desired standards. More junior executives or those in smaller companies, on the other hand, probably entered the government with fewer firmly held convictions and less public exposure. It is possible, too, that big business executives are accepted for status reasons, while lesser known men are much more carefully evaluated.

Ratings According to Age and Education Level

Since the job of a political executive requires both physical stamina and imagination, Bayless Manning contended that men in middle life are to be preferred since they are then at the height of their vigor and powers.[3] Marion Folsom enlarged this idea, stating, "The persons really needed for many of these positions are men in their late thirties or forties with 10 or 15 years of business experience and with several years in important administrative positions, especially in large organizations."[4]

The raters appeared to agree with these opinions and considered that there is no serious risk in employing the services of men below sixty years of age but that the risk progressively increases from that age on. While relatively few executives below the age of forty turned in excellent performances, a very large percentage were above average and would appear to be good risks. The relative youth of political executives apparently was no indication of a lack of mature judgment. But advancing age appeared to take a serious toll in their capacity to shoulder heavy responsibilities.

There was little correlation between the level of education and performance, according to the raters, as the proportion of political executives who were considered to be above average was approximately the same at every level of educational attainment. Those with master's degrees perhaps did slightly better than others, whereas men with doctorates were rated no higher than those who were only college graduates or who had not attended college at all.

Not without interest is the fact that those holding doctoral degrees and those who had no college education were the two groups having the highest percentage of political executives with below average ratings. The attainment of a doctor's degree in itself probably does not impair capacity for performing high level political executive service, but such specialization does not lead to the experience or develop the necessary personal characteristics for successful executive performance. On the other hand, men who have not had the advantage of higher education, unless they have outstanding personal qualities and a great deal of experience, may find executive service extremely difficult.

Ratings by Administration and Agency

There was little variation in rating either by party or administration. Truman executives did as well as Eisenhower appointees; Democrats

[3] *Organizing for National Security,* Inquiry of the Senate Subcommittee on National Policy Machinery of the Committee on Government Operations, 86 Cong. 2 sess. (1961), Vol. 1, pp. 457, 479-80.
[4] *Ibid.,* pp. 479-80.

were considered to be as good—or as bad—as Republicans in office. Neither was there much difference in the overall evaluations of executives who served in the domestic and security fields and in the independent agencies. Perhaps the most important agency variation occurred in the Treasury Department where responsible officials who rated their subordinates were satisfied that they had obtained the services of very competent and effective executives. On the other hand, those in Interior and Health, Education, and Welfare were much more critical, the notable exceptions rated highly only proving the rule.

In the area of foreign policy and defense, officials of the State Department were particularly pleased with the general level of performance of their political executives, including former Foreign Service officers. Raters in military services and the Department of Defense, on the other hand, were far from happy; only in the Department of the Army were the executives generally felt to be competent.

The polarization of the ratings in some domestic departments—particularly the high incidence of extreme incompetence—reflects recruiters' uneasy compromises in criteria for selection between administrative and policy competence and accommodation to political pressures, the latter more often than not being the deciding factor.

Background and Personal Characteristics Related to Performance

Businessman, banker, professor, or lawyer—which one is likely to make the best political executive? What special personal attributes are most useful to the able assistant secretary? When reviewing the individual performances of men they had known and worked with, the raters gave their opinions on relative advantages of certain career experiences and on the types of people who had proved most successful in office.

Importance of Occupational Background

The raters were mixed in their opinions, dividing almost evenly between those who saw some relationships between occupational background and efficiency in office and those who thought such background factors were only of minimal importance. The latter who rejected such occupational typing generally stressed personal characteristics, such as intellectual capacity or ability to get along well with people.

The relatively high assessments of men from the financial world is not easily explained but their success may lie in the breadth of outlook they must have to develop in dealing with the wide range of problems involving many industries and all levels of government. One investment banker who spent many years in the government explained the success of bankers as well as lawyers in the following way:

> Investment bankers and lawyers have a number of advantages which prepare them to do good work in the government. They're used to a variety of problems and a variety of subjects, in contrast with people who are experts in selling refrigerators, for example. They're used to working with big people. When they have business to do they go directly to the presidents of the firms rather than work through the lower hierarchy. These kinds of backgrounds give them an advantage in dealing with the multitude of problems one finds in government service and with the multitude of different participants in making any decision. In essence, then, their backgrounds equip them more adequately for "the art of the possible."

Another factor may be that a banker is used to making his own decisions and having to abide by them. One cabinet member, a former lawyer, observed that a particular investment banker was an effective political executive because he had had to make up his mind on how to use his own money. His were quite different—and individual—responsibilities from those facing businessmen in large organizations where decisions are essentially corporation products.

The ratings for businessmen recruited from nonfinancial institutions, particularly from manufacturing enterprises, were somewhat contradictory. Some raters considered that this group made poor executive material, construing it to be a result of training in big industrial enterprises. One investment banker who served in the Department of Defense observed:

> Competence and incompetence are found in business as in other professions. Businessmen are often the worst possible choice for some posts. Consider [a large corporation official]. There's no bigger stuffed shirt in the country and few people more gauche in their relations with Congress. There's nothing sacrosanct about businessmen, for God's sake, even though military generals seem to be in great awe of them.

And another with long government experience considered that:

Businessmen are often the hard-boiled type who are like ducks out of water in the government. They always made their own decisions in their companies even when opposed by their associates. They are not used to situations which require consensus.

There were other raters who agreed with the important Eisenhower official with many contacts in the business community who observed that "the chances of finding a good political administrator in the field of business are as good or bad as they are elsewhere."

Men who rise to the top of big business are generally very well equipped. They must be very broad men. Their companies become so complex that they tend to be like governmental units. People on Wall Street also tend to have broader thinking than those who come, say, from a small town in Illinois. They get a flood of information from all over the world which helps them overcome their parochial views.

Contrary to the general consensus, this Eisenhower official found big business to be the most fruitful recruiting ground.

The manager of a smaller or a family business tends not to be so good. He is too independent because he is a self-made man and looks down on anyone who is not. The businessmen who are in right-wing politics are typically from this background.

An official of a trade association argued that businessmen from large enterprises were more effective political executives than those who came from small firms because of the narrower experience range. He asserted: "General Electric and General Motors have big staffs with highly trained, competent people. People who are in big business are better equipped to serve in the government since they are emotionally in tune to a big operation."

The legal profession is often considered a "natural" for those interested in a political career. But whether this predilection for politics makes lawyers more effective executives is a matter for conjecture. Lawyers, of course, believe their legal training to be one of their biggest assets, even if they are appointed to positions where such a background is unnecessary. One lawyer—a cabinet officer—observed that his coprofessionals were particularly effective political executives because (like investment bankers) they were accustomed to working alone and using their own initiative. A career officer corroborated this view, considering the law basically the best training for most assistant secretary positions, especially if combined with a broader range of other interests. He cited the case of one highly regarded executive in his own agency who had had legal experience in all three branches of the government: as a law clerk with a justice of the Supreme Court, in a congressional office, and as an official in the executive branch. One non-lawyer political executive equivocated on this particular point, however. Lawyers, he said, may be effective "because they are used to fighting their way through a variety of forces in reaching consensus. On the other hand, they are not likely to be good administrators since they are not good at foreseeing future events. They can straighten out messes but have no capacity for predicting events or forces in the future."

Other raters regarded legal experience from a different perspective—as being helpful primarily in terms of substantive knowledge acquired rather than in skills developed. One deputy in a defense agency stated:

> Professional experience, primarily in the fields of business and corporation law, but also as a trial lawyer, give a breadth of knowledge and exposure which enables [a political executive] to understand many facets of this agency.

In spite of the generally high ratings given political executives whose primary occupational experience had been in the federal government, there was considerable disagreement about the role of career executives in politically sensitive positions. A few believed that the career service provided one of the best sources for federal executive recruitment. Others, while crediting civil servants with complete loyalty to the administration in power and with the capacity to deal adequately with policy issues, felt that their performance was less than adequate in practice because they feared that the publicity to which they were subjected as political executives might threaten their future careers. The debate centered on the Foreign Service, since it was the career group most frequently asked to supply political executives.

All of the Foreign Service officers who served as assistant secretaries and who were rated on their performance were given passing marks; none was rated below average or poor and nearly 70 percent were rated good or excellent. They were praised on ability in general terms, although the raters had some reservations as to the types of posts which Foreign Service officers could fill most effectively. They were considered particularly good as assistant secretaries and heads of geographical desks where they could use their expert knowledge of regional affairs derived from long years in the field. Moreover, it was felt that they could handle certain administrative or management posts which were nonsensitive. (This most decidedly did not include the Bureau of Security and Consular Affairs which was under constant congressional scrutiny.) Those posts which required maximum political exposure, particularly before Congress, such as under secretary or assistant secretary posts responsible for policy planning, were often considered unsuitable for Foreign Service officers.

On the other hand, some observers were doubtful of their suitability as a matter of general principle. One former Secretary of State observed that these career men were "pretty good" but nevertheless he preferred noncareer people in political executive posts.

It's too bad to use them in Washington when they can be put to better use out in the field. I would prefer to have noncareer people as assistant secretaries. Very often Foreign Service Officers don't have the breadth of experience required by these jobs. Also, noncareer people tend to have more fight and I wanted "no" men, not "yes" men in the department. I wanted men who were willing to leave if they had to because of the positions they took.

A key State Department recruiter had strong feelings against placing Foreign Service officers in political executive positions.

When you put a Foreign Service Officer in a political job he becomes a defender of the administration's point of view after awhile. He can't approach problems freely because he has argued for and defended the administration's policies. Even if they are bright and have great integrity, which they usually do, they are conditioned by their previous experience.

A Foreign Service Officer who is in his forties is likely to say to himself, "The top people presently in the Department will be gone in a few years and their successors will look back and want to know why certain things were done and who was responsible." Foreign Service Officers who are in responsible positions therefore tend to play it conservative and avoid taking risks.

Besides, Foreign Service Officers are far happier being ambassadors and they hate being assistant secretaries since it does involve them in politics.

An assistant secretary must be tough, expendable, willing to take risks and force the implementation of decisions down through the departmental desks. Look at [a newly appointed noncareer assistant secretary]. He has moved into his job like a breath of fresh air. He's not worried about political attacks or about being a hostage to anyone.

Personal Characteristics of the Able Executive

Some lawyers have made very successful political executives, some have not. So it is with investment bankers, Foreign Service officers, and those in other occupations and professions. Although raters were in disagreement as to whether a candidate's background and experience had any specific relationship to his successful performance in office, they held fairly positive views on the personal characteristics they would look for in the individuals they themselves would like to recruit or work with. It could be anticipated that some occupations lend themselves more directly to the development of skills and abilities directly related to the functions of a political executive than others.

Subject matter competence, for example, kept recurring as a deciding factor in the respective ratings of executives in the Departments of State and Health, Education, and Welfare; and it was foremost in the raters' eyes as an essential attribute for the successful candidate. Admittedly, ability to assimilate new knowledge quickly and usefully might be a substitute for experience in some instances—and it also was rated very high. So also were creativity, imagination, and initiative; cooperative attitude, trustworthiness, and loyalty; a broad perspective, and the ability to make quick decisions.

In their evaluations of under secretaries, assistant secretaries, and others of equivalent ranks, agency heads, fellow executives, and top career officials were asked to identify the characteristics with which they associated success or failure. Every effort was made, however, to relate their analysis of these characteristics to specific individuals in order to avoid parroting of clichés or vague, imprecise answers which conveyed little specific behavior content.

SUBJECT MATTER COMPETENCE. Twenty-one of the forty-three raters identified successful performance with substantive competence and sixteen considered that its lack had been the main cause for inadequate performance. The most frequently mentioned explanation for success was that executives had had previous experience in the general area of their responsibilities—that they had, in fact, been former civil servants or followed an appropriate profession or occupation outside the government.

When speaking in general terms, however, the raters tended to deprecate the importance of specialized knowledge and they praised the "generalist" with a knowledge of broad outlines of policy or procedures as the most effective executive. At times, detailed knowledge was considered a positive hindrance. The raters argued in the abstract that the necessary background and information could be acquired quickly when the executive came on the job. Nevertheless, despite this impersonal leaning toward the generalist, when it came down to personalities, both career officials and political executives alike emphasized the need for substantive knowledge. Where they tended to differ was in the degree of specialization and knowledge of minutiae. To illustrate, one career official with long experience in foreign affairs explained the relatively low rating he had given an under secretary because of his ignorance of foreign policy issues: "You can't run the Department of State without knowing the subject matter." Defense career executives shared this view in relation to their Department, stressing the need for a broad grasp of Defense issues rather than for detailed knowledge. They attributed the success of Donald Quarles, for example, in part to his work with the Sandia Corporation.

Officials in other departments also stressed the need for generalized experience. A Secretary of the Treasury listed some of the prescribed qualifications for the assistant secretary in charge of international affairs. The appointee would need understanding of monetary affairs, know where and from whom to borrow money, and what price to give to potential borrowers. Moreover, he should have some foreign experience and some language capability.

Justice officials emphasized the importance of certain types of legal knowledge in certain assistant attorney general posts. In the criminal division, for example, one deputy attorney general observed that a candidate must have criminal law experience. Such experience—particularly in the division itself—was important because of the significance of precedent and procedures in dealing with criminal cases. Similarly, the success of an assistant attorney general in the tax division was attributed in part to his previous experience as a tax lawyer. This assistant attorney general was considered to be "three jumps ahead" of someone who had not had such a background.

Only a few raters emphasized relatively narrow technical competence, such as knowledge of banking laws or agricultural stabilization programs. The majority stressed the importance of contact and familiarity with public affairs in general and specific areas of policy-making in particular. For example, a State Department official was critical of successful businessmen because of their concentration on business affairs to the exclusion of public problems: "Often they haven't read anything in history or economics." The problem for businessmen was that, if they broadened their interests to include public affairs, their energies were not, in his view, sufficiently narrowly channeled for them to succeed in the business world.

INNATE CAPACITY. Innate capacity, usually meaning intellectual ability, was considered second only to substantive competence in explaining the successful performance of political executives. It was clear that the raters were emphasizing a fundamental quality which went beyond the mere capacity to acquire information and technical data. It was possessed by individuals who could grasp basic issues quickly and who were able to adapt themselves to new, constantly changing situations. These men were able to perceive interrelationships clearly. They were able to take necessary steps to arrive at and implement a decision.

Both supervisors and career officials were conscious of the importance of these qualities in the men they recruited or worked for. One career officer described an assistant secretary in the following terms: "He could look at any issue and with his incisive mind ask the right questions which got to the heart of the matter. He knew the exact depth to which he should go in exploring any issue. He never made any decisions based on superficial knowledge." And, in speaking of another assistant secretary whom he had also highly rated, he explained, "He had the same incisive mind but he was too young to know the proper depth to which he should explore problems. Also he tended to make judgments too quickly."

Another career official thought highly of those who "had the ability to grasp and analyze problems and to see the pitfalls and advantages in various solutions. They were sharp intellectually and could analyze and synthesize a solution from differing positions." He considered that management ability was important but that it could be developed on the job by an able person. One secretary gave high ratings to two assistant secretaries because of their "intelligence, imagination and capacity to tackle new and challenging problems," and he gave a very low rating to another subcabinet officer because "he did not give any evidence of a real concentration of intelligence."

Other characteristics closely associated with basic intelligence and which raters related to success were creativity, imagination, and initiative. Successful executives had to be able to shoulder responsibilities independently and arrive at solutions without "handholding by the agency chief." Conversely, a serious criticism of the less able was their inability to make decisions. They always wanted to pass the buck. One under secretary was described as being "too soft-hearted. He simply found it impossible to make a tough decision, although in many other ways he was a superb appointee." Another under secretary was described by his chief as always trying to get along very well with everyone. It was almost impossible to pin him down to a problem; he was always "flitting around in a breeze."

RAPPORT WITH ASSOCIATES. The ability to work effectively with others in a large organization was considered essential for the able appointee. He had to learn to use his staff to advantage and to develop a relationship of mutual trust and cooperation with career officials.[5]

Inability to get along with those around him considerably diminished the effectiveness of an assistant secretary described by an under secretary as a "table pounder" who tended to grate on other people's nerves. Another assistant secretary was talked of by his agency chief—a close friend—as being "like sandpaper." His "analyses were good but were executed in a brutal and ruthless manner which was calculated to cause trouble and did so."

The need for close rapport with members of Congress and congressional committees was also frequently mentioned by raters as essential for the successful political executive.

PERSEVERANCE. Career officials required long hours and devotion to duty of their political executives, and considered that many had failed because they were unwilling to exert themselves. Defense career officials were particularly critical. Political appointees "came primarily

[5] On this point it is perhaps important again to note that both career officials and agency heads recognized this factor as important.

for prestige and for the social life. They seemed to be most concerned with their status in the department, with their titles and car privileges, and so forth." Another appointee in a domestic agency was called "a complete bust." He was unwilling "to do a single solitary thing to earn his money. He apparently felt that he was lending his great name to the government and that was all he had to do." And an assistant attorney general who was given a very low rating was spoken of as a member of the "Two T" club. He worked in Washington from Tuesday to Thursday and spent the rest of the time in his home town engaged in private law practice. "An ordinary guy who was just fooling around in the government" was the description of an assistant secretary of Commerce. "He had retired and wanted something to do. He'd put in eight hours but he certainly didn't lose any sleep worrying about departmental problems." The same type of thing was said of an assistant attorney general. "All he did was wait to get appointed to the federal bench. He didn't really knuckle down to his job and he relied on his subordinates too much. He was really just a figurehead."

OBJECTIVITY AND SELF-RELIANCE. Many of the raters, both political executives and career officials, were particularly critical of executives whom they described as excessively partisan, narrow in approach, lacking in objectivity, and inordinately responsive to the pressures of special interests, whether within or outside the department.

A career officer described several assistant secretaries who were less than adequate for these reasons. Of these, one was "primarily a politician who was interested in Washington's social life." Another was a good administrator but at the same time, "some of his decisions were straight political"; for example, when he shifted the location of a field office at the request of a powerful senator.

A senior civil servant in a politically sensitive agency gave his lowest ratings to men who "knuckled under to political pressure." In his view, the effective political executive had to have "political savvy" but he also needed political independence. Although he believed that most of the men in that agency obtained their positions through their party affiliations, the able appointee had to develop a sense of detachment to withstand the pressures to which he would be subjected. This career officer's agency head was also aware of the fine line that had to be drawn between political sensitivity and excessive partisanship. In rating one subordinate he commented that he was "too political; he had many friends on the Hill and elsewhere in political circles who subjected him to political pressure." Excessive attention to political pull was considered to be particularly characteristic of Truman appointees in the domestic departments.

Narrowness and pettiness appear in many agencies. One career officer in the Defense establishment rhetorically asked the question concerning a political executive he rated: "Did you ever hear of [the political executive] doing anything in the Department except in terms of what was good for him? He never once considered what might be the interest of the Department." And in another department, a career officer was vehement in his criticism of an assistant secretary who was later under public attack because of his left-wing politics. "He was the very worst of all appointments, not only because of his left-wing ties and sympathies, but because he was egotistical and believed he knew everything. At the same time he surrounded himself with the damnedest bunch of hacks the department ever had." Again, an appointee was viewed with disfavor because he continually acted as if he was being discriminated against because of his nationality. "He always thought he was being persecuted. He was very high-strung and had a bad temper and was just generally hard to get along with. His attitude toward the use of official cars indicated his problem. He always wanted a car available the minute he asked for it and he wanted it to stay with him whenever he left the department, rather than allowing it to return according to departmental policy."

A number of raters were critical of executives who were "captured" by units in their own agency or by outside interest groups. One assistant secretary, in their view, carried such partiality for certain divisions too far. If one of his favorites sponsored a cause, he would support it and would refuse to listen to arguments from any other side. Another political executive apparently conceived his role as chairman of the board and concerned himself chiefly with public relations.

> He developed confidence in the staff of the office of the secretary and therefore would sign anything that was put in front of him. He simply refused to go into any subject of internal management. When he left, one of the staff made a comment to the effect that "there goes our automatic signature."

A Defense Secretary, while generally approving the performance of an assistant secretary in one of the military services, criticized him for his indulgence toward his own service which he would support in controversies over military roles without really taking a careful look at the issues involved. In the same context, a Defense assistant secretary was described as a spokesman for the American Legion, and another in a domestic agency, who later was severely censured for favoritism, was spoken of by his chief as "inherently honest but [he] permitted himself to be used by people who were interested in influencing his decisions."

LOYALTY. Some agency heads were particularly concerned about the question of loyalty, considering that an effective political executive should have "the moral courage to express an opinion which might be contrary to his chief's, but be willing to carry out a decision even though it was not in conformity with his own views." One secretary gave high ratings to men who "did everything they were asked in full and undiminished measure," such as defending highly controversial programs; another in the same department emphasized "complete loyalty" in making his evaluations. The most effective executives were "good team players who were able to get others to cooperate with them while the less effective were those who were anxious to please others and were a little too ready to sacrifice principle for expedience."

ATTITUDE TO POLICY. Conforming to the party line on policy issues was remarkable by its absence in the raters' catalog of personal characteristics likely to produce the most effective political executives. Its nonappearance in the ratings is all the more significant when it is considered that the political nature of these appointments is in part justified by the administration's need to maintain control of policy at all times and in all areas.

First of all, it may be noted, the party line is frequently hard to define. The chances, of course, of recruiting appointees who have conscious aims on the overall program and specific issues akin to the administration's are small. And, perhaps, within the relatively narrow confines of the average assistant secretary's range of decision-making, adherence to a general political platform—if there is one—may be irrelevant. In any event, not all political executives have strong views on policy; many join the government with no clear perception of their agency's past or future doctrine and willingly adopt the current departmental position. Many, too, may have helped to develop agency policy from a lower level.

Whatever the explanation, conformity and acceptance of existing policy are not considered essential to success.

In effect, however, regardless of the above obviously desirable attributes, recruiters are still faced with the problem of finding men with the proper qualifications for specific positions. Reference to generalized lists of qualifications may impede rather than facilitate recruitment. The satisfaction of only a few of the criteria may qualify a man for a specific post under a given set of circumstances. Furthermore, the man who, on paper, has the appearance of an ideal background may be a total failure in a crisis. The prior assessment of a man's capacity, given his unique set of personal experiences, temperament, values and attitudes—particularly when entering an entirely new environment like the federal government—remains an Olympian task.

10

Reviewing the System

THE SELECTION OF MEN for the second echelon of the President's executive team reflects many of the basic characteristics and values of the American political system. Having responded over the years to the cross-pressures of conflicting interests—executive and legislative, business and professional, public and private—the process appears to be haphazard, for no standard formal procedure has been devised for locating, classifying, and enticing qualified men into these positions. An even more important point is that no system has been evolved for preparing potential candidates adequately for their duties in office. As a result, the government is largely dependent on untrained people to fill its policy-making positions. A relatively small proportion of the appointees have held more than one appointment at the federal political level (less than one-fifth between 1933 and 1961); and although those who have moved up from the career ranks are better versed in government than their counterparts from the private sector, they have often had a different orientation which, in the eyes of some recruiters, is definitely a drawback in political decision-making.

Yet, as the case studies have established, this odd assortment of methods and practices (termed somewhat euphemistically the selection process) produced many able and experienced assistant secretaries and under secretaries during the Truman, Eisenhower, and Kennedy administrations, the period under review. It also produced others who were less than able and who reflected no credit either on their administration or on the executive branch of the government. There is no telling how many good executives turned down appointments later filled by less competent individuals—or how many good executives were unable to qualify for a variety of extraneous reasons other than ability. But it is obvious that many of the 108 appointments studied were filled by compromise candidates: the recruiters' third or fourth choices.

What then are the major findings of this study and how best may the appointment system be modified in order to attract and retain in office the best qualified presidential management team?

Summary of Major Findings

Selection for the subcabinet echelon is a highly decentralized and personalized process revolving around the respective department and agency heads. It is pluralistic and inconsistent, varying over time during the course of an administration and from department to department. Since each cabinet officer relies to a large extent on his own circle of acquaintances, his subordinates tend to mirror his own image: businessmen look for businessmen; men with long experience in public affairs require a similar background of their assistants; and lawyers look for likely recruits in the legal community. The President is relatively inactive in the search for second-level executives, particularly after the first round of appointments have been made. The White House, however, has attempted to establish standards, especially in regard to political background. In addition, it has resisted the nomination of those considered to be politically unacceptable. The department and agency heads have been given wide latitude in their selection of subordinates and have, therefore, tended to pick men who subscribe to their own way of thinking, whether or not this diverges from the official presidential approach.

The traditional patronage interests play relatively modest roles. The two most common routes to appointment, via the intercession of congressmen and political party organizations in the recruitment process, have to a great extent atrophied, in part because secretaries and administrators largely supervise their own staffing efforts and often set greater store on relevant experience than on political dexterity. The clientele to which congressmen and party officials have access tend to have impeccable political credentials but usually lack the grounding and perspective necessary in the management fields. The third traditional source of patronage—the interest groups—generally restricts its role to setting the metes and bounds within which recruiters must operate. All three patronage groups can, and do, exercise an effective veto over objectionable candidates.

Deviations in the career lines of individuals appointed to the various departments demonstrate the secretary's increasing emphasis on specialized abilities for certain positions. In effect, there are "natural" sources of specific political executive talents. The fact that bankers are prominently represented in the Treasury and Westerners in the Interior indicates, of course, an attempt to win interest group support. But it is also an endeavor to obtain appointees with a sufficient commitment to the appropriate area of public policy, if not actual experience in that area.

A substantial number of the under secretaries and assistant secretaries serving during the last few decades have had some form of government administrative experience before appointment. Many among them have also some prior knowledge of their respective departments' activities, often in other appointive positions. Nevertheless, too many recruits arrive from the private sector who are totally unfamiliar with their work as political executives; and too many appointees leave their secretarial positions before they have been able to contribute effectively to the presidential program—some even before one year is up.

On the whole, secretaries, administrators, and senior career officials tend to be reasonably well pleased with their subordinates or political superiors. But there are marked variations in the assessments of executive performance among departments: those positions demanding greater expertise tend to be filled by men of considerable ability, probably because of the greater care taken in their selection. Expertise, as such, however, is valued less highly than a broad general background in the policy area; and, in fact, personal attributes seem to contribute more to success than occupational history. The man with some government experience is considered to be more likely to succeed than his colleague without such experience; and, more often than not, former career executives are highly favored by their superiors, even by those recruiters who confess to considerable prejudice against career civil servants playing a political role.

Appointees themselves are, for the most part, extremely well satisfied with their lot as assistant secretaries and under secretaries. They consider that the rewards of service quite definitely outweigh the many disadvantages: only two of the 108 interviewed wished that they had not served. The majority leave their appointments for a number of personal reasons related to financial loss, job tenure, or career advantage. Seldom are conditions of service more than an aggravating factor. To be sure, most appointees complain about certain features of their work, such as too heavy a workload, long hours, and public exposure. Quite a few of these complaints, whether warranted or not, cannot and presumably should not be allayed since they are directly related to a political system which is dependent on the administration's managerial team to implement party programs at the departmental level.

Candidates who accept assistant secretaryships and undersecretaryships must expect to be politically exposed; they must expect to be chosen in part because of their political connections, if they have them; and they must often expect to shoulder the heavy responsibility of top-level decisions without adequate training and policy-making experience.

Implications for the Recruitment Process

The modification of an appointment process inextricably intertwined with the total political system is a perilous undertaking. Existing appointment procedures for political executive office are the result of decades of practice and reflect the configuration of interests concerned with the operation of the federal government. Moreover, the present system reacts to pressures and distributes benefits among the contending participants and to the public at large: benefits which may be sacrificed by ill-considered changes. The adoption of new ways of doing things can often lead to untoward consequences as the total political organism accommodates to a new component. Nevertheless, it is obvious that changing times call for changes in the system. Nothing radical is envisaged; but the case studies have highlighted certain remediable defects. The fact that they have already been the subject of serious reappraisal is illustrated by the direction of President Johnson's 1965 recruitment drive.

Based on this review of practices during the past two decades, there are several recommendations which while not new should certainly be reexamined with greater care. Modifications along these general lines have been apparent in the 1965 reorganization and staffing of the White House personnel office, but the findings of this study have brought the need for change into sharper focus.

A More Active Presidential Voice

In only eight of the 108 appointments studied did the President and White House staff play a dominant role in second-level recruitment. In twenty-four additional instances, the secretary cooperated closely with the presidential recruiting team but nevertheless retained the deciding vote.

Whatever the merits of such a system, the President has a legitimate stake in these subcabinet appointments which was obviously not met during the period under review. He could spare relatively few hours for the incessant scramble that characterizes the selection process and therefore delegated authority to his department and agency heads.

The typical secretary's approach to recruitment remains distinctly personal. For example, as opposed to the twenty-four cases in which the secretary or administrator relied on the advice of White House staff, there were sixty instances in which he worked through his own circle of acquaintances. This heavy reliance on personal relationships, induced very often by ignorance of departmental operations, led to restricted utilization of available recruitment sources and poor representation of the variety of skills required to run the federal establishment. In addition, too, the case studies showed that this freedom in staffing subcabinet posts can, on certain occasions, buttress policy positions and programs the President may be trying to alter or modify.

To meet the problems resulting from such haphazard recruiting, a more effective White House recruiting operation should be organized. Close proximity with the President himself should emphasize an important aspect absent during these three administrations: these appointments are and must remain *presidential* in character; they should not be held by departmental attaches. An effective White House organization will ensure that the President's standards of performance and qualifications for service will be met more appropriately. Concentration on selection here allots more time and continuity to a task which normally receives only intermittent attention from secretaries harassed by myriad duties seemingly more important than filling a vacant office.

In effect, it is recommended that the concentrated effort in recruiting that has worked most successfully at the beginning of the Eisenhower, Kennedy, and Johnson administrations be continued throughout the duration of each administration. Instead of allowing the dissolution of the "talent hunts," as these impromptu recruiting efforts have been called, these searches should be institutionalized, not in the sense that they become routine, but in the sense that the effort is persistent, recognized, and given adequate support by those centrally involved.

PRECEDENTS FROM PREVIOUS AND CURRENT ADMINISTRATIONS. In the Truman administration a personnel office was set up for the first time in the White House under Donald Dawson, an assistant to the President. Its work was primarily that of a clearinghouse, receiving the names of candidates from all sources but doing little in the way of active recruiting or evaluation. Moreover, it focused attention on meeting the demands of those whose stakes were political in nature rather than on the promotion of effective policy leadership. Dawson's operation saw to it, however, that many qualified career people were appointed to political executive positions.

In the Eisenhower administration, a slightly more ambitious attempt was made under Sherman Adams. But it, also, was little more than a distribution center because of the large number of candidates who were being considered for a wide variety of positions before they had been appropriately evaluated. The office's effectiveness was further damaged by an early attempt to impose political criteria in the selection of men for career positions, bringing down the wrath of those who saw this as a partisan raid on the classified service.

The Kennedy administration tackled the problem in a different manner. A special assistant to the President, Dan H. Fenn, Jr., formerly of the Harvard Business School, organized a limited presidential recruiting program which concentrated solely on the highest policy-making positions in the government, for the most part at the appointive level. The office set up a roster of men who were considered qualified for various types of positions and who had been found acceptable on political grounds. It was anticipated that this roster would not exceed 500 in number. The office also began creating a network of "contact men" who could be relied on to provide names of potential candidates and to give frank evaluations of those who were under serious consideration. These contact men were chosen because of the range of their acquaintance and their presumed capacity to judge the qualities necessary for high public office; they were, more often than not, former federal officials themselves. Fenn's operation also recognized the importance of close working relationships with agency heads who would in most instances make the final decision on appointments.

The appointment of John W. Macy, Jr., as the key man in President Johnson's 1965 recruitment drive and the adoption of systematic and codified procedures in the countrywide search for talented men for political executive office perhaps forecasts a continuous, coordinated personnel effort at the White House. However, without a detailed review of specific Johnson appointments similar to those undertaken for the three preceding administrations, it is impossible to foretell the direction of this Johnson-Macy "quest for quality." Appointments at this level still retain their political character but Macy's dual role as chairman of the Civil Service Commission and the President's chief personnel adviser has led to a more centralized operation and a more thoroughgoing appraisal of potential candidates for political positions in the government. About half of the first round of 1965 presidential appointments were filled by men with some form of public service background; and the others were filled by men drawn in almost equal proportions from industrial, labor, academic, and legal sources.

Expanding Recruitment Sources

The selection process for second-echelon executives must of necessity remain political both in form and fact. Given this determinant and the broad range of skills and abilities required, there is no single career line which apparently develops better candidates for executive office than any other. Each has its advantages and disadvantages in the political, management, or substantive realms. However, the drawbacks in appointing political executives with certain occupational backgrounds have perhaps been overemphasized. Career civil service sources, state and local government, Capitol Hill, and certain professions, for example, have been regarded with mixed emotions as potential recruiting grounds during preceding administrations. The case studies, although not representative of the total group, showed a growing tendency to use more diversified fields of selection which may be reflected in future administrations. Kennedy's small sample of twenty-four, for instance, included representatives of the press, labor unions, political parties, and nonprofit organizations, as well as a fairly equal number from the business, legal, public service, and academic fields. The case studies also showed that Kennedy had a greater inclination to use men with strong political affiliations.

PROFESSIONAL AND BUSINESS CIRCLES. The key to any improved recruitment from the private sector is White House involvement in selection. Few are likely to refuse office if the President says, "I need YOU." Such a personal appeal will redound to the candidates' credit in their own occupational circles and lead to far less opposition from corporation chairmen, law partners, university administrators, and the like. Apart from this crucial, yet relatively modest, current adjustment in the selection process, better understanding in professional quarters of what executive service entails and a better public image of the federal service itself would broaden the scope of choice considerably. More business and professional sources would be open to the recruiter, too, if certain conditions of service were adjusted so as not to impose too great a personal sacrifice on those who agree to serve the government as opposed to their colleagues who remain in the private sector. These aspects are discussed later in the chapter.

CAREER CIVIL SERVICE. The career service has been, and still is, a major source of recruitment for undersecretaryships and assistant secretaryships. (Among the case studies about a quarter had had such careers.) The Johnson administration has made a deliberate effort to make effective use of this recruiting ground. Some observers have urged the inclusion of certain positions at the assistant secretary level within the career service while others have simply urged greater utilization of career men in what are openly political posts. It is evident, however, that a closer scrutiny needs to be made of this rich reservoir of experience.

Except in the Department of State, there has been extremely limited use of career executives in subcabinet posts. Occasionally, as in the case of Jesse Donaldson and Bert Barnes in the Post Office Department, Dale Doty in Interior, Daniel Bell in Treasury, and Thomas Blaisdell in the Department of Commerce, career men have advanced to the rank of assistant secretary or under secretary. In many instances, experienced career men, having the confidence of their superiors and the temerity to move into the unprotected ranks, have performed extremely effectively.

A major deterrent to increased recruitment from the career area is the impact of executive office on later service. At the end of the Truman administration, for example, Vernon Northrop was appointed Under Secretary of the Interior after working several decades in that department. Whatever his hopes about being retained, he found that the Eisenhower team no longer wanted his services. On the other hand, some career executives outside the State Department have been able to maintain their positions. In addition to Foreign Service officers who survived transitions, Wilfred McNeil stayed on as Assistant Secretary of Defense from 1947 through 1959, weathering the 1953 transition. Lyle Garlock, the Assistant Secretary of the Air Force under Eisenhower, remained on in the Kennedy administration, retiring only because of ill health.[1]

In the Department of State, there has been a traditional practice of appointing career diplomats to secretarial positions. Since 1853, when the first assistant secretary post was established, over one-third of the appointees at that level have come from the career service. After the initial wave of appointments in the Eisenhower administration, an equal balance was maintained between career service officers and noncareer appointees at the secretarial level, but the Kennedy administration did not follow this practice. Kennedy's recruiting officials deliberately sought noncareer people for secretarial posts and appointed career Foreign Service officers only as a last resort; they felt that these career men could not serve with sufficient enthusiasm in a new administration.

Nevertheless, in the belief of John Macy's recruiting team and on the evidence of the case studies, there seems to be no reason in terms of experience or temperament to bar career officials from political executive positions in any department. Improvement in the treatment of the career service to fit men for high policy responsibilities as well as the more routine managerial tasks will perhaps make it an even more attractive recruitment source.

POLITICAL SOURCES. Political parties are unlikely to play a more useful

[1] See Paul T. David and Ross Pollack, *Executives for Government* (Brookings Institution, 1957), pp. 143-44, for a positive view of the possibilities of career men returning to career ranks after serving in sensitive posts.

role in the near future despite urging that they should do so. They tend to see recruitment as a means of ensuring the next election, and are more interested in patronage which, to them, seems "like bread and butter, or like a shelter in a car—a place to stay and a means of getting somewhere."[2] They are less concerned with management as an essential element in an administration's success and less devoted to the substantive aspects of government programs.

Party organizations are based on a substantially different substructure of American society than that from which political executives are recruited. The national and state committees and their functionaries tend to be concerned with rewarding individuals like themselves—men and women who have worked hard at various political levels to achieve victory for their party. Few of the assistant and under secretaries appointed during the Truman and Eisenhower administrations owed their appointments primarily to their influence within the Democratic or Republican National Committees or with state and local party organizations.

Despite this somewhat negative view of the party organizations as recruiting machinery, there are some hopeful signs. The Democratic Advisory Council, an adjunct of the Democratic National Committee, provided a significant source of manpower at the beginning of the Kennedy administration. In large part, the members were men with a presidential and national orientation rather than a congressional and local outlook, and many had earlier held positions at the federal level. Eighteen Council members were selected for appointments by President Kennedy: three cabinet officers (Orville Freeman, Arthur Goldberg, and Abraham Ribicoff); two agency heads (Robert C. Weaver and James E. Webb); three under secretaries (Chester Bowles, Henry Fowler, and Charles Murphy); five assistant secretaries (Archibald Cox, Averell Harriman, Paul Nitze, George L. P. Weaver, and G. Mennen Williams); and five in other positions (Adlai Stevenson, Thomas Finletter, Walter Heller, Arthur Schlesinger, Jr., and J. Kenneth Galbraith). Obviously, many of these men were sufficiently prominent to have been on any list of eligibles. Council membership for others, however, was a significant factor in their later political appointments.

[2] Harvey C. Mansfield, "Political Parties, Patronage, and the Federal Service," in The American Assembly, *The Federal Government Service: Its Character, Prestige, and Problems* (1954), p. 90.

In 1961, the Republican National Committee established the National Republican Citizens Committee. Under it, the Critical Issues Council was headed by Dr. Milton Eisenhower. The council had twenty-two prominent Republicans as members, many of whom were former officeholders in the Eisenhower administration. It was responsible for developing Republican positions on major public issues prior to the 1964 presidential campaign. In many ways, this Council paralleled the Democratic Advisory Council; its membership (or that of any successor organization) could be utilized in a similar manner—as a possible source of political executive recruitment when a Republican administration again comes to power.

Political sources at the state and local levels have produced a number of top-level executives during the course of the three preceding administrations. Men such as Abraham Ribicoff, Orville Freeman, Luther Hodges, Douglas McKay, Paul McNutt, and Frank Murphy have moved from state governorships to the key posts in their various departments and agencies. Others (although a small proportion of the total group) have become assistant secretaries and under secretaries. Former mayors, tax commissioners, and the like have also been appointed and there has been a fair sprinkling of legislative assistants from the Hill; the latter were particularly noticeable in Kennedy's entourage. Elective government officials at all levels have not been too popular as a potential source of executive recruitment in the past; but it may well be that political acumen and the legislator's perspective will be found more desirable by future Presidents.

Understanding the Role of the Public Service

Men in private occupations seldom have a clear picture of the public service. Dedicated to their professions or their business activities, they have little time to develop either an awareness of the complexities of government work or of the challenges it presents. They have general impressions, often negative, but these impressions are frequently lacking in specific content.

EARLY GOVERNMENT EXPERIENCE. Some of the best political executives have learned their jobs from the ground up, advancing from assistantships step by step to the second echelon; but few followed this route between 1945 and 1961. More accepted junior positions for a short period and then returned to the private sector with a fairly good working knowledge of the government which stood them in good stead when they ventured into public office again. Lately, a conscious effort has been made to develop apprenticeship schemes along these lines which will at the same time provide a reservoir of qualified executives and expand the sources of recruitment.

Such devices have considerable merit, but some of the suggestions to date have been overly elaborate and are therefore not likely to attract support. Moreover, their proposed use as recruiting systems, at least as it applies to political executive positions, ignores the crucial personal and political considerations which must enter every selection decision. Nevertheless, some of these programs, if simplified and properly planned, could perform a useful function.

One device suggested by George McGhee, a political executive with experience in both the Truman and Kennedy administrations, is the creation of a "National Reserve List" comparable to military reserve corps. Under the direction of national and local boards of leading citizens, many of whom should have had federal experience themselves, young men and women would be enlisted to receive training both through study materials and in-service activities. They would be obligated to undertake two years' full-time employment during their first five years in the Reserve. These reservists would then make up a permanent roster of individuals available to the government in an emergency. In McGhee's view, the results would be threefold: better prepared executives, greater public confidence in executive ability, and better geographic distribution of potential recruits.

Other programs actually established in recent years supply formal training for people of all ages. One of these is the National Defense Reserve administered by the Office of Emergency Planning (OEP) in the Executive Office. Started in 1956, this roster is composed of men from various elements of the civilian economy who have indicated a willingness to accept executive positions during emergencies. In late 1961 this roster included the names of 2600 individuals who were designated to serve in seventeen different agencies. OEP has attempted to enlist men who have top-grade management skills suitable for positions just below the political level. Men with a government background are considered particularly desirable, and a number with extensive senior career or political executive experience were found in the 1960 roster, including Charles Coolidge, Struve Hensel, Najeeb Halaby, Vincent Burke, Jr., William Benton, Paul Hoffman, Brian Holland, Edward W. Barrett, Tracy Voorhees, Lothair Teetor, Theodore Streibert, Mansfield Sprague, John M. Redding, Philip Ray, Robert Ramspeck, and Thomas Pike.[3]

OEP and the other agencies needing manpower in emergencies provide training through biennial conferences, regional conferences, and through appropriate materials describing current developments. As yet, there has been no attempt to recruit from such a reserve. Agency interest has varied; some, such as the Business and Defense Services Administration, have taken the program seriously, while others have given it only lip service.

In 1961 the Brookings Institution inaugurated a Public Affairs Fellowship Program designed to give representatives of business, labor, agriculture, and the professions a combined program of intensive education and actual working experience at decision- and policy-making levels in federal agencies. The program lasts five months during which the interns are allocated projects which make positive contributions to the work of the agency to which they are assigned. The fellows, usually relatively young men, are destined for private careers, but it is hoped that they will be more favorably inclined toward the public service as a result of their internship.

Opportunities for more mature men from the private sector are increasingly available as the relationships between public and private institutions become closer. Advisory boards and committees have proliferated as federal programs have expanded. Businessmen, scientists, and engineers especially have had a closer view of government methods through government contracts dealing with many vital functions. Take, for example, the research and development contracts of the Department of Defense and the military agencies, and the complete outside management of certain activities in the Atomic Energy Commission.

A BETTER PUBLIC IMAGE. Nearly all the appointees who were the subject of case studies derived considerable satisfaction from their federal service. Most of them considered that it had either had no effect on their private careers or that it was a material asset to them later in life,

[3] Executive Office of the President, Office of Civil and Defense Mobilization, *The National Defense Executive Reserve: Directory* (April 15, 1960).

while only four thought that the experience had been detrimental. Appointees may have had to change jobs in returning to private life—and many of them did—but it was generally to their career advantage. This favorable majority experience is in sharp contrast to the substantial number who originally hesitated to accept appointment because it might harm their private careers or personal circumstances. The gap between preconceived, somewhat pessimistic ideas about federal employment and later reactions would seem to be the result of a general lack of communication between the public and the private worlds on the realities of federal office.

This popular misconception of the political appointee's role does not mean that men in private professional circles think poorly of their government colleagues. On the contrary, the most likely potential recruits in all occupations—those at relatively senior management levels—have more respect for federal executives than the less well-educated or those in lower grade positions.[4] But public office stands poorly in comparison to their own jobs, and senior executives are not particularly willing to trade the private for the public sector.

It is therefore to be hoped that some measures will be taken to improve the knowledge which private individuals have of government employment. It should also be possible to capitalize on the generally favorable attitude of many top-grade professional and business people to promote interest in political assignments. No amount of attention to the procedures for selecting political executives will overcome impediments to recruitment rooted in the features of public office which are unattractive to otherwise eligible men. President Eisenhower emphasized this rather strongly when he called for an end to the belief that "political life was somewhat degrading—that politics was primarily a contest, with the spoils to the victor and the public paying the bill."[5] The later Fenn operation under President Kennedy was a positive effort to take advantage of wider sources of recruitment and to assist in overcoming the reluctance of qualified people to serve.

High-powered public relations campaigns to improve the "image" of political executives are unnecessary for knowledgeable executives and scientists. Among them are men who have served in appointive posi-

---

[4] See Franklin P. Kilpatrick, Milton C. Cummings, Jr., and M. Kent Jennings, *The Image of the Federal Service* (Brookings Institution, 1964).

[5] Address delivered at the commencement exercises, University of Notre Dame, South Bend, Indiana, June 5, 1960.

tions and who can provide first-hand information. The Task Force on Personnel and Civil Service of the Second Hoover Commission recommended that such ex-political executives "keep their hands in" public affairs at the state and local level in order to encourage others by precept and example to take a positive attitude toward the public service. Both potential candidates and their employers need such reeducation.

Removing Obstacles to Acceptance

Although it must be conceded that preoccupation with private careers is a major deterrent to the recruitment of able political executives, it is by no means the only serious factor. Dedication to private interest certainly precludes public office for many men, but there are a number of others greatly attracted to the federal service who find the terms under which they would have to accept appointments very difficult to stomach. Some of these conditions, such as possible harassment by Congress and the unwieldy, slow-grinding wheels of bureaucracy, are inherent in the political system. But others are not congenital defects and could be modified without upsetting the intricate balance of the system itself. Such are problems relating to salary, conflict of interest, inadequate orientation, and job security.

Salary

In spite of the substantial 1964 pay raises and President Johnson's determination to close the gap between salaries in the public and private sectors, inadequate compensation is still a deterrent to acceptance of political executive positions. It is also a factor in the decisions of many men to leave the government.

Virtually every group that has studied the problem of high-level staffing in the executive branch has concluded that, because government salaries tend to lag, the disparity between public and private salaries remains of decisive importance. If an effort is made to recruit men for even longer periods of service, the problem of compensation will become more serious. Successful executives and professional men have been willing in the past to leave their businesses and professions for a limited period of time; but they frequently observed upon leaving that they had had to return to their private occupations to recoup their losses, which were often considerable.[6]

The impact of relatively low salaries is felt most keenly by those who are at midcareer. Such men have substantial obligations: mortgage payments, educational expenses, insurance premiums, medical costs, and the like. In the opinion of the Jackson Subcommittee, a man at this stage makes the best political executive in that he is "bold and innovative" but "he may be at the point where he can least afford additional expenses or a reduction of income."[7] Therefore the recruiters must seek their candidates among those who are already beyond the height of their powers and are preparing for retirement, or they must rely on younger men who are perhaps less experienced and less mature in their judgment.

At the time the appointees were interviewed in 1960 and 1961, over three-quarters said that they had hesitated to accept because of personal difficulties; at least half of them emphasized the financial aspect. These interviews took place before the 1964 federal pay raises were enacted; and it is possible that, as a result, financial questions are now no longer as great an obstacle to some assistant secretaries and under secretaries as they once were. Nevertheless, the pay raises and compensation are still far less than those recommended by the Randall Commission whose arguments for adequate reimbursement are hard to dispute in light of the case study findings.[8]

The Randall Commission did not adopt the principle of comparability between federal political executive salaries and high-level business

[6] In general, the pattern of federal executive salaries has been as follows: At the beginning of the Truman administration cabinet secretaries received $15,000, under secretaries $10,000, assistant secretaries $9,000. A general executive salary readjustment in October 1949 raised secretaries to $22,500, under secretaries to $17,500, and assistant secretaries to $15,000; intermediate steps were created for the Deputy Secretary of Defense at $20,000 and for the three military secretaries (now subordinated to the Secretary of Defense) at $18,000. The next general salary increase came in July 1956; this raised secretaries to $25,000, the Under Secretary of State and Deputy Secretary of Defense (also the Directors of the Budget Bureau and the Office of Defense Mobilization and the Comptroller General) to $22,500, the military secretaries to $22,000, under secretaries to $21,000, and assistant secretaries to $20,000. Increases enacted in 1964 are summarized in the text. For full details, see P.L. 81-359 (63 Stat. 880), P.L. 84-854 (70 Stat. 736), and P.L. 88-426 (78 Stat. 416).

[7] *Organizing for National Security,* Inquiry of the Senate Subcommittee on National Policy Machinery of the Committee on Government Operations, 86 Cong. 2 sess. (1961), Vol. 3, p. 68.

[8] Report of the Advisory Panel on Federal Salary Systems, June 12, 1963. The chairman was Clarence Randall.

executives, but it did recognize that the adoption of that principle for career officials made upward revision of political executive salaries imperative. The commission urged restoration of a substantial differential between congressional and political executive salaries (which has not been effected), although recognizing at that time the obvious need for some increase in congressional salaries. The following are the changed salaries according to the Federal Executive Salary Act of 1964, with commission recommendations in parentheses:

Cabinet Secretaries	$35,000	($50,000)
Deputy Secretary of Defense, Under Secretary of State; heads of the most important agencies; military secretaries	$30,000	($45,000)
Under Secretaries, regulatory commission chairmen; heads of six other large agencies; some deputy heads	$28,500	($40,000)
Assistant Secretaries, regulatory commission members, deputy heads of large agencies; remaining agency heads; outstanding bureau chiefs; general counsels	$26,000-$27,000	($30,000-$35,000)

The commission also recommended reimbursement of full costs of moving to and from Washington, an increase in the per diem travel allowance, reimbursement for reasonable expenses in the official line of duty, and separation pay.

The authors heartily endorse such steps to remove the inequities in compensation. This step alone will not solve the recruitment problem for the federal government but it will reduce one of the important elements in a complex of elements which deter some men from accepting service.

Conflict of Interest

Conflict of interest laws and regulations, necessary as they are, have been a hindrance in the selection process because of their archaic formulation and application. Evidence obtained during the course of this study indicated that conflict of interest problems did not constitute a barrier to recruitment in any way comparable to other barriers such as inadequate compensation and unwillingness to interrupt a career. On the other hand, some experienced recruiters and the Bar Association of the City of New York considered these restraints among the most important limitations in the selection process.

The problems of conflict of interest derive from the fact that the basic statutes were written for quite different purposes over a span of more than one hundred years. The statutes have a reasonable purpose: to ensure the undivided loyalty of an employee to the government, unalloyed by any personal interest in the decisions he may make or the influence he may wield. But these statutes were formulated before the age of the "mixed economy" in which the interests of the public and private groups and individuals are inextricably interrelated.[9] This situation was further exacerbated by the Senate Armed Services Committee which forced presidential appointees to divest themselves of stocks or any other interest in a company doing business worth $10,000 or more a year with military departments.

The effect of these conflict of interest problems during the period under review has been dealt with in earlier chapters. Some of the difficulties encountered by case study appointees have been remedied by Public Law 87-849, enacted during the last days of the 1962 session of Congress. This law was a major step forward in rationalizing standards, although it did not solve all of the questions raised by the existing outdated and uncoordinated statutes.

Perhaps the most significant change is in the provision which forbids an employee to participate "personally and substantially" in any decision in which he or his family or any organization to which he belongs or with whom he is negotiating for employment has a financial interest. The only exception to this rule is in those instances where the employee in advance receives a determination by his appointing officer that his interest is not so substantial that it will affect the integrity of the employee's services.

The act continues the prohibition against outside compensation in spite of the fact that many who first encounter it consider the rule "unnecessary, insulting, costly and absurd."[10] The act exempts from its prohibition, however, participation in "bona fide pension, retirement, group life, health or accident insurance, profit-sharing, stock bonus, or other employee welfare or benefit plan maintained by a former employer."[11] Thus, an executive does not have to sacrifice his security

---

[9] For a complete analysis of the background of the conflict of interest statutes, see The Association of the Bar of the City of New York, *Conflict of Interest and Federal Service* (Harvard University Press, 1960).

[10] *Ibid.*, p. 211.

[11] 76 Stat. 1125.

program as well as his current income as the price of public service. Other provisions attempt to reconcile various other conflict of interest statutes including those relating to a former employee's relationships with the United States government; these are particularly relevant to agents and attorneys.

The Bar Association of the City of New York traced much of the difficulty with conflict of interest to lack of an established role for the presidency. At present the attention devoted to the conflict of interest problem depends on agency interest and action, which is sporadic and limited to only a few. But the problem is constant and day-to-day. "It is not a single dragon to be slain and then enshrined in song; it is a nagging harpy constantly near at hand."[12] The Association therefore recommended the creation of centralized machinery, probably under the direction of the President's administrative assistant for personnel, to coordinate the various phases of the program. It would develop and prepare for promulgation regulations applicable throughout the government, assist the agencies in preparing their own regulations, collect information and experience with the problem which could be shared with each agency, assist appointees and the Senate in preparing for confirmation proceedings. For actual enforcement of the program each agency would continue its primary responsibility.

However, the problem of conflict of interest cannot be solved entirely by statute or formalized procedures, since other alleged conflicts loom large in the minds of many critics of political executives, particularly in Congress. As the Bar Association of the City of New York pointed out, "The hearings clearly show that the [Senate Armed Services] Committee's preeminent concern is the appearance of impropriety."[13] The fact that an executive has residence in a particular area where a base is established or a contract let may be sufficient grounds for a conflict of interest allegation. The hearings before the Senate Government Operations Committee on the TFX contract award to General Dynamics Corporation resulted in such allegations with regard to Fred Korth, Secretary of the Navy, because he lived in Fort Worth, Texas, the site of a major installation of that company. He had also been an officer of a bank which had earlier made a loan to General Dynamics, although the loan was comparatively small.

It is doubtful that the legal change will have a marked effect on re-

[12] *Conflict of Interest and Federal Service,* p. 189.
[13] *Ibid.,* p. 108.

cruitment of political executives. Nevertheless, the action taken by Congress is justifiable on grounds of equity. In addition, it does remove an unnecessary barrier to acceptance of political executive positions, thus reducing the cumulative effect of many discouraging features of American politics.

Possibly some of the difficulties encountered by potential candidates could be avoided if the Department of Justice provided advice on conflict of interest questions to incoming personnel in order that they understand the requirements of the law and regulations before they appear before the Senate committees.

Job Security

Political appointees who undertake what are necessarily short-term assignments are likely to have somewhat dubious future career prospects. If, however, a more favorable business and professional climate existed, employers might be willing to grant longer leaves of absence for their subordinates (preferably four years). The large number of case study appointees, who said that they had never intended to stay long in government, feared to remain longer lest they sacrifice their pension rights or promotion. Often they had to return to their former jobs within a specified time or lose them altogether. The cultivation of a better public image, already referred to, might perhaps bring about a change of heart among employers.

Adequate Orientation

Senior career officials in the majority of departments and agencies supply their incoming political superiors with extremely well-documented dossiers on departmental and agency activities. The problem political recruits most generally complain of is not having enough time to digest the information. Nevertheless, there were some appointees interviewed during the course of the study who hesitated to accept assistant secretaryships because they felt they lacked the necessary qualifications. Others, looking back, felt their ignorance to be a serious deterrent to effective performance during the first few months in office. This, they considered, was a poor environment in which to weigh the pros and cons of important policy decisions. As Rufus Miles wrote, "A good start may have a marked effect on how long an official is willing to stay, and whether he subsequently refers to his experience as a 'rat race,' without smiling, or an experience he will never regret."[14] It may also affect his decision to accept or reject further political assignments.

President Eisenhower approved in 1957 a policy paper establishing a systematic plan for the orientation of newly appointed political executives, the first effort of its kind in American history. Each department was to provide a program for its executives, utilizing its own resources and those of other agencies, including the Executive Office of the President. The program was to cover major aspects of the department's activities: its organization, procedure, and program; its external relationships, including the organization and functions of agencies with which the executive would have to deal; and the authority and responsibilities of his own position. The merit system and conflict of interest problems relating to the department were to receive special attention, and individuals in the Office of the President, Bureau of the Budget, Civil Service Commission, Departments of State and Justice would be used for specific discussions.

Unfortunately, this systematic orientation program never got off the ground. In any event, there were relatively few incoming officials during the second term of the Eisenhower administration, most political executive appointments being filled by men already in the government. Thus, the program was instituted during a period when there was little need for it.

Both in 1952-53 and 1960-61, the outgoing administrations and the bureaucracy made extensive efforts to prepare incoming officials of the new administrations for their responsibilities.[15] The Bureau of the Budget took the lead in both efforts and was assisted by each of the departments. Documents were prepared outlining the organization and program of each department and agency, its budget, and legislative proposals. Briefing sessions were conducted by career officials and occasionally the new appointee met with his predecessor, obtaining a review of the operating responsibilities of the office and its problems. While these efforts were generally considered useful, there were limitations also. Incoming officials were often suspicious of materials pre-

[14] "The Orientation of Presidential Appointees," *Public Administration Review*, Vol. XVIII (Winter 1958), p. 1.

[15] See Laurin L. Henry, *Presidential Transitions* (Brookings Institution, 1960), pp. 470-73.

pared by a previous administration and tended to discount them. Often, too much material was presented too fast so that it completely overwhelmed the neophyte. And, in an essentially decentralized operation, some agencies did effective work, permitting individuals to spend full time on the preparation of materials, whereas in others, time was devoted to the project only when available.[16]

Thus, in spite of the usefulness of the programs set up at the beginning of the Eisenhower and Kennedy administrations, effective planning for a continuing government-wide systematic orientation for new political executives is still needed.

Summary of Recommendations

Several positive courses of action must be continued and strengthened under White House leadership if the government is to attract and retain top-quality political executives:

1. Selection decisions must continue to reflect the active influence and participation of the President or his staff. The Johnson-Macy operation for recruiting and screening candidates should be regarded as a minimum. Continuous efforts should be made to develop its scope and methods. Active search within the government should continue to find career employees who are qualified and willing to assume the prestige, burdens, and risks of political executive positions.

2. Every effort should be made to provide opportunities for men in private life to have direct experience either in or with the public service at a relatively early age.

3. To increase the attractiveness of these positions in a society where success is measured in part by the level of income, President Johnson's projected annual review of salaries paid political executives would help, if continued, to attract ambitious talented men to the public service.

4. Advice on conflict of interest problems to incoming personnel might be provided by the Department of Justice in order that candidates may understand the requirements of the law and regulations before they appear before the Senate committees.

[16] See Rufus Miles, in *Public Administration Review* (Winter 1958), for some of these limitations.

5. Orientation for new executives must be tailored to individual needs. Many appointees need little more than an intensive briefing on current programs. Others, with little or no experience, will require extensive assistance.

6. It is imperative that further measures be taken to improve the knowledge which men in private life have of government service and its rewards, and to exploit the already favorable image that most senior professional men have of their government colleagues.

The adoption of any or all of these recommendations is not likely to effect any radical change in the existing system of recruitment and selection. The basic factors which contribute to difficulty in finding suitable candidates for political executive service will remain strong: an economy that rewards private activity far more than public service; a political system in which high executive office is held for a relatively brief period of time; and a society which has been slow to accord government service the honor which it deserves. In spite of the obstacles to acceptance under the present system, however, it is obvious that the United States has obtained the services of a legion of dedicated, public-spirited men. They have dealt with enormous problems and have acquitted themselves generally very well, and often with real distinction.

APPENDIXES

APPENDIX A

Tables on 108 Political Executives
Selected for Case Studies

TABLE A.1. *Legal Residence When Appointed, Compared with Birthplace, by Administration (Birthplace in Parentheses)*

Geographic Region[a]	Administration						Total	
	Truman		Eisenhower		Kennedy			
Northeast	7	(6)	16	(9)	3	(8)	26	(23)
South	17	(17)	6	(7)	13	(8)	36	(32)
North Central	6	(10)	15	(22)	6	(7)	27	(39)
West	7	(2)	10	(7)	2	(1)	19	(10)
Foreign and territories	—	(2)	—	(2)	—	—	—	(4)
Total	37	(37)	47	(47)	24	(24)	108	(108)

[a] The United States Census sets up the regions as follows:
Northeast: Maine, New Hampshire, Vermont, Massachusetts, Rhode Island, Connecticut, New York, New Jersey, Pennsylvania.
South: Delaware, Maryland, District of Columbia, Virginia, West Virginia, North Carolina, South Carolina, Georgia, Florida, Kentucky, Tennessee, Alabama, Mississippi, Arkansas, Louisiana, Oklahoma, Texas.
North Central: Ohio, Indiana, Illinois, Michigan, Wisconsin, Minnesota, Iowa, Missouri, North Dakota, South Dakota, Nebraska, Kansas.
West: Montana, Idaho, Wyoming, Colorado, New Mexico, Arizona, Utah, Nevada, Washington, Oregon, California.

289

TABLE A.2. *Residence in Washington D.C., or Immediate Vicinity at Time of Appointment, by Administration*

Residence	Administration		
	Truman	Eisenhower	Kennedy
Total Washington, D.C. legal residence	10	4	10
Actual residence because of government service	18	8	1
Subtotal	28	12	11
Out of Washington, D.C.	9	35	13
Total	37	47	24

TABLE A.3. *Age to Nearest Birthday at Time of Appointment, by Administration*

Age	Administration		
	Truman	Eisenhower	Kennedy
30–39	10	4	6
40–49	16	8	11
50–59	9	28	7
60 and over	2	7	—
Total	37	47	24
Medians	43	53	$45\frac{1}{2}$

TABLE A.4. *Level of Education, by Administration*

Level of Education	Administration			
	Truman	Eisenhower	Kennedy	Total
No college degree	8[a]	5	1	14
Bachelor's degree	23[b]	39	23	85
Law degree only	6[c]	3	—	9
Total	37	47	24	108
Law degree in addition to bachelor's degree	11[d]	14[e]	9[f]	34
Other collegiate work beyond bachelor's degree:				
Some graduate study	3	9	2	14
Master's degree	5	6	2	13
Doctor's degree	2	—	4	6
Total of those with studies beyond bachelor's degree	21	29	17	67

[a] One had no degrees but had been admitted to the bar.
[b] One had no law degree, but had been admitted to the bar.
[c] One also had a master's degree.
[d] In addition one had some graduate study, two had master's degrees, and one had a doctor's degree.
[e] Three also had some graduate study.
[f] One also had some graduate study, one a master's degree, and one a doctor's degree.

TABLE A.5. *Appointees with and without Legal Training,*
by Administration and Occupational Background

Legal Standing	Administration			
	Truman	Eisenhower	Kennedy	Total
With legal degree or training				
Law	4	13	5	22
Business	2	2	—	4
Public service	9	—	1	10
Other	1	—	2	3
Multiple occupations	3	2	1	6
Subtotal	19	17	9	45
Without legal degree or training				
Business	5	17	4	26
Public service	7	4	3	14
Other	6	7	8	21
Multiple occupations	—	2	—	2
Subtotal	18	30	15	63
Total	37	47	24	108

TABLE A.6. *Previous Major Occupations, by Administration*

Occupation	Administration			Total
	Truman	Eisenhower	Kennedy	
Law	4	13	5	22
Business	7	19	4	30
Public service	16	4	4	24
Other[a]	7	7	10	24
Multiple occupations[b]	3	4	1	8
Total	37	47	24	108

[a] Nine from the academic world, 4 trade unionists, 3 farmers, 3 newsmen, 5 miscellaneous.

[b] Men who had moved from one career field to another and sometimes to a third—chiefly law, business, and public service.

TABLE A.7. *Previous High-level Public Service, by Administration and Occupational Background*

Status	Administration			Total
	Truman	Eisenhower	Kennedy	
With service[a]				
Law	4	6	2	12
Business	3	4	2	9
Public service	2	2	2	6
Multiple occupations	—	1	—	1
Other	2	—	2	4
Subtotal	11	13	8	32
Without service				
Law	—	7	3	10
Business	4	15	2	21
Public service	14	2	2	18
Multiple occupations	3	3	1	7
Other	5	7	8	20
Subtotal	26	34	16	76
Total	37	47	24	108

[a] Includes service as: executive assistant to secretary or undersecretary; assistant secretary; ambassador; general counsel; administrator; deputy administrator.

TABLE A.8. *Appointees Having Minor or No Previous Federal Government Experience, by Administration and Occupational Background*

Experience	Administration			Total
	Truman	Eisenhower	Kennedy	
Minor experience[a]				
Law	—	4	2	6
Business	1	4	—	5
Multiple occupations	1	—	—	1
Other	—	—	2	2
Subtotal	2	8	4	14
No experience				
Law	2	3	1	6
Business	2	6	1	9
Multiple occupations	—	1	1	2
Other	1	6	3	10
Subtotal	5	16	6	27
Total with minor or no experience	7	24	10	41
Major experience				
Law	2	6	2	10
Business	4	9	3	16
Public service	16	4	4	24
Multiple occupations	2	3	—	5
Other	6	1	5	12
Subtotal	30	23	14	67
Total	37	47	24	108

[a] Either of brief duration or at very low level.

TABLE A.9. *Previous Political Experience, by Administration*

Type of Experience[a]	Administration			Total
	Truman	Eisenhower	Kennedy	
Presidential campaign	2	5	8	15
National convention	—	6	—	6
National Committee	2	3	1	6
Other	—	5	2	7
Total	4	19	11	34

[a] Some appointees belonged in more than one category; in order to avoid duplication, they have been placed in the most relevant. "Other" includes state chairmen, men who had run for Congress, and other political activists. In Addition to the 34 tabulated, there were three who had participated in state politics only and two whose wives were active politically.

TABLE A.10. *Major Reasons Mentioned for Accepting Appointment*

Reasons for Accepting	Percentage (N = 106)[a]
Public service	45%
Career advancement	28
Influence on policy	27
Service to new administration	27
Attraction of public life	23
Prestige	23
Appeal of Washington	22
Drawing power of recruiter	19
Personal appeal from President	9
Good of the department	9
Challenging job	8
Higher pay	3
Emergency in government	2

[a] Percentages do not add to 100 because of multiple responses.

TABLE A.11. *Drawbacks Mentioned to Accepting Appointment*

Drawbacks	Percentage (N = 68)[a]
Personal difficulties	
Financial	21%
Other (Move to D.C., schools and children, leave friends, etc.)	25
Both	31
Subtotal	77
Job-related difficulties	
Conflict of interest	13
Loss to organization	12
Unfavorable publicity or criticism	10
Current status preferable	10
Doubt of own qualifications	9
Loss of advancement	7
	61
No drawbacks	6

[a] Of the 108 case study appointees, only 68 were asked this question. Percentages do not add to 100 because of multiple responses.

TABLE A.12. *Sources of Satisfaction Mentioned*

Sources of Satisfaction	Percentage (N = 89)[a]
Challenge and responsibility of the job	67%
Utilization of previous experience and contacts	62
Policy achievement	33
Good personal relations with leaders	27
Respect for civil servants and/or military personnel	19
Good relations with Congress	15
Attraction of Washington environment[b]	15
Freedom from interference on job	11
Increased knowledge of government	11
Career advancement	7
Ability to work under pressure	4

[a] Of the 108 case study appointees, only 89 were asked this question. Percentages do not add to 100 because of multiple responses.

[b] Only two specifically mentioned social life.

TABLE A.13. *Sources of Dissatisfaction Mentioned*

Sources of Dissatisfaction	Percentage (N = 78)[a]
Pressure of work[b]	47%
Long hours	29
Heavy responsibility	24
Widely varied activity	24
Effect on health	3
Legal and political restrictions	23
Frustrations—red tape—multiple clearance	18
Personal financial loss	17
Policy disputes	8
Difficulty in communication with colleagues or Congress	8
No way to measure effectiveness	5
Job different from anticipation	5
Social routine	4
Lack of experience and substantive knowledge	3
No dissatisfactions	5

[a] Of the 108 case study appointees, only 78 were asked this question. Percentages do not add to 100 because of multiple responses.
[b] Five others mentioned the pressure of work, but not as a dissatisfaction.

TABLE A.14. *Reasons for Departure from Case Study Position (Truman and Eisenhower Cases Only), by Administration*

Reasons for Departure	Percentage[a] Administration Truman	Eisenhower	Total
Acceptance of another government position	35%	26%	30%
No intention of remaining long	14	38	27
Change of administration	32	21	26
Frustrations in job	8	13	11
Attractive job offer	16	4	10
Financial reasons	5	11	8
Disappointment over promotion	8	6	7
Concern for private business or own career	—	13	7
Congressional harassment	3	9	6
Policy disputes within government	5	4	5
Desire to run for political office	3	2	2

[a] Percentage base = 37 for Truman, 47 for Eisenhower, 84 for total. Percentages do not add to 100 because of multiple responses.

TABLE A.15. *Next Position Taken upon Departure from Case Study Post (Truman and Eisenhower Cases Only), by Occupation*

Position	Occupation				Total
	Law	Business	Public Service	Other	
Return to					
Same business	—	9	1[a]	—	10
Same law practice	5	—	—	—	5
Other organization	—	—	—	8	8
Subtotal	5	9	1	8	23
Move to					
New business	2	9	—	1	12
New law practice	4	1	3	—	8
Other organization	—	1	3	4	8
Subtotal	6	11	6	5	28
Move to other federal government post	6	6	11	8	31[b]
Retire	—	—	2	—	2
Total	17	26	20	21	84

[a] This man had spent most of his career in public service but had retired and taken a business position about a year before accepting the political executive post.

[b] Fifteen of these thirty-one federal political executives returned eventually to the private sector: 4 lawyers, 5 businessmen, 3 public servants, and 3 miscellaneous. Of the lawyers, two returned to their old law practices, one set up a new practice, and one made a new business connection. Of the businessmen, three returned to their former businesses and two retired. Two of the public servants entered new law practices and one retired. Two of the three in other occupations set up new businesses and one went into a new law practice.

TABLE A.16. *Next Position Taken upon Departure from Case Study Post (Truman and Eisenhower Cases Only), by Administration*

Position	Administration		Total
	Truman	Eisenhower	
Return to			
Same business	4	6	10
Same law practice	1	4	5
Other organization	2	6	8
Subtotal	7	16	23
Move to			
New business	3	9	12
New law practice	4	4	8
Other organization	6	2	8
Subtotal	13	15	28
Move to other federal government post	16	15	31
Retire	1	1	2
Total	37	47	84

APPENDIX B

Tables on Performance Ratings of Political Executives, 1933-61

TABLE B.1. *Evaluation of Political Executives by Occupation*

Occupation	Number	Ratings[a]				
		Excellent	Good	Fair	Below Average	Poor
Business	98	24%	27%	21%	7%	20%
Law	66	29	26	18	12	15
Other professions	20	25	25	10	30	10
Government, elective	6	17	17	17	17	33
Government, nonelective	77	32	31	26	4	6
Other	16	12	31	31	25	—
Total	283					

[a] In Appendix B tables percentages may not add to 100 because of rounding.

TABLE B.2. *Evaluation of Political Executives by Federal Public Service Background*

Federal Service Background[a]	Number	Ratings				
		Excellent	Good	Fair	Below Average	Poor
Executive, noncareer	169	33%	27%	21%	6%	12%
Executive, career	27	30	37	26	4	4
Congress, part-time and party	26	15	35	19	15	15
No service	60	15	22	20	22	22
Total	283					

[a] Only the most significant background of each appointee was tabulated here, in order to avoid duplication.

300

TABLE B.3. *Evaluation of Political Executives by State and Local Background*

State and Local Background	Number	Ratings				
		Excellent	Good	Fair	Below Average	Poor
Governor and other elective state executive	18	33%	17%	11%	17%	22%
State legislature	13	15	31	23	23	8
Local elective	10	20	20	10	10	40
Other state, local nonelective	26	15	46	35	4	—
Total	67					

TABLE B.4. *Evaluation of Political Executives by Years of Prior Government Administration Experience*[a]

Years	Number	Ratings				
		Excellent	Good	Fair	Below Average	Poor
No service	83	18%	24%	17%	19%	22%
0–2	42	31	29	14	12	14
3–5	58	29	26	21	9	16
6–10	48	33	33	27	2	4
11–15	26	27	19	35	4	15
16 or more	26	30	38	27	4	—
Total	283					

[a] Administrative experience is defined as previous administrative experience in federal, state, or local governments.

Table B.5. *Evaluation of Political Executives by Type of Business*

Type of Business	Number	Ratings				
		Excellent	Good	Fair	Below Average	Poor
Manufacturing	43	20%	25%	18%	9%	27%
Finance	27	32	36	21	4	7
Other business	28	21	14	34	17	14
Total business	98	24	25	24	10	18

Table B.6. *Evaluation of Political Executives by Age at Time of Appointment*

Age	Number	Ratings				
		Excellent	Good	Fair	Below Average	Poor
Below 40	41	20%	49%	20%	—	12%
40–49	124	32	28	23	8%	9
50–59	79	28	25	19	13	15
60 and over	38	16	8	26	21	29
Total	282					

TABLE B.7. *Evaluation of Political Executives by Level of Education*

Level of Education[a]	Number	Ratings				
		Excellent	Good	Fair	Below Average	Poor
Doctorate	25	24%	32%	4%	12%	28%
Master's degree	27	30	37	11	11	11
Law degree	108	30	24	21	11	14
Some graduate work— no degree	27	30	26	33	—	11
Bachelor's degree	57	26	28	33	7	5
Some college— no degree	25	12	32	24	16	16
All other	13	31	23	—	23	23
Total	282					

[a] Highest level of education only tabulated. The doctorate is judged the highest and so on down the list in the above table.

TABLE B.8. *Evaluation of Political Executives by Type of Agency*

Type of Agency	Number	Ratings				
		Excellent	Good	Fair	Below Average	Poor
Domestic departments	145	26%	28%	19%	12%	16%
Security departments	107	28	29	22	6	14
All departments	251	27	28	20	10	15
All agencies	32	28	22	31	12	6
Total	283					

Index

Drawbacks to acceptance, 176-89; career implications, 183-86; conflict of interest, 186-87; finances, 179-81; personal considerations, 178-79; public criticism, 188-89; family, 181-83
Dulles, John Foster, 36, 68, 94, 99, 200
Duncan, John, 50, 131
Dungan, Ralph, 72, 74
Durkin, Martin, 54, 68, 69

Eastland, James, 142
Eisenhower, Dwight D., administration of: Agriculture, 49-50; appointment process, 67-71, 78, 85, 88, 90, 92; career service advancement, 233n; confirmation hearings, 138-39, 140, 141; Commerce, 54-55; Defense, 34-35, 36-37; Health, Education, and Welfare, 57-58; Interior, 51-52; Justice, 40, 41, 42, 43, 44; Labor, 53-54; political considerations in appointment, 80, 125-31, 134; Post Office, 46-47; State, 35, 36; tenure, 228-30; Treasury, 38-39, 40. *See also* Administrations, comparisons of
Eisenhower, Milton, 274
Engle, Clair, 139
Estes, Billie Sol, 108
Experience, political, 23-25
Evaluation of political executives. *See* Performance ratings

Fay, Paul B., 145
Fenn, Dan H., 269-70, 277
Finletter, Thomas, 273
Flemming, Arthur, 233n
Floberg, John F., 36
Folsom, Marion B., 38, 70, 183, 227, 233n., 250
Ford, Peyton, 43-44
Foreign Policy Association, 82, 83, 133
Forrestal, James V., 34, 94, 113, 156, 233n
Foster, William C., 24, 29, 56, 229
Fowler, Henry H., 39, 140, 273
Franke, William, 233n
Freeman, Orville, 50, 131, 273, 274

Galbraith, J. Kenneth, 273
Garlock, Lyle S., 36, 272

Gates, Artemus L., 94
Gates, Thomas, 29, 113, 229, 233n
General Services Administration, recruitment, 59
George, Walter F., 203
Gilhooley, John, 54
Gillette, Hyde, 47
Goldberg, Arthur, 273
Gray, Gordon, 233n

Halaby, Najeeb, 276
Hall, Leonard, 125
Hansen, Victor, 42
Harriman, W. Averell, 156, 273
Harris, Joseph, 152
Hartigan, William J., 45
Harvard Business School Club of Washington, 162
Health, Education, and Welfare, Department of, recruitment, 57-58
Heller, Walter, 273
Henderson, Loy, 169
Hensel, Struve, 113, 276
Herter, Christian, 233n
Hook, Charles, 46-47
Hickerson, John D., 36
Hodges, Luther, 274
Hoffman, Paul, 276
Holland, Brian, 276
Holt, Rush, 138
Holum, Kenneth, 132
Howard, Katherine, 17
Hughes, Rowland, 233n
Humelsine, Carlisle H., 33
Humphrey, George, 38, 39, 78
Hunter, Floyd, 15
Hutchinson, Knox, 49
Hyneman, Charles S., 15

Ickes, Harold, 149
Interior, Department of: policy views, 198; recruitment, 50-53, 107-08, 132
Jackson, Henry. *See* Senate Subcommittee on National Policy Machinery
Jeffers, William M., 156
Johnson, Earl, 36
Johnson, Louis A., 213, 233n
Johnson, Lyndon B., administration of, 77, 270, 271, 278
Jones, Roger, 7, 60, 226